THE JOHNS HOPKINS UNIVERSITY PRESS

BALTIMORE AND LONDON

Amish Society

THIRD EDITION

☙

John A. Hostetler

Originally published, 1963
Johns Hopkins Paperbacks edition, 1970
Third edition, 1980
85 86 87 88 89   7 6 5 4

The Johns Hopkins University Press
701 West 40th Street
Baltimore, Maryland 21211
The Johns Hopkins Press Ltd., London

Title-page illustration courtesy of Bill Coleman

Library of Congress Cataloging in Publication Data

Hostetler, John Andrew
  Amish society.

  Bibliography: pp. 385–401
  Includes index.
  1. Amish in the United States—Social life and customs.
2. Amish—Social life and customs. I. Title.
E184.M45H63 1980   301.45′28′87   79–23823

ISBN 0–8018–2333–1
ISBN 0–8018–2334–x pbk.

To the memory of

MOSES LAPP,

an inspiring man of the Amish faith,

and

ABDUL HAMID M. el-ZEIN,

a Temple University colleague who, in the search for
social reality, combined the love of knowledge
with humility

Contents

✣

PART II. STABILITY AND FULFILLMENT

PART III. PATTERNS OF CHANGE

PART IV. SURVIVAL

Preface

॥

THIS, THE THIRD edition of *Amish Society*, is a completely rewritten volume. While the best has been retained from the previous editions, not a single chapter or page remains the same. This new book was made necessary by changes in Amish society, by new discoveries from research, and by changes in my own point of view. At mid-century, sociologists predicted that the Amish would be absorbed into the larger society within twenty-five years. It was thought that once the vitality of the European tradition was exhausted the Amish would be assimilated by the larger social forces of the dominant society. The predictions were wrong. The Amish population has since doubled and the assimilation rate has not changed significantly. The cultural energy of the Amish is healthy.

Popular misconceptions still abound as they did twenty-five years ago, all in spite of more research and widely available publications. Two extreme views still prevail. One is the traditional view of pity for persons who will not modernize and ease the burdens of life through the convenience of twentieth-century ways and who will not be enlightened by the creativity of individual self-determination. The other extreme is embodied in the comment of the industrialist who insisted that "the Amish are the only honest Christians left in the modern world." Because of the qualities of sainthood ascribed to them, the Amish are viewed by some as a rare species, a people who raise their crops "naturally," who live by extraordinary standards of honesty and uprightness.

Any society that is perceived as "standing still" will soon become a tourist attraction. The Amish are viewed as a slow-changing people, but they are not an "archaeological discovery." The paradigm they have worked from is different from that of the larger culture; therefore they have reached different conclusions about how to live in the modern world. The present revitalization of ethnic and religious groups calls for a reevaluation of traditional social theories. Amish communities are not relics of a bygone era. Rather, they are demonstrations of a different form of modernity.

The first edition of *Amish Society* was preceded by ten years of preparation and appeared in 1963. It was slightly enlarged in 1968. These earlier editions embody the perspectives of the times in which they were written. It is time for a new interpretation. The Amish have changed, world society has changed, and Americans generally have shifted their thinking about culturally diverse peoples within their borders. Modern scholarship has refocused its method of inquiry, resulting in new perspectives.

The clash of "civilized ways" with "Amish ways" is still as apparent in Amish settlements as it was several decades ago. The notion that the Amish suffer from more human stress by denying themselves or their children the uses of modern technology and convenience or by living a more austere life than others is today in serious doubt. Civilization has indeed taught us how to survive in large numbers, how to prolong life, how to transform tribal societies into urban ones, and how to ease the burdens of labor. American rural communities generally have been transformed into landscapes for development, investment, and commercial gain. Without preachment the Amish have taught us something of the human cost when old values are cast away, when parents are alienated from children, when neighbors are treated as strangers, and when man is separated from his spiritual tradition.

This book provides a context for evaluating technical change, human values, and the alternatives confronting human communities in many parts of the world. The purpose is to communicate a knowledge of Amish life to the inquiring reader. The scope of the material is comprehensive rather than regional, integrative rather than specialized or esoteric. Although the special terms of the social sciences are in evidence, it is hoped that such terms will serve as a structure for the description of the people. A discussion of the origins, values, maintenance, and social relationships of the Amish community will be followed by a consideration of the problems, conflicts, and costs of being Amish. The book attempts to widen our knowledge of the diversity of human cultures—their customs and conflicts—and to convey the depth of human experience.

How did the Amish formulate their beliefs and develop their community life? How have the Amish managed to circumvent the forces of mainstream civilization? What is the character and scope of personal, family, and community life? What are the consequences of living in a slow-changing culture? What is the logic of introducing more efficient technology if in the process the human qualities of *Gemeinschaft* (the "natural groupings") are cut into shreds? These and other questions have relevance for human communities anywhere, from university and municipal communities to the small villages in Africa and Asia that are faced with radical change in their age-old customs.

The ethnographic material in this volume is based on the three largest Amish settlements, which are located respectively in Pennsylvania, Ohio, and Indiana. Many smaller settlements also were visited. I have conducted research on socialization, schooling, family patterns, population trends, and occupational patterns since the first edition of *Amish Society* was published. Mifflin County, Pennsylvania, where I lived as a member of an Amish family, and Washington and Johnson counties, Iowa, where I spent my youth until the age of twenty-two, taught me much about the depth and diversity of Amish culture. I have experienced the ties of kinship and faith, but I have also seen the tragedies of division, exclusion, and fragmentation.

The natural history of the Amish people has been enriched by the discovery of new sources. Some have come to light through the efforts of the Amish people themselves, who have taken a vital interest in their own heritage. Other sources have emerged through the research and publications of European scholars who have subsequently "discovered" the Amish. My understanding of Amish origins was greatly aided by a stay in Alsace, France, Switzerland, and Germany, where I visited villages, families, and congregations of descendants from the first followers of Jacob Ammann.

The specialized studies of others, both colleagues and students, have helped to round out the description of agriculture, demography, education, geography, medical studies, and tourism. These contributions are acknowledged and appreciated, for they add significant knowledge to the total perspective. All the chapters have been rewritten. Where enlightening, new material has been added, while some of the more dated technical terminology has been removed. The organization of the material, as in previous editions, is grounded in a holistic understanding of the small society.

Any society that falls under the scrutiny of scientific investigation is liable to have its internal strengths and weaknesses exposed. The risks of discovery become the responsibility of the investigator. To any reader who may feel that the strengths and weaknesses of Amish society have been disproportionately emphasized here, and especially to Amish readers, I extend the assurance that there has been no ill intent.

Acknowledgments

FOR THE FINANCIAL support that made possible my archival and European field studies, as well as the basic research essential to this volume, I thank the National Endowment for the Humanities. For assistance in the collection of data I thank many of the Amish people.

I also wish to thank Jean Jacques Hirschy, Rene Hege, Willy Hege, Claude Jerome, Willy Nafziger, André Nussbaumer, Prof. F. Raphael, and Prof. Jean Séguy of France; Paul Ammann and Dr. Theo. Gantner of Switzerland; and Edwin Hochstättler, Paul Schowalter, Gary Waltner, and Dr. Karl Scherer of Germany.

For critical readings of one or more sections of the manuscript, often involving engaging discourses, I thank in addition to many unnamed Amish informants, Allen Alexander, Richard Beam, John W. Bennett, Roy Buck, Eugene Ericksen, Julia Ericksen, Joshua Fishman, Ivan Glick, Thomas Gallagher, Hugh Gingerich, Leonard Gross, Paul Herr, Gertrude Enders Huntington, James Hurd, Victor A. McKusick, Mervin Smucker, Don Yoder, John H. Yoder, and the late Abdul Hamid M. el-Zein. Elizabeth Horsch Bender translated many German sources, Nancy Gaines provided bibliographic help, and Doris Weiland drew the maps and charts.

I am greatly indebted to Beulah Stauffer Hostetler, my wife, for thinking out with me many of the ideas of the book. Ann Hostetler, my daughter, performed commendable editorial work on the entire manuscript.

Part I

Foundations

CHAPTER 1

Models for Understanding Amish Society

SMALL COMMUNITIES, with their distinctive character—where life is stable and intensely human—are disappearing. Some have vanished from the face of the earth, others are dying slowly, but all have undergone change as they have come into contact with an expanding machine civilization. The merging of diverse peoples into a common mass has produced tension among members of the minorities and the majority alike.

The Old Order Amish, who arrived on American shores in colonial times, have survived in the modern world in distinctive, viable, small communities. They have resisted the homogenization process more successfully than others. In planting and harvest time one can see their bearded men working the fields with horses and their women hanging out the laundry in neat rows to dry. Many American people have seen Amish families, with the men wearing broad-brimmed black hats and the women in bonnets and long dresses, in railway depots or bus terminals. Although the Amish have lived with industrialized America for over two and a half centuries, they have moderated its influence on their personal lives, their families, communities, and their values.

The Amish are often perceived by other Americans to be relics of the past who live an austere, inflexible life dedicated to inconvenient and archaic customs. They are seen as renouncing both modern conveniences and the American dream of success and progress. But most people have no quarrel with the Amish for doing things the old-fashioned way. Their conscientious objection was tolerated in wartime, for after all, they are meticulous farmers who practice the virtues of work and thrift.

In recent years the status of the Amish in the minds of most Americans has shifted toward a more favorable position.[1] This change can scarcely be attributed to anything the Amish have done; rather, it is the result of changes in the way Americans perceive their minority groups. A century ago, hardly anyone knew the Amish existed. A half-century ago they were viewed as an obscure sect living by ridiculous customs, as stubborn people who resisted education and exploited the labor of their children. Today the Amish are the unwilling objects of a thriving tourist industry on the eastern seaboard. They are revered as hard-working, thrifty people with enormous agrarian stamina, and by some, as islands of sanity in a culture gripped by commercialism and technology run wild.

In the academic community several models have been advanced for understanding Amish society. Social scientists, like other Americans, have been influenced by the upward push of an advancing civilization and changes in the social discourse between the dominant society and its minorities. University teachers have traditionally taught their students to think of the Amish people as one of many old-world cultural islands left over in the modern world. The Amish have been considered "a sacred society," a "familistic society," as maintaining "organic solidarity," an "integrative social system," "primary" (face-to-face) rather than "secondary" relationships, and "Apollonian" instead of "Dionysian" orientations to life. They may be viewed from any one of these perspectives, but such objective models and abstractions leave out things that are important for understanding the whole perspective of Amish society.

The Amish are a church, a community, a spiritual union, a conservative branch of Christianity, a religion, a community whose members practice simple and austere living, a familistic entrepreneuring system, and an adaptive human community. In this chapter

---

1. In selecting a theme for the bicentennial of the founding of the United States of America, the *Michigan Farmer* chose to feature the Amish when only a few years previously the state had prosecuted them for maintaining uncertified schools. The narrative was written by an Amish girl, Mary Miller, and appears in the July 1976 issue.

several models will be discussed in terms of their usefulness and limitations as avenues for understanding Amish society as a whole. By models I mean structured concepts currently used by anthropologists to characterize whole societies. The serious reader will want to transcend the scientific orientation and ask, What is the meaning of the Amish system? What, if anything, is it trying to say to us?

A COMMONWEALTH

The Amish are in some ways a little commonwealth, for their members claim to be ruled by the law of love and redemption. The bonds that unite them are many. Their beliefs, however, do not permit them solely to occupy and defend a particular territory. They are highly sensitive in caring for their own. They will move to other lands when circumstances force them to do so.

Commonwealth implies a place, a province, which means any part of a national domain that geographically and socially is sufficiently unified to have a true consciousness of its unity.[2] Its inhabitants feel comfortable with their own ideas and customs, and the "place" possesses a sense of distinction from other parts of the country. Members of a commonwealth are not foot-loose. They have a sense of productivity and accountability in a province where "the general welfare" is accepted as a day-to-day reality. Commonwealth has come to have an archaic meaning in today's world, because when groups and institutions become too large, the sense of commonwealth or the common good is lost. Thus it is little wonder that the most recent dictionaries of the American English language render the meaning of commonwealth as "obsolescent." In reality, the Amish are in part a commonwealth. There is, however, no provision for outcasts.

It may be argued that the Amish have retained elements of wholesome provincialism, a saving power to which the world in the future will need more and more to appeal. Provincialism need not turn to ancient narrowness and ignorance, confines from which many have sought to escape. A sense of province or commonwealth, with its cherished love of people and self-conscious dignity, is a necessary basis for relating to the wider world community. Respect for locality, place, custom, and local idealism can go a long way toward checking the monstrous growth of consolidation in the nation and thus help to save human freedom and individual dignity.

2. For a discussion of wholesome provincialism and community self-consciousness, see Josiah Royce, *Race Questions, Provincialism, and Other American Problems* (n.p., 1908), p. 62.

The Amish world view is reflected in the orderliness,
careful maintenance, and simplicity of the home.

A SECTARIAN SOCIETY

Sociologists tend to classify the Amish as a sectarian society. Several
European scholars have compared the social structure of "sect" and
"church" types of religious institutions.[3] The established church was
viewed as hierarchic and conservative. It appealed to the ruling
classes, administered grace to all people in a territorial domain, and
served as an agency of social control. The sect was egalitarian. Essentially a voluntary religious protest movement, its members separated
themselves from others on the basis of beliefs, practices, and institutions. The sects rejected the authority of the established religious
organizations and their leaders. The strains between sect and church
were viewed as a dialectic principle at work within Christianity.
The use of an ideal type helped to clarify particular characteristics of
the sectarian groups. The Anabaptists, for example, were described
as small, voluntary groupings attempting to model their lives after
the spirit of the Sermon on the Mount (Matt. 5,6,7) while also

3. Ernst Troeltsch, *The Social Teachings of the Christian Churches*, 2 vols.
(New York: Macmillan, 1931). Troeltsch, the pioneer in this field, drew his observations from the sects arising out of medieval and modern Christianity before 1800.

exercising the power to exclude and discipline members. Absolute separation from all other religious loyalties was required. All members were considered equal, and none were to take oaths, participate in war, or take part in worldly government.[4]

Sects have employed various techniques of isolation for maintaining separateness. Today the extreme mobility of modern life brings people together in multiple contexts. The spatial metaphors of separation (i.e., valley, region, sector, etc.) are fast becoming obsolete. Nevertheless, modern sectarians turn to psychic insularity and contexts that protect them from mainstream values and competing systems.[5] Members of the sect remain segregated in various degrees, chiefly by finding a group whose philosophy of history contradicts the existing values so drastically that the group sustains itself for a generation or more. To the onlooker, sectarianism, like monasticism, may appear to serve as a shelter from the complications of an overly complex society. For its participants, it provides authentic ways of realizing new forms of service and humility as well as protection from mainstream culture.

Sectarians, it is claimed, put their faith first by ordering their lives in keeping with it. The established churches compromise their faith with other interests and with the demands of the surrounding environment. Sectarians are pervasively religious in that they practice their beliefs in everyday life. Sects are often considered marginal or odd groups of alienated people with fanatic ideas. Yet the sects have had an immense influence in shaping the course of history. The British sociologist Bryan Wilson has observed that sects are "self-conscious attempts by men to construct their own societies, not merely as political entities with constitutions, but as groups with a firm set of values and mores, of which they are conscious."[6] The growth of religious toleration in America has resulted in the development of religious pluralism in a manner that has not been realized in Europe. Wilson, who has characterized modern Christian sects into several types, classes the Amish as *introversionist* rather than *conversionist* or *reformist*. "Salvation is to be found in the community of those who withdraw from involvement in the affairs of mankind."[7] The Amish recognize the evil circumstance of man, attempt to moderate its influence upon them, and retreat into a community to

4. Ibid., 2:705.
5. Martin Marty, "Sects and Cults," *Annals of the American Academy of Political and Social Science* 332 (1960): 125–34.
6. Bryan Wilson, *Religious Sects* (New York: McGraw-Hill, 1970), p. 22.
7. Ibid., p. 39.

experience, cultivate, and preserve the attributes of God in ethical relationships.

The sectarian model lends itself to a historical, religious context. As a model, it offers some insight into the proliferation of groups with a negative orientation during a specific time period. Today there are many types of movements that did not exist in the early stages of industrialization. Sects may lose their spontaneity in a variety of ways. While the model may teach us something of how sects originate and grow from a protest movement to a separate religious entity, it does not provide us with a knowledge of the dynamics of the group. The Amish, for example, are not sectarians in the sense that they demand that others conform to their practices. Nor do they claim to base all actions on holy writ. They are not in conflict with the dominant culture in the same way, or with the same intensity, as are a number of sects such as the "apocalyptic" or "manipulationist" types.[8]

Many sectarian societies, including the Amish, make little or no attempt to communicate their message. They recognize instinctively that authentic communication would mean greater literacy, education, and sophistication, and this would mean the beginning of the end. "The contribution of the sect to the larger society is," according to Martin Marty, "made best through the sympathetic observer who carries with him a picture of the advantages or particularity and assertiveness back to the world of dialogical complexity."[9] In the Amish case, the message of the sectarian society is exemplary. A way of living is more important than communicating it in words. The ultimate message is the life. An Amish person will have no doubt about his basic convictions, his view of the meaning and purpose of life, but he cannot explain it except through the conduct of his life.

A FOLK SOCIETY

Anthropologists, who have compared societies all over the world, have tended to call semiisolated peoples "folk societies," "primitives," or merely "simple societies." These societies constitute an altogether different type in contrast to the industrialized, or so-called civilized, societies. The "folk society," as conceptualized by Robert Redfield,[10] is a small, isolated, traditional, simple, homogeneous society in which

8. Ibid.

9. Marty, "Sects and Cults." p. 134.

10. Robert Redfield, "The Folk Society," *American Journal of Sociology* 52 (January 1947): 293–308. See also his book *The Little Community* (Chicago: University of Chicago Press, 1955).

oral communication and conventionalized ways are important factors in integrating the whole of life. In such an ideal-type society, shared practical knowledge is more important than science, custom is valued more than critical knowledge, and associations are personal and emotional rather than abstract and categoric.

Folk societies are uncomfortable with the idea of change. Young people do what the old people did when they were young. Members communicate intimately with one another, not only by word of mouth but also through custom and symbols that reflect a strong sense of belonging to one another. A folk society is *Gemeinschaft*-like; there is a strong sense of "we-ness." Leadership is personal rather than institutionalized. There are no gross economic inequalities. Mutual aid is characteristic of the society's members. The goals of life are never stated as matters of doctrine, but neither are they questioned. They are implied by the acts that constitute living in a small society. Custom tends to become sacred. Behavior is strongly patterned, and acts as well as cultural objects are given symbolic meaning that is often pervasively religious. Religion is diffuse and all-pervasive. In the typical folk society, planting and harvesting are as sacred in their own ways as singing and praying.

The significance of the Amish as an intimate, face-to-face primary group has long been recognized. Charles P. Loomis was the first to conceptualize the character of the Amish. In his construction of a scale he contrasted the Amish as a familistic *Gemeinschaft*-type system with highly rational social systems of the *Gesellschaft*-type in contemporary civilization.[11]

The folk model lends itself well to understanding the tradition-directed character of Amish society. The heavy weight of tradition can scarcely be explained in any other way. The Amish, for example, have retained many of the customs and small-scale technologies that were common in rural society in the nineteenth century. Through a process of syncretism, Amish religious values have been fused with an earlier period of simple country living when everyone farmed

11. Charles P. Loomis and J. Allan Beegle, *Rural Social Systems* (Englewood Cliffs, N.J.: Prentice-Hall, 1951), pp. 11–30. Further refinements on the Amish as a social system appeared in subsequent publications. See also Ferdinand Toennies, *Community and Society*, ed. and trans. Charles P. Loomis (East Lansing: Michigan State University Press, 1957).

The self-imposed isolation of Amish society suggests that they are neither folk nor peasant but "a voluntary contrived folk society," says Gertrude Enders Huntington in what is the most discerning dissertation ever written on an Amish community ("Dove at the Window: A Study of an Old Order Amish Community in Ohio" [Ph.D. diss., Yale University, 1956], p. 107).

with horses and on a scale where family members could work together. The Amish exist as a folk or "little" community in a rural subculture within the modern state, as distinguished from the primitive or peasant types described in anthropological literature. Several aspects of Redfield's folk-society model and features of the Toennies-Loomis *Gemeinschaft* aid us in understanding the parameters of Amish society. They are *distinctiveness, smallness of scale, homogeneous culture patterns,* and the *strain toward self-sufficiency.*

Distinctiveness. The Amish people are highly visible. The outsider who drives through an Amish settlement cannot help but recognize them by their clothing, farm homes, furnishings, fields, and other material traits of culture. Although they speak perfect English with outsiders, they speak a dialect of German among themselves.

Amish life is distinctive in that religion and custom blend into a way of life. The two are inseparable. The core values of the community are religious beliefs. Not only do the members worship a deity they understand through the revelation of Jesus Christ and the Bible, but their patterned behavior has a religious dimension. A distinctive way of life permeates daily life, agriculture, and the application of energy to economic ends. Their beliefs determine their conceptions of the self, the universe, and man's place in it. The Amish world view recognizes a certain spiritual worth and dignity in the universe in its natural form. Religious considerations determine hours of work and the daily, weekly, seasonal, and yearly rituals associated with life experience. Occupation, the means and destinations of travel, and choice of friends and mate are determined by religious considerations. Religious and work attitudes are not far distant from each other. The universe includes the divine, and Amish society itself is considered divine insofar as the Amish recognize themselves as "a chosen people of God." The Amish do not seek to master nature or to work against the elements, but try to work with them. The affinity between Amish society and nature in the form of land, terrain, and vegetation is expressed in various degrees of intensity.

Religion is highly patterned, so one may properly speak of the Amish as a tradition-directed group. Though allusions to the Bible play an important role in determining their outlook on the world, and on life after death, these beliefs have been fused with several centuries of struggling to survive in community. Out of intense religious experience, societal conflict, and intimate agrarian experience, a mentality has developed that prefers the old rather than the new. While the principle seems to apply especially to religion, it has also become a charter for social behavior. "The old is the best, and the

A white-top carriage along a back mountain road
in Pennsylvania.

new is of the devil," has become a prevalent mode of thought. By
living in closed communities where custom and a strong sense of
togetherness prevail, the Amish have formed an integrated way of
life and a folklike culture. Continuity of conformity and custom is
assured and the needs of the individual from birth to death are
met within an integrated and shared system of meanings. Oral tradition, custom, and conventionality play an important part in maintaining the group as a functioning whole. To the participant, religion

and custom are inseparable. Commitment and culture are combined to produce a stable human existence.

These are some of the qualities of the little Amish community that make it distinctive. "Where the community begins and where it ends is apparent. The distinctiveness is apparent to the outside observer and is expressed in the group consciousness of the people of the community."[12] The Amish community is in some aspects a functional part of modern society but is a distinctive subculture within it.

Smallness of Scale. The basic social unit of the Amish community is small. Wherever the Amish live, this primary, self-governing unit is the "church district." The rules of life are determined by this face-to-face group, which is kept small by the ceremonial functions of assembling in a single household and by the limitation imposed by horse-and-carriage travel. In most places the Amish live adjacent to non-Amish farm neighbors, but all Amish households in a geographic proximity form a unit. This small unit, from thirty to forty households, is the congregation. Households take turns hosting the biweekly religious services in their homes as there is no central building or place set aside for ceremonial functions. Families may migrate from one settlement to another, or from one state to another, but in so doing they affiliate with a local district. A settlement may be large, but the basic social unit remains small and indigenous.

The rules that are formulated by each district cover the range of individual experience. In this little community, which survives by keeping the world out, there are many taboos, and material traits of culture become symbolic. Conformity to styles of dress is important.

Smallness of scale is assured in Amish life by the multiple functions of the family. When asked about the size of his congregation an Amish bishop thinks in terms of families, not individuals. Persons who make up the society are associated with genealogical position. Most people in this society have orderly kinship and coherent social connections with one another so that virtually the whole society forms a body of relatives. Outsiders who join the Amish community —although in fact very few do—identify with the ethnic and kinship values of Amish life. Persons who defect from the little community break not only with Amish beliefs but also with normal ties with their relatives.

The Amish people maintain a human rather than an organizational scale in their daily lives. They resisted the large, consolidated school and the proposition that big schools (or farms) were better than small

The Amish farm: a blending of human labor, stewardship,
and diligence with nature

ones. A bureaucracy that places pupils together within narrow age
limits and emphasizes science and technology to the exclusion of
sharing values and personal responsibility is not tolerated. The
Amish appreciate thinking that makes the world, and their own lives,
intelligible to them. When human groups and units of work become
too large for them, a sense of estrangement sets in. When this happens
the world becomes unintelligible to them and they cease participating
in what is meaningless.

Each Amish community exhibits a local culture, though in its
basic orientation it is like other Amish communities. Organization,
roles, authority, sanction, facility, and controls governing relations
with the outside world are much alike in all Amish communities.
Smallness in the Amish community is maintained by a functional
unit no larger than a group of people who can know one another
by name, by shared ceremonial activity, and by convention. Like the
Redfield model, the Amish community "is small, so small that either
it itself is the unit of personal observation or else, being somewhat
larger and yet homogeneous, it provides in some part of it a unit of
personal observation fully representative of the whole."[13]

13. Ibid.

Homogeneous Culture Patterns. The Amish community is homogeneous in the totality of its culture and psychology. Ways of thinking and behaving are much alike for all persons in corresponding positions of age and sex. "States of mind" are much alike from one generation to the next. Egalitarian patterns are manifest in socially approved means of subsistence, production, and consumption. Physiological homogeneity among the Amish has been recognized by persons who associate inbreeding with facial types. The first American Mennonite historian, C. Henry Smith (1875–1948), who earned a Ph.D. from the University of Chicago in 1907, was born of Amish parents. He says: "My ancestors were of Mennonite faith and race. I say race deliberately, for like the Jews they had developed in the course of time not only spiritual homogeneity, but a physical solidarity as well, which, through a process of inbreeding, had accumulated many of the characteristics of a distinct human type."[14]

Psychological homogeneity finds expression through preference for traditional and shared knowledge. All have the same amount of education, and the aspirations of one generation repeat those of the preceding one. Critical thought for its own sake has no function in the little community. Agricultural lore and tradition still provide potent sources of knowledge. Science is "worldly" wisdom, although in his farming operations the Amishman cannot help being influenced by outside knowledge.

Amish communities constitute some of the most productive and stable agricultural societies in the United States. The Amish have no great desire for wealth other than owning family-size farms that serve the purposes of the community. Their rejection of trends that characterize other rural communities, such as migration to the cities, consolidation of schools, and urban recreation and associations, is a function of cohesive homogeneity. Placing a high value on farming and farm-related occupations has tended to preserve a total way of life in a little community.

Homogeneous patterns in the Amish community can be observed in the parts that people play, their activities, and the roles that govern life. Such functions correspond with those of the preceding genera-tions. The infant born into an Amish home is received with joy; his given name will be similar to that of his grandparents, cousins, uncles, and aunts. His last name will, of course, be the same as his father's, which will be one of several common family names. He will grow up conforming to patterns of life like his older brothers and sisters,

14. C. Henry Smith, *Mennonite Country Boy* (Newton, Kans.: Faith and Life Press, 1962), p. 12.

playing and experimenting with things within the Amish farm environment.

Wisdom accumulates with age, and with age comes respect. Old people retain the respect of children and grandchildren. Obedience to parents is one of the most common themes in Amish preaching— in family relations in particular, and in extended kinship relations generally—so that it becomes a life principle. Those who honor father and mother have the biblical promise of long life. Since the wisdom of the aged carries more weight than the advice of younger men, the conservation of the entire community is assured and the religious ideals are protected from too much change. The aged father and mother are content if their children are all married in the Amish faith, if they are all located on farms, and if they abide by the rules of the church. They may confidently face a sober death knowing that their children and a large group of relatives will continue to live a stable, believing life according to the Amish pattern. In the Amish community, the career of one generation repeats that of the preceding.

Strain toward Self-sufficiency. Although Amish communities are highly integrated, they are not economically self-sufficient. In the everyday operations of the farm, total separation is neither sought nor desired. The communities are dependent on local markets, merchants, hospitals, and medical services. The Amish community is self-sufficient in its religious life, socialization patterns, and educational functions. The basic needs of the individual are met within the community.

The attempt to retain self-sufficiency is associated with agrarianism and occupations close to nature. Closeness to the soil, to animals, to plants, and to weather is consistent with the Amish outlook on life and with limited outside contact. Hard work, thrift, mutual aid, and repulsion of city ways such as leisure and nonproductive spending find support in the Bible and are emphasized in day-to-day experience. With practical knowledge and hard work, a good living can be made from the soil; and this, the Amish contend, is the only fit place for a family.

The Amish woman's sphere and work are at home, not in the factory or in a paid profession. Cooking, sewing, gardening, cleaning, whitewashing fences, tending to chickens, and helping with the milking keep her occupied. Caring for the children is, of course, her principal work. Her place in the religious life of the community is a subordinate one, though she has voting rights in congregational meetings and in the nomination of persons for the ministry. An

Amish woman's work, like the work of any American woman, is never done. But she is always with her children, and to break the monotony, there are weddings, quiltings, frolics, auction sales, and Sunday services. For her satisfaction in life she turns to brightly colored flowers in the garden, or in the winter, to rug-making, embroidery work on quilts, pillowcases, and towels, and to shelves of colored dishes in her corner cupboard. Some the work of her hands, these are her prized possessions, made for the enjoyment of the household and her host of relatives. Within her role as homemaker she has a greater possibility of achieving status recognition than the suburban housewife; her skill, or lack of it, has direct bearing on her family's standard of living. She sews all their clothes; plants, preserves, and prepares the food her family eats; and adds beauty to life with quilts, rugs, and flowers. Canning her own food, making her chow-chow, and spreading the dinner table with home-prepared food are achievements that are recognized and rewarded by her society.

The Amish have no schools of higher learning, but they have built elementary schools to avoid the external influence that comes with the centralized school system. As soon as the law will allow, Amish children are taken out of school for work at home. The Amish viewpoint is that "if a boy does little hard work before he is twenty-one, he probably never gets to like it afterward. In other words, he will not amount to much as a farmer."[15]

The need for leisure and social enjoyment is met by informal institutions within the community. Kinship duties require extensive visiting. Recreation consists primarily of meaningful social experiences, group solidarity, and rites of passage within the community. Work bees, such as barn-raisings, woodcuttings, husking bees, quiltings, preparations for church services, weddings, and funerals (including casket-making), all combine work and recreation. The social life of the young people is centered in the Sunday evening singing. One of the most important life ceremonies is the wedding, which calls for a large amount of festivity, food, kinship duties, and ritual. What matters most about the prospective bride and bridegroom is not whether they come from a wealthy family, but whether they show promise of being a good housekeeper and a good farmer, respectively, within the bounds of the community.

The little Amish community is not a communal society with an exclusive economic system, and property ownership is not unlike that in the dominant society. However, the Amish have been able to maintain patterns of mutual aid and ways of sharing economic re-

15. Anonymous Amish comment.

wards and misfortunes. Their vital linkages with outside institutions are conditioned by their distinctive core values and by the special rules that govern such relationships. By making agriculture a sacred occupation, the Amish avoid the drift toward the complex world of labor relations and the professions. Farm produce may not be delivered or picked up on the Lord's Day. Religion prevents members from taking an active part in activities that are beyond "necessity" on Sunday. Amish farmers are not integrated with farm organizations, local political groups, or consolidated schools.

Self-sufficiency is the community's answer to government aid programs such as farm subsidy and social security benefits. The Amish are opposed to receiving direct government aid of any kind, whether old-age pension, farm subsidy, or compensation payments, and to having their children and grandchildren fall heir to such handouts. To admit that the government has a responsibility for Amish members is to deny the faith. This, they say, would undermine their own stable community and their form of mutual aid. Amish security requires a high degree of personal relations and responsibility in times of stress, fire, sickness, old age, or death. Strictly commercial or federal means of providing for these needs are regarded as secular, if not sinful. Amish life is not segmented into cliques, clubs, or special-interest groups, but approximates a cradle-to-the-grave arrangement as an integral whole; the little community "provides for all or most of the activities and needs of the people in it."[16]

Amish society, developed along the lines of the folk model of Robert Redfield, is a type of human community that is realized in many parts of the world. These "little" communities that remain at the edges of expanding civilizations share certain characteristics. The Amish, however, are neither primitive nor peasant in the manner of the older and more geographically isolated groups.[17] The Amish derived from the Reformation, which in itself was a liberating and self-determining movement. Amish life is permeated with the Christian tradition and its codifications of reality. The folk model demonstrates the structure of Amish society, its tradition-directed quality, and the variety of its interpersonal relationships. To understand the inner dynamics of Amish society, however, we must look elsewhere. The model that follows will attempt to illuminate some of the problems of social discourse between the Amish community and mainstream American culture.

16. Redfield, *The Little Community*, p. 4.
17. For a classification of folk types, see Elman Service, *Profiles in Ethnology* (New York: Harper & Row, 1963).

A HIGH-CONTEXT CULTURE

Cultural anthropologists have demonstrated enormous variations between cultures and a significant degree of elasticity within a single culture. Culture patterns determine what people pay attention to and what they ignore. What people feel, think, and do varies from one culture to another. Edward T. Hall has distinguished between "high-" and "low-context" cultures, illustrating different but legitimate ways of thinking and perceiving.[18]

A high-context culture is one in which people are deeply involved with one another. Awareness of situations, experience, activity, and one's social standing is keenly developed. Information is widely shared. Simple messages with deep meaning flow freely. There are many levels of communication—overt and covert, implicit and explicit signs, symbols, and body gestures, and things one may and may not talk about. Members are sensitive to a screening process that distinguishes outsiders from insiders.

The models created to explain nature are rooted in culture—are very much a part of life—but are unavailable for analysis except under very special circumstances. The nonverbal, or unstated, realms of culture are extremely important as conveyors of information. High-context cultures are integrated, for members are skilled in thinking comprehensively according to a system of the common good. Loyalties are concrete and individuals work together to settle their problems. If one person has a problem, others are expected to know what is bothering him.

Low-context cultures emphasize literacy and rationality. Highly bureaucratized segments of culture within American life are "low" in context because information is restricted primarily to verbal communication. Other levels of awareness are underdeveloped or dormant. Ways of perceiving are restricted primarily to a linear system of thought, a way of thinking that is considered synonymous with truth. Logic is considered the only road to reality. Low-context cultures use primarily mathematical models to explain nature and environment. People are highly individualistic and somewhat alienated in contexts that require little involvement with other people. Low-context culture is fragmented rather than integrated, and people live more and more like machines. The contradictions that compartmentalize life are carefully sealed off from one another. Persons in

18. Edward T. Hall, *Beyond Culture* (Garden City, N.Y.: Doubleday, 1976). Grateful acknowledgment is made for permission to use excerpts from pp. 74–77 and 91–93.

low-context cultures are prone to use manipulation to achieve their goals and are also prone to be manipulated. Failures are blamed on the system. In times of crisis, individuals expect help from institutions, not from persons.

High- and low-contexting cultures emerge not through conscious design or because people are not intelligent or capable but because of the way in which deep cultural undercurrents structure people's lives in subtle ways that are not consciously formulated. It is the hidden currents of culture that shape the lives of people living under its influence. These differences are rooted in how people express themselves, the way in which they think, how they move, how problems are perceived and solved, how transportation systems function, and how people arrange their time and space. Edward Hall does not discuss high- and low-contexting within a single culture (American culture as a whole), but his scheme appears to allow for such comparisons.

What are the consequences when the Amish (a high-contexting culture) and low-contexting segments within mainstream America come together? There is no indication that they cannot cooperate in certain ways, but there are likely to be structured misunderstandings. Two illustrations will suffice to indicate some possibility consequences. One is based on information systems and the other on methods of training the young.

Information overload is a technical term applied to information-processing systems in which the system breaks down because it cannot properly handle the large amount of information to which it is subjected. Hall illustrates this with the case of the mother who in trying to cope with the demands of small children, run a house, live with her husband, and carry on a normal social life is suddenly faced with the feeling that everything is happening at once and that everything seems to be closing in on her. This American mother is experiencing the same information overload that afflicts business managers, administrators, physicians, attorneys, and air controllers. How the Amish and persons in mainstream American culture cope with information overload has important consequences. Amish culture provides a highly selective screen between itself and the outside world. The flow of information into the Amish community is highly selective. Furthermore, the Amish are keenly aware of their own screening process. Direct exposure to mass communication systems is greatly reduced. This screening protects members, and their nervous systems, from information overload. What the Amish pay attention to (contexting) and what they ignore are different from the choices of low-contexting cultures. Information overload is handled differently in the two cultures. Most Americans are exposed to large amounts of information daily and are scarcely aware of a screening process between themselves and the outside world.

The way children are treated in school will vary according to high- and low-contexting cultures or settings. In high-context cultures like the Amish, the young are effectively prepared for adult life by the family and community, and formal schooling is a minor part of their lives. The Amish teach their children social cohesion, practical skills, and social responsibility. This is accomplished in small groups, in small country schools where persons learn to know one another well. Each recognizes and knows the talents of the others. Learning is always interspersed with liberal periods of work and play. Children form close and lasting friendships, and they communicate well with one another and are effective in group processes. Studies of children in small schools (in groups of from eight to twelve members) show that the children are absent less frequently, are more dependable and more articulate, and find their work more meaningful than children in large schools.[19]

In the large American public schools children are subject to massive learning situations. It is well known that in such large groups natural leadership patterns suffer and that it becomes necessary to choose leaders by manipulation and political process. Children in low-context cultures suffer from overstructuring, overbureaucratization, and the compulsive need to consolidate and coerce social structures to fit budgets. According to Hall, organized public education in the United States has managed to "transform one of the most rewarding of all human activities into a painful, boring, dull, fragmenting, mind-shrinking, soul-shriveling experience."[20]

Whether one accepts this judgment of the quality of learning in the public schools or not, it is clear that preparation for life is very different in these two contexts. Both social cohesion and technical competence are essential for any society. The Amish emphasize values that generally supersede the emphasis on facts. By design, Amish schools are not suited for training artists, musicians, painters, and actors. The Amish school does not function as an institution for upward mobility in the modern industrial complex. By design, public schools do not teach children simplicity, humility, and the fear of God. State regulations for the approval of schools in American society take for granted the practices important to verbal articulation (low-

19. Ibid., p. 183. See also Jonathan P. Scher, ed., *Education in Rural America: A Reassessment of Conventional Wisdom* (Boulder, Colo.: Westview Press, 1977), p. 96.

20. Hall, *Beyond Culture*, p. 96.

contexting situations). The long conflict between state departments of education and the Amish is rooted in these deep undercurrents of culture.

THE VIEW FROM THE INSIDE

The Amish are real people, not simply an ideal type or a theoretical construct. Like all human beings, they use signs and symbols to cope with everyday life in order to make their world more meaningful and desirable. They are engaged in a social discourse with reality, the meaning of which is revealed in the analysis of the "unconscious" structure of their religious ideology. Such an analysis takes into account the mythological, the ritual process, and the charter of the community, and thus opens doors that aid us in comprehending how the Amish view themselves as a people and how they regard their mission in the world.

The Amish view themselves as a Christian body suspended in a tension-field between obedience to an all-knowing and all-powerful Creator on the one hand and the fear of disobedience on the other. The setting is the story of Creation in the Genesis account. God made all things, including the physical world, the animals and plants, dry land and sea, and after God had made man and woman he placed them in a perfect garden as stewards. Satan, the evil one, who himself had been cast out of heaven for his "pride," in a cunning way tempted Eve into taking a position of "knowing better than God." Through the temptation, both Adam and Eve fell into the sin of disobedience, and consequently all mankind acquired a disobedient or carnal nature which is under the curse of death. Meanwhile, man must suffer the consequences of having to earn his living "by the sweat of his brow" and woman must suffer the pain of childbirth (Gen. 3: 16–19). God provided a way of escape, however, for the spiritual side of man. He took pity on man in his sinful plight and provided hope by offering his son as a gift. By becoming a human being and suffering crucifixion and death at the hands of disobedient men, the Son of God became the medium of escape from spiritual death. Whoever believes and lays claim to the gift (the substitutionary suffering and death of the Son of God) can be restored to a spiritual or right relationship with God—he can attain eternal life after death of the body. The individual must acknowledge his natural state of disobedience, declare his helplessness without the Son of God, and surrender his will to the community of the believing.

This basic religious mythology, so common to the Semitic tradition, is, however, very different from that of other Christian groups. The

Amish have retained certain elements from biblical tradition and have combined them into a system that is relevant for them. Let us examine two of the important paradigms: *pride vs. humility* and *love vs. alienation.*

Pride leads to knowledge that is counterproductive to the knowledge of God. The knowledge that comes from disobedience to God comes from the "evil one" and will lead to the broad path of distruction. By contrast, the knowledge of God comes from obedience, and obedience leads to the narrow path of redemption. The Amish people's educational goals for their childen and their antipathy toward philosophical and worldly knowledge are grounded in this dialectic.

The love of God for sinful man requires an appropriate response. That response is "a brotherly community" living in obedience. The model for this "love community"—the life and teachings of the Son of God—emphasizes sacrificial suffering, obedience, submission, humility, brotherly love, and nonresistance. Not only is this community made up of surrendered members, but Christ himself is incarnated into the community, or "body." As a corporate offering to God, the brotherly community must be "without spot or blemish" (Eph. 5:27; I Pet. 1:19; II Pet. 3:14) and must be "a light to the world" (Matt. 5:14). Living in a state of unity and constant struggle to be worthy as "a bride for the groom" (Rev. 21:2), the community must be vigilant, living on the edge of readiness. Within the community the "gift" of God is shared and reciprocated among the members, for since God loves all, "we ought also love each other" (John 3:23). This reciprocation commits the members to an indivisible unity according to which each lives in harmony with all other members.

Separation must naturally exist between those who are obedient to God and those who are proud and disobedient. There is, therefore, a continuous tension between the obedient and the disobedient. The Amish are mandated to live separate from the "blind, perverted world" (Phil. 2:15) and to have no relationship with the "unfruitful works of darkness." The Amish are "in the world but not of it" and hence claim the status of "strangers" and "pilgrims" (I Pet. 2:11). As a believing community, the Amish strive to be "a chosen generation" (I Pet. 2:9), "a congregation of the righteous," and a "peculiar people" (Tit. 2:14) prepared to suffer humiliation or persecution.

Aside from the usual acts of admonition, indoctrination, and worship, ritual in the Amish community consists of maintaining the purity and the unity of the community. Unworthy members and those who are disobedient or cause disunity must be expelled, for they cannot be part of the "bride" offered to God. The "old leaven" must be purged from the group (I Cor. 5:7). Twice each year the church-community enacts the necessary ritual to cleanse and purify the corporate body through the observance of communion.

The charter of the Amish community, insofar as it affects the behavior of individuals, has great significance in everyday life. Loyalty to God is judged by obedience and conformity to the community's rules of discipline. These rules, enacted by the church-community, stipulate the ways in which members may interact with worldly and disbelieving members. The overriding principle is that members must not be "unequally yoked with unbelievers" (II Cor. 6:14). On such grounds business partnerships or conjugal bonds with outsiders are forbidden. Strife, war, and violence have no place in the community or in the life of the member. Members of the community cannot function as officers or caretakers of the political or world society. The community is guided by the teachings of the Son of God, by the recorded stories of the people of God from the time of creation, and by the rules of discipline.

The structural implications of Amish mythology and religious ritual are discussed in greater detail under "The Charter" in Chapter 4. The relations between language, though, and social action lie within the scope of structural analysis. The same myth may have different meanings for different groups. The significance of symbols so pervasive in Amish life, e.g., soil, preparation and fertilization of the soil for planting, manual work, fertility, "plain" living, productivity associated with animals, and the ritualization of the calendar year, has yet to be fully analyzed.

Myth in Amish society serves as a charter for social action, i.e., it becomes a by-product of a living faith and hence takes on a sociological character requiring group consensus, moral rule, and sanction. Myth institutionalizes the behavior of a society by enforcing traditions and norms. Acting as a charter, myth endows the society's values with prestige and supernatural force. It is not only a conservative force, perpetuating the status quo with powerful integrative functions as indicated by Malinowski, but it is also a language of social discourse which provides the members with purpose.[21] In times of social conflict and change, myth provides a language of argument using signs and symbols to establish meaningful distinctions from those of other groups.

21. Bronislaw Malinowski, *Magic, Science, and Religion* (New York: Anchor Books, 1954), pp. 144–46. For insights on myth as a social discourse, I am indebted to Abdul Hamid M. el-Zein, *The Sacred Meadows: A Structural Analysis of Religious Symbolism in an East African Town* (Evanston, Ill.: Northwestern University Press, 1974), pp. 195–98.

The models introduced here are offered as aids for comprehending the whole of Amish life. It is hoped they will help to place in perspective the complexity of the society and serve as a benchmark for some of the more detailed analyses that follow. The effectiveness of these models must be judged on how well they encompass and explain the material.[22] The description of Amish society is not limited to one or any of these models. All such models are incomplete and most elicit answers to objective questions asked from the outside. The view from the inside is offered throughout the ethnography so that the reader may come to understand the logic of Amish society.

22. The Amish as an ethnic group and as a minority group are discussed elsewhere. See Calvin Redekop and John A. Hostetler, "The Plain People: An Interpretation," *Mennonite Quarterly Review* 51 (October 1977): 266–77.

CHAPTER 2

The Birth of Amish
Society

🌿

THE AMISH are direct descendants of the Anabaptists of sixteenth-
century Europe and were among the early Germanic settlers in Pennsylvania. As part of a widespread counterculture movement of religious
reform, the Anabaptist movement[1] produced three groups that survive
to this day: the Mennonites of Dutch and Prussian origin, the Hut-
terian Brethren of Austria, and the Swiss Brethren. Named after their
leader, Jacob Ammann, the Amish are a branch of the Swiss Brethren.
In order to understand the origins of the Amish it is first necessary to
understand the role of the Anabaptists in the social context of religious
reform.

THE SOCIAL CLIMATE OF REFORM

Fundamental changes had been taking place in European society
long before the outbreak of the Reformation in the sixteenth century.
This unrest was articulated by able and dedicated spokesmen. Among

1. The literature on the Anabaptists is voluminous. I recommend first the
magnum opus by the Harvard church historian George H. Williams, *The Radical
Reformation* (Philadelphia: Westminster Press, 1962); and then the shorter, more
readable accounts of Walter Klaassen, *Anabaptism: Neither Catholic nor Protestant*

the prophets of a new way were Peter Waldo in Italy (founder of the Waldensians), John Wycliffe in England, and John Huss in Bohemia (forerunner of the Moravians), all of whom helped to set the stage for popular reform. Discontent was widespread. Traders and peasants found themselves displaced by the growing commerce with other parts of the world. People who had lost faith in the traditional institutions were ready to become followers of radical religious movements. For them, the old church was legalistic, irrelevant, and exploitive. The Catholic church had become the scapegoat for the social ills of society.

The astonishing variety of nonconformists in the sixteenth century demonstrates the seriousness with which people sought solutions leading to a better life. Following the invention of the printing press, people began reading the Bible for the first time. Some turned to following the teachings of the Gospels literally: because Jesus taught that a person must become as a little child to enter the Kingdom of God, some people literally behaved like children, playing with toys and babbling like babies.[2] One source lists the heretics of the period, and among them were the Adamites, who ran naked in the woods; the Free-livers, who had wives in common; the Weeping Brothers, who held highly emotional prayer meetings; the Blood-thirsty Ones, who drank human blood; the Devil-worshippers, who praised the devil ten times daily; and the Hypocritical Ones, who were indifferent to all liturgical ceremonies.[3]

Rebellion against old systems of authority gave rise to religious wars, to new territorial boundaries, and to a general reorganization of religious groups ranging from "right" to "left" in their attitude toward social reform. When Martin Luther wanted to discuss some of the practices of the established church, the church took a rigid position against changes. Following Luther's excommunication from the church, he found himself the leader of a group that later became the Lutheran church. Reforms more liberal than those of Luther were instituted by Ulrich Zwingli and John Calvin, who founded the Reformed church in Switzerland. Both of these Protestant groups, however, retained the concepts of a united church and state and infant baptism, and Luther

---

(Waterloo, Ont.: Conrad Press, 1973); and C. J. Dyck, *An Introduction to Mennonite History* (Scottdale, Pa.: Herald Press, 1967). The idealism of the Anabaptists is described in Harold S. Bender's classic "The Anabaptist Vision," *Church History*, March 1944, also published in pamphlet form by Herald Press, Scottdale, Pa.

2. Klaassen, *Anabaptism*, p. 2.

3. Henry A. DeWind, "A Sixteenth Century Description of Religious Sects in Austerlitz, Moravia," *Mennonite Quarterly Review* 29 (January 1955): 44. For a longer history of revolutionary millenarianism, see Norman Cohn, *The Pursuit of the Millennium*, rev. ed. (New York: Oxford University Press, 1970).

retained the mass in a modified form. These changes were still unsatisfactory to those who wanted more far-reaching reforms. Those seekers who wanted to take a more radical position and "reform the reformers" were called Anabaptists.[4]

The rejection of infant baptism became a symbol of the Anabaptist movement, a movement the authorities considered seditious. The term *Anabaptist* originated as a nickname meaning "rebaptizer." Rebaptizing was practiced by sincere seekers who felt that baptizing babies could not be supported by the Scriptures. They argued that sin entered the world with a knowledge of good and evil (Gen. 3). Since an infant does not have this knowledge, it cannot have sin. Thus, children do not need baptism for the removal of sin. Those who refused to baptize their infants were also seeking new ways of reforming the church. They expressed their displeasure with economic and social injustices.

Diverse groups of nonconformists flourished throughout Western Europe at this time, but the authorities did not distinguish between militant anarchists and pacifist believers. Both groups were labeled as seditious Anabaptists, as worthy of arrest, torture, exile, or death. To its enemies Anabaptism appeared to be a cancerous growth that would destroy Europe's religious and social institutions. The Anabaptists' beliefs were regarded as devil-inspired; their practices, odd and antisocial.[5]

THE SWISS BRETHREN

A small group of dedicated persons in Zurich, Switzerland, began to study the Gospels seriously and to propose reforms to the heads of state churches. Conrad Grebel, a nobleman by birth, had attended the universities of Basel, Paris, and Vienna. Felix Manz knew Latin, Greek, and Hebrew and spent much of his time preaching without authorization from the state, an action for which he was often put in prison. George Blaurock was educated for the priesthood. These men came to believe that the name "Christian" should be applied only to those who truly practiced the teachings of Jesus, and not indiscriminately to all who observed such state church rituals as infant baptism and the mass. Their reforms were rejected first by Ulrich Zwingli, head of the Swiss state (Reformed) church, and later by the Zurich City Council, and they were ordered not to disturb the unity of the church. But the small

---

4. The nature of this radicalism is set forth by Franklin H. Littell in *Origins of Sectarian Protestantism* (New York: Macmillan, 1964). See also Williams, *Radical Reformation*, chap. 11.

5. Klaassen, *Anabaptism*, p. 1.

group continued to meet secretly for Bible study and prayer. With full knowledge that they might be brought to trial by state authorities, they baptized one another into a new church-community, and commissioned one another as missioners to proclaim their newly founded "believers' church."[6] This church was to be separate from the state and membership was to be voluntary, free from the hierarchy and coercive power of the old church. Strong emphasis was placed on obedience to the words of Jesus, his teaching of love and nonresistance, and the imitation of his life and character. Christ was present not in the sacraments, they said, but in the body of believers who lived redemptive lives and practiced his teaching.

The small group in Zurich was arrested, imprisoned, and banished. Manz was publicly executed by drowning for the crime of rebaptism, Grebel died of the plague at the age of twenty-seven in exile, and Blaurock was burned for his heretical beliefs.

Another important leader, Michael Sattler, left his post as prior of a Benedictine monastery to become an Anabaptist evangelist. He presided over a secret conference of Anabaptist leaders in February 1527. The conference issued a declaration of "Brotherly Union" (since called the Schleitheim Articles) which became instrumental in structuring the character of the movement.[7] Its seven articles (abridged below) embody the Swiss Anabaptists' view of a Christian brotherhood living in a viable community.

THE SCHLEITHEIM ARTICLES

1. *Adult baptism*

Baptism shall be given to all who have been taught repentance and the amendment of life, who believe that their sins are taken away through Christ, and who desire to walk in the resurrection of Jesus Christ. This excludes all infant baptism.

2. *The ban*

After taking baptism as a sign of commitment to the fellowship, if any inadvertently slip and fall into error and sin, the ban shall be employed. First they shall be warned twice privately, and the third time publicly before the congregation (according to Matthew 18). This shall be done before the breaking of bread, so that all may in one spirit and in one love, break and eat from one loaf and drink from one cup.

---

6. For a detailed account of the founding of the first Swiss Brethren congregation in 1525, see Fritz Blanke, *Brothers in Christ: The History of the Oldest Anabaptist Congregation* (Scottdale, Pa.: Herald Press, 1961).

7. The conference was held in the town of Schleitheim on the Swiss-German border. For the text and critical discussion, see John Y. Yoder, *The Legacy of Michael Sattler* (Scottdale, Pa.: Herald Press, 1973).

3. *Concerning the breaking of bread*

Those who partake of the bread (the Lord's Supper) must beforehand be united in the one baptism and one body of Christ. Those who desire to drink in remembrance of the shed blood of Christ, cannot be partakers at the same time of the table of the Lord and the table of devils. All who have fellowship with the dead works of darkness have no part in the light. We cannot be made one loaf together with them.

4. *Separation*

We have been united concerning the separation that shall take place from the evil and wickedness which the devil has planted in the world, simply in this; that we have no fellowship with them, and do not run with them in the confusion of their abominations. . . .

Thereby shall also fall away from us the diabolical weapons of violence— such as sword, armor, and the like, and all of their use to protect friends or against enemies—by virtue of the words of Christ: "You shall not resist evil."

5. *Shepherds*

The shepherd in the church shall be a person of good report according to the rule of Paul, who can read, exhort, teach, warn, admonish and properly preside in prayer and in the breaking of bread. If he has need, he shall be supported. If he is driven away or martyred, another shall be installed immediately.

6. *The Sword*

The sword [government] is an ordering of God outside the perfection of Christ. It punishes and kills the wicked, and guards and protects the good. . . .

Within the perfection of Christ only the ban is used for the admonition and exclusion of the one who has sinned—without the death of the flesh— simply the warning and the command to sin no more.

The rule of government is according to the flesh; that of Christians, according to the spirit.

7. *Rejection of oaths*

The oath is a confirmation among those who are quarreling or making promises. In the old law it was permitted in the name of God. Christ, who taught the perfection of the law, forbids all swearing. One's speech shall be yea or nay. Anything more is evil.

Within a few years most of the leaders of the Swiss Brethren had died or been martyred. But the seven articles on which they had agreed are still basic guidelines in the lives of the Swiss Brethren and the Amish today.

Several years after the Schleitheim meeting, a priest in the Netherlands began to doubt whether the bread he held in his hands turned into the flesh of Jesus every time he recited the mass. He soon had second thoughts about infant baptism. By 1536, Menno Simons felt he had to choose between the authority of church tradition and the authority of the Scriptures.[8] The courageous example of the suffering and death of the Anabaptists around him was so compelling that he joined them. He preached, admonished, argued, and wrote long explanations of the Scriptures for the rest of his life. The high and learned doctors of the church, he said, were blinded to the simplicity and directness of the Gospels by many trappings: "legends, histories, fables, holy days, images, holy water, tapers, palms, confessionals, pilgrimages, masses, matins, and vespers . . . , purgatory, vigils, and offerings."[9] He felt that the observance of these matters was trivial and kept the people in ignorance of the real Christ. Menno Simons became the most important Anabaptist leader in the Netherlands in the sixteenth century. His followers were called "Mennists" or "Mennonites," and the name was later adopted by descendants of the Swiss Anabaptists who came to America.

Among Menno's friends who had turned Anabaptist were two brothers, Dirk and Obbe Philips. Dirk, like Menno Simons, wrote many tracts. Trained as a Franciscan monk, he had had a good education and had an excellent command of classical languages. In the interest of strengthening the new brotherhoods he wrote eloquently on church discipline, the ban, spiritual avoidance, and order within the church. His lengthy volume *Enchiridion or Hand Book*,[10] as well as *The Complete Writings of Menno Simons*, is prized and read by Amish and Mennonites today in both German and English editions. The Anabaptists were not content with merely changing a few rituals or with surface reforms. The newly formed movement was concerned with restructuring the religious order and creating its own cosmos. The Catholic church had maintained a social-religious structure that was built on the observance of the sacraments. The grace of God, dispensed through the proper hierarchy, was necessary for salvation. The Protestants—the Lutheran and Reformed state churches—emphasized creed and doctrine. Both Catholic and Protestant churches closely coordinated their religious structures with the political structure of a territory or region. The Anabaptists rejected such an alliance as un-Christian. For the Anabaptists, being a Christian meant voluntarily yielding one's sovereignty to a committed community, a spiritual brotherhood

8. For an evaluation of the teaching of Menno Simons, see Franklin H. Littell, *A Tribute to Menno Simons* (Scottdale, Pa.: Herald Press, 1961).

9. Menno Simons, *The Complete Writings of Menno Simons*, ed. J. C. Wenger, trans. Leonard Verduin (Scottdale, Pa.: Herald Press, 1956), p. 165.

10. Dietrich Philip, *Enchiridion or Hand Book* (1910; reprint ed., Aylmer, Ont.: Pathway Publishers, 1966).

of believers. The process of redemption required not only personal repentance and yielding to God but also forsaking "the works of darkness": wrongdoing, self-assertiveness, greed, and the uses of retaliation. As Christ suffered and died, so his followers must be ready to suffer. The qualities taught by Jesus in the Sermon on the Mount (Matt. 5,6,7) were to become the model in this redemptive community. The authorities perceived that the Anabaptists were building a new social order that was undermining their control. As Anabaptist groups sprang up in many places, imprisonment, torture, and harassment followed. The authorities argued that the Anabaptists refused to obey the constituted, God-ordained government. Protestant reformers, including Martin Luther, were disturbed by the irresponsible acts of the peasants, which culminated in 1525 in the Peasants' War and which were indeed a basic threat to a unified and orderly society. Panic provoked the Catholic and Protestant states to use military force against the peasants as well as the Anabaptists. For the Anabaptists, a martyr's death represented the supreme identification with Christ's "death on the cross."[11]

Living in a country dominated by the Reformed church, the Swiss Mennonites suffered persecution and oppression for at least two centuries. With the original leadership gone, succeeding generations settled into the hinterlands and valleys of the Jura and the Vosges Mountains and pursued an agrarian life. Here they managed to exist as conservative islands of sectarianism.[12]

THE AMISH BRANCH

The Amish division of the Swiss Mennonites owes its existence as well as its name to the elder of Markirch (Sainte Marie-aux-Mines), Jacob Ammann (Figure 1).[13] Little is known of him except that he was born in Switzerland and later migrated to Alsace, where he became an elder and spokesman for Anabaptists who had moved to that region.

11. See the enormous martyr book, *The Bloody Theatre; or, Martyrs Mirror*, comp. Thieleman J. van Braght (Scottdale, Pa.: Mennonite Publishing House, 1951). Originally published in Dutch (Dordrecht, 1660); also published in German.

12. For the agricultural and rural character of these communities, see Ernst Correll, *Das schweizerische Täufermennonitentum* (Tübingen: Mohr, 1925); and Jean Séguy, *Les Assemblées anabaptistes-mennonites de France* (The Hague: Mouton, 1977).

13. Ammann's role in the division is treated by Harold S. Bender in the *Mennonite Encyclopedia*, s.v. "Ammann, Jacob," and known facts about his person are discussed by Delbert Gratz in "The Home of Jacob Amman in Switzerland," *Mennonite Quarterly Review* 25 (April 1951): 137–39.

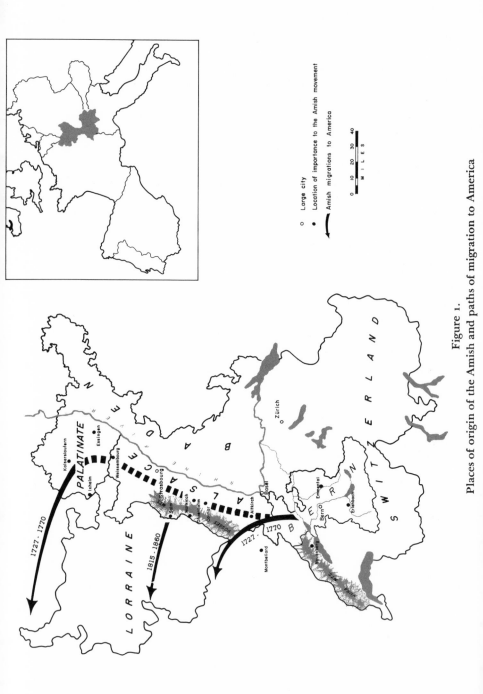

Figure 1.
Places of origin of the Amish and paths of migration to America

He is presumed to have left Switzerland in 1693 or earlier.[14] In a state document of 1696 he is cited as the spokesman for a group of members in the Alsatian area who were seeking exemption from military service. Compared with the major reforms that grew out of the Reformation, the division of the Swiss Brethren was a family squabble. The French sociologist Jean Séguy holds that the division grew out of certain tensions between the "mother" group in Switzerland and the "diaspora" in Alsace.[15] The chain of events leading up to the schism can be reconstructed from a number of letters that have been preserved, most of which were written after the events themselves had taken place.[16] According to the letters, the sequence of events was as follows:

Probably in July or August 1693, Jacob Ammann of Markirch advocated that communion should be observed twice each year instead of once as had been the custom. News of this innovation spread rapidly, and the majority of the congregations, including those in Switzerland, were faced with the question of whether to reprove or follow Ammann. When the issue was discussed in a meeting, the senior Swiss elders, Benedict Schneider and Hans Reist, did not squarely oppose the suggestion. They replied that the high priest in Old Testament times had entered the holy place yearly and that if anyone was worthy and could prepare himself twice, then twice was not too often. On the other hand, they said, if one is deserving, then yearly communion would seem to be sufficient.[17]

Ammann then turned from the observance of communion to the subject of social avoidance (*Meidung*). He insisted that members who had been excommunicated should also come under the censure of

14. An extant letter by Ammann states that he was in Alsace in 1693. See John B. Mast, ed., *The Letters of the Amish Division* (Oregon City, Ore.: C. J. Schlabach, 1950), p. 41.

15. Séguy, *Les Assemblées*, p. 256. I am indebted to Jean Séguy for important cultural insights, both from personal conversations in 1977 and from his comprehensive work, coming as they do from a prodigious scholar in the country where the Amish division occurred.

16. The letters are listed and discussed by Milton Gascho in "The Amish Division of 1693–1697 in Switzerland and Alsace," *Mennonite Quarterly Review* 11 (October 1937). The texts were published in German by Joseph Stucky in *Eine Begebenheit* (1871), by Johannes Moser in *Eine Verantwortung* (1876), and by the *Christliche Gemeinde Kalender* in 1908 (pp. 138–51), 1909 (pp. 134–41), and 1915 (pp. 121–24). L. A. Miller of Arthur, Illinois, published the Stucky edition with new material in 1936. English translations appear in John B. Mast, ed., *The Letters of the Amish Division* (Oregon City, Ore.: C. J. Schlabach, 1950). Several of the letters were translated into English (with comment) by C. Henry Smith in *The Christian Exponent* (April 11, May 9, June 6, and July 1, 1924).

17. Peter Geiger letters, in Mast, *Letters*, p. 69.

social avoidance. The Swiss Anabaptists had practiced excommunication in keeping with the Schleitheim Articles of Faith. But the Alsatians, unlike the Swiss, had accepted the Dutch or Dordrecht Confession of 1632, which in addition to excommunication also upheld social avoidance (*Meidung*) and the practice of foot washing. Articles 11 and 17 from the Dordrecht document[18] read as follows:

Article 11, Of the Washing of the Saints' Feet

We also confess a washing of the feet of the saints, as the Lord Jesus did not only institute and command the same, but did also Himself wash the feet of the apostles, although He was their Lord and Master; thereby giving an example that they also should wash one another's feet, and thus do to one another as He did to them; which they also afterwards taught believers to observe, and all this is a sign of true humiliation; but yet more particularly as a sign to remind us of the true washing—the washing and purification of the soul in the blood of Christ. John 13:4–17; I Tim. 5:9, 10.

Article 17, Of the Shunning of Those Who Are Expelled

As regards the withdrawing from, or the shunning of, those who are expelled, we believe and confess, that if any one, whether it be through a wicked life or perverse doctrine—is so far fallen as to be separated from God, and consequently rebuked by, and expelled from the church, he must also, according to the doctrine of Christ and His apostles, be shunned and avoided by all the members of the church particularly by those to whom his misdeeds are known, whether it be in eating or drinking, or other such like social matters. In short, that we are to have nothing to do with him; so that we may not become defiled by intercourse with him, and partakers of his

18. The Dordrecht Confession originated in Holland in 1632 as an ecumenical statement by a number of Dutch and Old Flemish Mennonite factions. (See *Mennonite Encyclopedia*, s.v. "Confessions of Faith," "Dordrecht Confession," and "Flemish Mennonites.") The document was printed and circulated widely outside the Netherlands in French and German. Thirteen of the Alsatian ministers and elders from eight congregations signed the Dordrecht Confession in 1660. (The document, with signatures, appears in J. C. Wenger, *History of the Mennonites of the Franconia Conference* [Telford, Pa.: Franconia Mennonite Historical Society, 1937], pp. 462–63.) Some signed it because they thought it was being universally accepted by their Anabaptist brethren (Jonas Lohr letters, in Mast, *Letters*, p. 18).

That it was signed by the Alsatian ministers does not necessarily indicate that they endorsed all its points, some of which differed from Swiss Mennonite practice. For example, Rudolph Egli signed it but spoke against social avoidance (Jacob Good letter, ibid., p. 58). Not all congregations that subscribed to the Confession practiced foot washing or social avoidance. Similarly, the Franconia Conference in America adopted the Dordrecht Confession in 1725 but never practiced social avoidance and began to practice foot washing only late in the nineteenth century. Because the document was printed and widely distributed, it was readily available for submission to governments that requested a statement of Mennonite beliefs. This fact may help to account for its popularity.

sins; but that he may be made ashamed, be affected in his ways. I Cor: 5:9-11; Rom. 16:17; II Thess. 3:14; Titus 3:10,11.

That nevertheless, as well in shunning as in reproving such offender, such moderation and Christian discretion be used, that such shunning and reproof may not be conducive to his ruin, but be serviceable to his amendment. For should he be in need, hungry, thirsty, naked, sick or visited by some other affliction, we are in duty bound, according to the doctrine and practice of Christ and His apostles, to render him aid and assistance, as necessity may require; otherwise the shunning of him might be rather conducive to his ruin than to his amendment. I Thess. 5:14.

Therefore we must not treat such offenders as enemies, but exhort them as brethren, in order thereby to bring them to a knowledge of their sins and to repentance; so that they may again become reconciled to God and the church, and be received and admitted into the same—thus exercising love towards them, as is becoming. II Thess. 3:15.[19]

Ammann advocated both avoidance and foot washing. Realizing that the congregations in Switzerland were not observing these practices uniformly, Ammann decided to visit their assemblies. He took with him three Alsatian ministers (Uli Ammann, Christian Blank, and Nicholas Augsburger). Ammann met with the Swiss elders rather hastily in a number of meetings. One of the senior elders, Hans Reist, had already decided not to practice *Meidung* and refused to take part in the meetings.

At each of the meetings the elders were asked to state their policies with respect to the practice of *Meidung*. If they agreed with Ammann's view, he demanded their attitudes on two other issues: whether true-hearted persons[20] would be saved, and whether persons who were guilty

19. J. C. Wenger, *The Doctrines of the Mennonites* (Scottdale, Pa.: Herald Press, 1950), pp. 80-83.

20. True-hearted persons were non-Anabaptist sympathizers called *Treuherzigen*, or "half-Anabaptist," and were nominal members of state churches. The controversy was whether these persons, because of their good deeds, would attain salvation. The German reads "Dass man die treuherzigen Menschen ausser Gottes Wort nich selig sprechen soll, die noch in den weltlichen Ordnungen stehen" (Ulrich Ammann letter, 1698). The true-hearted people aided the Anabaptists, giving them food and shelter, protecting them from the official "Anabaptist hunters," and in so doing endangered themselves, for Swiss mandates threatened and condemned these sympathizers. One observer wrote in 1690: "Great is the number of those who are suspended between heaven and earth, and know not what to do" (*Mennonite Encyclopedia*, s.v. "Half-Anabaptists"). Hans Reist composed several prayers for the true-hearted, "who love us and do good unto us and show mercy, but have little strength to come unto the obedience of God." See Robert Friedmann, *Mennonite Piety through the Centuries* (Goshen, Ind.: Mennonite Historical Society, 1949), p. 185; see also John Horsch, *Mennonites in Europe* (Scottdale, Pa.: Mennonite Publishing House, 1950), pp. 394-97. To Ammann, however, the true-

of telling a falsehood should be excommunicated. Ammann demanded unconditional answers, and he succeeded in polarizing the churches. At their first stopping place, Friedersmatt (near Bowil), minister Nicholas Moser agreed to the ban, but he advised Ammann to go and see Elder Schneider. Instead the delegation went to Reutenen (near Zaziwil), which was near the home of minister Peter Geiger. There Ammann called a meeting without notifying Geiger, who had retired for the night. When Geiger arrived later that evening, the meeting was about over. At neighboring Habstetten, minister Nicholas Baltzi was summoned and accused of teaching that true-hearted persons would be saved. Baltzi asked that the delegation be patient.

The investigating group then went to Eutigen, where it summoned Hans Reist to declare his position on *Meidung*. He answered, "What one eats is no sin; Christ also ate with publicans and sinners."[21] Avoidance at the table was wrong, according to him, for it is not what goes into a man's mouth that defiles him. His answers to this and other questions were unsatisfactory to Ammann.

At their next stop, Eggiwil, Ammann was informed by two elders that it would be best if the entire ministry would assemble and decide upon a general rule. Forthwith Ammann summoned the Swiss ministry to a meeting in Nicholas Moser's barn. Given such short notice, not all the ministers could be present, and when pressed for their attitudes on *Meidung*, some said they could not come to a decision until after the entire ministry had met. The only conclusion they reached was to call another meeting of all the ministers. Ammann wanted to hold the meeting in eight days, but Geiger wanted it in three weeks. Meanwhile, Ammann sent two men to visit Reist to ask him a second time about his stand on the *Meidung*. Reist stalled in giving a reply, but wrote a letter to several ministers saying he could not accept the *Meidung* and that "in matters concerning doctrines and church rituals, not too much attention should be given younger men."[22] He obviously meant Jacob Ammann.

While waiting for Reist to come to the second meeting in Moser's barn, Geiger again quoted the Scriptures: "What enters the mouth does not defile a man, but what goes out of the mouth."[23] Ammann replied that the quotation had nothing to do with the issue. Geiger then quoted another passage: "If ye bite and devour one another, see

---

hearted were "thieves and murderers" who were being admitted "by another way into the sheepfold, without the cross and without tribulation" (Mast, *Letters*, p. 38).

21. Mast, *Letters*, p. 69.
22. Ibid., p. 29.
23. Ibid., p. 71.

that ye be not consumed of one another."[24] He pleaded with Ammann not to bring about a division in the church. Meanwhile, some women were instructed to go and tell Reist and others to come to the meeting, but they returned saying that it was harvest time and these men could not come. Ammann interpreted their absence as an indication of their indifference.

Ammann, according to the account, became enraged. Taking a letter from his pocket, he read six charges against Reist, declaring him and six other ministers excommunicated. One of the women fell on her knees and in tears begged Ammann to be patient. He turned to Moser and asked his opinion of the *Meidung*, but Moser said he could not speak for his congregation since he had not asked their counsel. Ammann turned to Geiger for his opinion, but he replied that he could not give his opinion until all the ministers were present. Ammann then charged both of them with falsehood and took upon himself the task of excommunicating them. He next turned to Habegger, Schwartz, and Gul, and when they could not accept the *Meidung*, he excommunicated them. The meeting broke up and the Ammann party left without shaking hands. Geiger pulled Ammann by the shirt sleeve, saying, "Let me present my word also," but Ammann jerked his arm away and departed.[25]

Shortly after the dramatic meeting in the barn at Eggiwil, Ammann wrote a warning letter to the Swiss ministers demanding that by a certain date they appear and yield to his interpretations or prove them false. His warning letter in English translation follows:

JACOB AMMANN'S WARNING MESSAGE

Together with the ministers and bishops, I, Jacob Ammann, am sending this writing to everyone who is not already expelled by judgment and resolution [*durch Urteil und Rat*], both men and women, ministers and lay members, to inform you that you shall appear before us on or before February 20th to answer whether you can confess these controversial articles with us namely: to avoid those who are expelled, and the liars shall be expelled from the church, and that no one shall be saved, apart from the Word of God. Or if you can instruct us of a better way, from the Word of God, we shall lend you our ear. If you are unable to report by this appointed date, to confess these articles with us, or to point out to us another way from the Word of God, then we shall appoint another date, namely, March 7th, on which you may present your answer. But if you fail to appear, and answer at this appointed time, then you shall according

24. Ibid.
25. Ibid., p. 73.

Present-day Markirch (Saint Marie-aux-Mines), in Alsace, France,
near where the first Amish churches were formed

to my teaching and creed [*nach meiner Lehr und Glauben*], be expelled by
us ministers and elders, especially by me, Jacob Ammann, as sectarians
[*als sektische Menschen*], and shall be shunned and avoided [*gescheut und
gemieden werden*] until the time of your repentance according to the
Word of God. This paper shall be sent from one person to another to
make it known to all.

A.D. 1693[26]

In Alsace most of the congregations supported Ammann. On hearing
about the dissension, the elders across the Rhine River in the Palatinate
arranged for a meeting of both sides of the dispute. The meeting was
held on March 13, 1694, at "Ohnenheim (Alsace) in the mill." Despite
the willingness of the Palatines to negotiate their differences, no agreement could be reached. The Ammann party refused to compromise on
any of its demands and left the conference. The Swiss and Palatine
ministers issued a statement telling why they were unable to agree with
Ammann.[27] Ammann then excommunicated the Palatine ministers,
including numerous persons he had never seen. Thus the Mennonites
of Switzerland, Alsace, and southern Germany were divided into two

26. Ibid., p. 49.
27. Ibid., p. 50.

factions. Of the sixty-nine ministers who took sides in the division, twenty-seven sided with Ammann. Twenty of the twenty-three ministers in Alsace supported Ammann. One in Switzerland and five in Germany were sympathetic to Ammann.

In 1700 the Ammann or "Amish" party, as it was called, admitted that its methods were too rash and hasty.[28] The Amish party made an overture toward reconciliation by revoking its excommunication of the Reist group. Furthermore, its members "excommunicated themselves," anticipating that the Reist party would be humiliated into offering some gesture of reconciliation.[29] When the two parties met in conference, however, the Amish group was not willing to surrender the doctrine of *Meidung*. The Swiss Brethren contended that if the Amish group were to be restored into their fellowship, foot washing, as Ammann wanted it, would still be an issue. Some of the congregation doubted the motive of the Amish party and advised against reunification. With so many hurt feelings, animosity continued between the factions.

After the initial confrontations on social avoidance, it became evident that Ammann also attached great importance to the wearing of traditional, simple clothing, and to the avoidance of the grooming styles of the world. Ammann condemned the trimming of the beard and the wearing of fashionable clothing, and "anyone desiring to do so," he said, "shall be justly punished."[30] Although the use of hooks and eyes was not part of the initial controversy, it later symbolized their differences. The Amish were known as *Häftler* ("hook-and-eyers") and the Mennonites were the *Knöpfler* ("button people"). Such material differences provided members with a constant stimulus for social distance and consciousness of their differences.

In retrospect, what were the real causes of the Amish division? Personal ambition for leadership, perhaps even jealousy, has been suggested as the main cause.[31] Jacob Ammann appears to have been particularly inflexible, stubborn, and extremely sure of himself and his judgments. His signature, it has been pointed out, was that of a tough, pretentious, and headstrong man.[32] To understand the causes, however, we must place the controversy in wider perspective. As has been suggested, neither a purely psychological explanation nor a moral judgment is adequate.

28. Ibid., p. 89.
29. Ibid.
30. Ibid., p. 42.
31. Gascho, "The Amish Division," p. 51.
32. Séguy, *Les Assemblées*, p. 258.

The Alsatian Mennonites, immigrants of Swiss background, were experiencing tensions that were different from those they had known in Switzerland. When Ammann arrived in the valley of Markirch in Alsace, he found several practices that were dissimilar from those in the "mother" community. Certain demands were being made on the local Anabaptists. They had been pressed for but had refused service in the militia and in the *Heimburg*. A *Heimburger* was a local office-holder, a civil servant who acted in the name of the community for the common good, e.g., in the surveillance of roads and in the administration of the village. Whether the office was an elective one or was filled by local family heads taking turns is not clear. The Anabaptists had also refused the duties of watchman, which involved guarding against marauders. At any rate, Ammann was emphatic in declaring that the Anabaptists in that area "were not in a position to have one single member serve in the *Heimburg* in any area of the valley, or for their young boys to serve in the militia as some had previously done."[33] Ammann arranged for an exemption fee to be paid each year by the Anabaptists so that they would be relieved of the duties in *Heimburg* and in the militia. Thus Ammann found himself in the middle of severe tensions between his Alsatian members and the local authorities, and between the Alsatian and the Swiss Anabaptists.

The Alsatian immigrants and their children appear to have been a well-integrated social and self-contained religious community. There was, however, a tendency among them to be loyal to the local lords and princes who had provided land and a means of livelihood. This alliance represented certain dangers, not of persecution, but of compromise. Some had frequented Lutheran worship services. Lutherans also were a minority in this region, or tantamount to a free church, and there were fraternal associations between the two groups. It was in this context that the question about the salvation of true-hearted persons had arisen back in Switzerland. Ammann drew a sharp line, excluding from congregations those who attended state churches or who attributed salvation to the true-hearted.

Both foot washing and *Meidung* were practiced by the early Mennonites in Holland and were included in the Dordrecht Confession of 1632. Neither was practiced by the Swiss, nor were they included in the Schleitheim Articles of 1527. The controversy between the two groups reflected differences in their understanding of exclusion. The

---

33. Ibid., p. 130. Because of the exemption fee a list of family heads (presumably newcomers and residents) in Ammann's region has been preserved (*Archives Haut Rhin* E 2014, E 2808). See Jean Séguy, *Les Assemblées*, p. 130 and p. 163, nn. 69 and 70.

Swiss called the *Meidung* "a new doctrine," and the elders admonished their members not to adopt the new teaching.[34] Ammann argued with his colleagues: "If you want to look to the forefathers, then look to the confession of faith made in Holland in the town of Dortrecht."[35] The Reist group flatly denied that avoidance was practiced by Christ or his apostles, and called the articles in the Dordrecht statement "a statute of mortal origin."[36]

In taking a firm position, Ammann was attempting to teach an uncompromising gospel. He had no patience with the deliberations of those who would not make up their minds immediately. Aware of the dangers of compromise faced by the Alsatian congregations, Ammann demanded that all return to a stricter discipline. One result of this position was the creation of a cohesive group with a particular ethnic composition. By instituting communion twice yearly, the Alsatian congregations were able to exercise greater discipline over the lives of their members. Ammann's emphasis on orthodoxy and on more frequent practice of the rituals led to stronger cohesion but also to greater legalism. Ammann was able to win the Alsatian congregations to his views most likely because they sensed that their ranks needed to be firmly tightened if they were going to retain their distinctive identity.

JACOB AMMANN, FOUNDER

Jacob Ammann has remained a mystery with respect to his birth, family line, and date of death. Except for his role in the division of the Swiss Brethren, little is known about him. Archival sources have indicated that he lived at Erlenbach in the Simme Valley south of Thun.[37] Whether he was born here or only served as an elder at this place is not known for certain. He lived in Alsace from about 1693, when he began to serve the Anabaptist groups. His name appears as a co-signer on lists of Anabaptists (required by the authorities) who resided in the area of Markirch. One of his grown daughters was admitted into the state church by baptism at Wimmis, near Erlenbach, in 1730. According to this baptismal record in the archives at Bern, Jacob died outside the Republic of Bern before this date. A psalm

34. Mast, *Letters*, pp. 53, 54.
35. Ibid., p. 40.
36. Ibid., p. 19.
37. Delbert Gratz has summarized what has heretofore been known about Ammann, and dates reported in this paragraph are based on his work. See his article "The Home of Jacob Ammann," pp. 137–39. An inventory of Anabaptist property (most likely made between 1703 and 1708) shows that Ammann owned two cows and three goats (*Archives Haut Rhin* E 2089).

book that once belonged to Jacob Ammann contains a note written by Baltz Ammann saying that he inherited the book from his father. It is possible that Jacob was the son of Michael and Anna Rupp Ammann, born February 12, 1644, but it is not probable; he was called "a young fellow" by Hans Reist at the time of the division, and at that time he would have had to have been forty-nine years of age. In 1712 an order of expulsion disbursed the Anabaptist community in Markirch, although all its members do not seem to have left the area at that time. What happened to Jacob Ammann in those circumstances is not known.

The publication of an Ammann family genealogy in Zurich in 1975 provides the documentation for a new thesis about the lineage of Jacob Ammann.[38] A Jacob Ammann was born on February 19, 1656, and baptized as an infant as the third son of Jacob and Katharina (Leuenberger) Ammann, a farming couple, in Steingasse of Madiswil. Madiswil lies between Langenthal and Huttwil, also an area of Anabaptist activity in the canton of Bern. The compilers of the genealogy did not find marriage or death dates for Jacob, or any record of wife and children. They found a notation in the records that he had vanished from the community. The notation states that he had been a very diligent student in the village school, especially zealous in religion, and that he was so industrious that he completed his work a year in advance of his class. For this he was given a Bible and was advanced to the adult age group. It was noted that he later went to Alsace.

At the onset of the Amish division, this Jacob would have been thirty-seven years old. That age fits the description of Hans Reist, who referred to Ammann as one of the younger ordained men. Ammann is a common name in the canton of Bern, as is Jacob, but few Ammanns appear in Anabaptist records. Of the Ammann families who came to America, none are known to have been Anabaptists.[39]

Was Founder Jacob a convert to Anabaptism and not born of Swiss Brethren parentage? If born at Madiswil, we may surmise that after completing his schooling, he vanished from his community and became

---

38. Paul Ammann and Hans Ammann, *Aus der Sippe Ammann von Madiswil, Stammregister, 1612–1955* (Zurich, 1975). This work represents the combined efforts of father (Hans, 1874–1959) and son (Paul, b. 1901) over many years. I am indebted to Paul Ammann for genealogic data as well as for insights gained from a personal interview in 1977.

39. Several Ammann families came to Pennsylvania as well as to North Carolina after 1730. See Ralph B. Strassburger and William J. Hinke, *Pennsylvania German Pioneers*, 3 vols. (Norristown, Pa.: Pennsylvania German Society, 1934), 1: 417, 643, 665. See also A. B. Faust and G. A. Brumbaugh, *Lists of Swiss Emigrants in the Eighteenth Century to the American Colonies*, 2 vols. in 1 (1920; reprint ed., Baltimore: Genealogical Publishing Co., 1968), 1: 30, 45, 195; 2: 35.

an Anabaptist. To become an Anabaptist would have been a criminal offense, and therefore it would have been necessary for him to leave his native town. There would have been no recording of his marriage or the birth of his offspring in state church records, and therefore the information would be lost for future generations.

There are clues in the letters exchanged by the Ammann and Reist parties which suggest that Founder Jacob may have been a convert to the Swiss Brethren. This information provides insights into the psychological causes of the Amish division. Jacob was zealous, and perhaps ambitious, as stated earlier. He pressed for observance of communion twice yearly. New converts to religious movements are frequently more deeply committed to the observance of forms and are more sensitive to inconsistencies than are members of long standing. One wonders who in a frontier community (Alsace) other than a novice would have had the audacity to confront the old bishops in the home community (Switzerland) with radical changes in ceremonies and basic practices and to call these elders liars.[40]

The two extant letters written by Jacob Ammann reveal an authoritarian policy of church government more typical of the Reformed church than of the Anabaptists. This, too, hints that he may have been a convert. In his letter to the Palatine ministers, he addresses himself

40. Letters of Peter Lehman and Rudolph Huszer (Mast, *Letters*, p. 61). Animosity between Reist and Ammann is evidenced by name-calling. Reist "was an eminent man of considerable influence at that time" (ibid., p. 77). Ammann accused Reist of pride. Legal claim to a meetinghouse also was in dispute. Nevertheless, knowing what havoc the practice of social avoidance had wrought in Holland, the senior elders were unwilling to give Ammann a serious hearing. They had knowledge of its adverse effects (Jacob Good letter, 1699, ibid., p. 59). Menno Simons had supported not only excommunication but also social avoidance on the grounds of excluding the "Münster fanatics" and "the abominations of the perverse sect [polygamy, violence, apolyptic tendencies, and coercion]."

In Holland the early Mennonites practiced marital avoidance, whereby married partners were required to cease cohabiting when one was excommunicated. Leenaert Bouwens and Dirk Philips carried the practice to the extreme. Wives who were uncertain whether they should leave their husbands or stay with them were forcibly taken from their homes at night by the strict party. While innocent children screamed, the husband pleaded with tears that his wife should be permitted to stay with the needy children, but there was no pity. Some spouses lived all their lives without ever finding their mates. Married couples divided their money and children and went their separate ways. Menno Simons grieved deeply over this excessive discipline and disapproved of attempts to enforce marital avoidance in cases where the couple was not convinced by conscience that it should be observed (*Complete Writings*, pp. 1050, 1060–63). The South German churches emphatically rejected *Meidung* in the sixteenth century and many Dutch Mennonites joined the Reformed church as a result of the bitter factionalism.

as "I, Jacob" sixteen times,[41] a practice that is out of character for an Anabaptist letter writer. He attached great significance to the office of elder and to his convictions, and lesser weight to the counsel of the brotherhood. Decisions in the Reformed church were made by synods. In Anabaptist churches, major decisions were made by counseling first with the ordained and then with the assembled members.

Two other incidents suggest a difference from Anabaptist practice. When Benedict Schneider asserted that no one should be excommunicated except by unanimous counsel of the entire congregation, Jacob Ammann said sarcastically: "[It appears] as though the keys [of the kingdom] were entrusted to all lay-members."[42] In another exchange, Nicholas Moser stated that for the acceptance of a new doctrine by the whole brotherhood, "toleration will be required."[43] Ammann questioned this procedure, charging: "You are a minister and want to learn your faith from the congregation!"[44] Today there are no Ammanns among the Amish. We do not know when the name disappeared among them. In her adult life one daughter of Jacob returned to the Reformed church. If a convert to Anabaptism, it is possible that Jacob Ammann felt emotionally rejected by the ethnic character of the Swiss group. The facts are suggestive but inconclusive for this new thesis.

Our final source of information on Jacob Ammann is his own handwriting, his signatures, of which four have been found in archival sources (see Figure 2). At that time many people could not write their names, and signatures varied. Ammann's name occurs in many variations, and his signatures for the years 1701, 1703, 1708, and 1709 were, respectively, "Jacob Amen," "I. Amme," "Jacob Ami," and "I.A." In keeping with the German custom at that time, no distinction was made between "J" and "I," especially when capitalized. There was no "en" ending, in keeping with the custom of using a printed "E" (or a script capital "E") for "en." The encircled signature "I A" (1709) with the words "Marque Jacob Aman" in the handwriting of the scribe of the text assures the reader that it was indeed the mark of Jacob Ammann. Co-signers with Ammann in 1701 were Hans Zimmerman and Jacob Hostetler, and in 1703, Hans Zimmerman and Nikolas Blank. The signature of 1703 is distinct from the text of the manuscript, and since the writer was presumably Swiss, the signature is likely that of Jacob Ammann. Swiss names often end in "i," as distinguished from German ones, which typically end in "e" or "en." Jacob wrote his name both ways, Amen as well as Ami.

41. Mast, *Letters*, pp. 28–49.
42. Ibid., p. 32.
43. Ibid., pp. 102–3.
44. Ibid., p. 103.

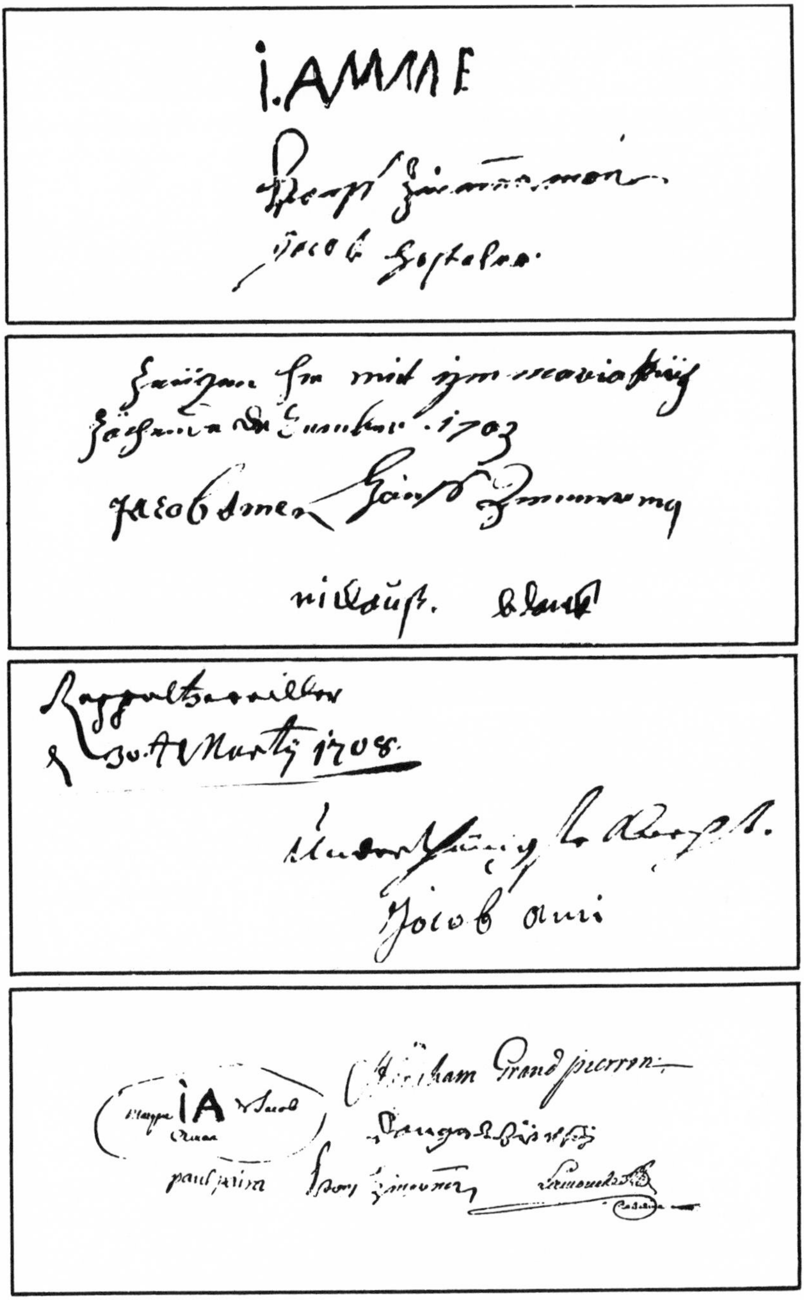

Figure 2.
Signatures of Jacob Ammann of Alsace

Jean Séguy, the French sociologist and researcher of Alsatian Mennonites, reviewed these signatures and offered the following comments in a letter: "Compared with the other signatures on the four documents, Jacob Ammann's own can be described as the most firmly written. Ammann makes his presence dramatically and theatrically felt in the way that he graphically manifests the consciousness he has of his own importance. He is a man who entertains outwardly no doubts as to his psychological and social identity. His signatures are of someone who claims leadership roles for himself, and tends to dominate over the people."[45]

Séguy also observed that only Ammann and the Alsatian officials used Latin. He says: "One cannot help asking the following question: Did not Jacob Ammann use the Latin rather than the Gothic script in order to convey the impression that he was culturally superior to his fellow Mennonites in Markirch, since he only could use the same script as the officials? Consequently, the use of Latin letters in his signature would mean that he was the man whom the local administration could trust. When he does use Gothic letters, as he partially does in the 1703 document, he still writes them in such a way as to make his signature appear in a class apart from that of the other Mennonite signers."[46]

With respect to the personality traits of Ammann, Séguy says: "The 1708 signature stands out as the least sophisticated." [Ammann is the only Anabaptist signer.] Could we say then, that when he did not feel competition around himself, Jacob Ammann could also be a simple, amiable person? It may have been the case after all. The variations and differences that can be observed in the four signatures of Jacob Ammann probably suggest that their author, on the one hand, was not a person given to the daily use of his writing pen; on the other hand, they also mean, I suppose, that the writer's personality was complex and contradictory."[47]

In view of the great emphasis placed on humility among the Amish, how do today's Amish regard the actions and innovations of Jacob Ammann? Some are frankly embarrassed by his harsh behavior and do not speculate further. Others regard him as a person who must have sensed the lukewarmness of his people and demanded a return to stricter rules. The social character of Amish life has much in common with the early Anabaptist practice of "brotherly love," which predated the Ammann era. This is evidenced by the books found in Amish homes today, e.g., the writings of Menno Simons and Dirk Philips, the *Martyrs Mirror*, and the *Ausbund*.

45. Personal letter, March 7, 1979.
46. Ibid.
47. Ibid.

Two Amishmen, Shem and David Zook, wrote in 1830: "The birth-place of Jacob Aymen we have not ascertained, nor yet the exact place of his residence—having never considered him a man of note, we do not deem the place of his nativity a matter of consequence."[48] In writing for his local newspaper in 1936, Eli J. Bontreger observed that the Amish church was observing its four hundredth anniversary.[49] The occasion was the year Menno Simons turned from the Catholic priest-hood to become an Anabaptist preacher.

The Amish people today regard themselves as Anabaptist, or *Wieder-täfer*, and most know nothing of Ammann. Through Ammann's influ-ence, however, they added foot washing, simple grooming styles, and social avoidance to the earlier basic Swiss tradition of brotherly love and brotherly union embodied in the Schleitheim Articles. The name given to the followers of Ammann was "Amish Mennonite" or "Amish," from the Swiss diminutive "Ami," though spellings vary in German and French sources. Early American usages such as "Aymennist" or "Aymeniten" were probably attempts to combine the phonetic features of "Amish Mennonite." The name "Old Order Amish" was never used in Europe but was a nineteenth-century label used in America to distinguish the traditional congregations from others.

THE DEVELOPMENT OF SEPARATISM

The Amish cleavage was not unlike the formation of other social movements. Certain characteristics are common to all leaders, prophets, or founders who establish dissenting movements.[50] Sectarian move-ments tend to emerge from the following conditions.

A *sectarian movement*[51] *must establish an ideology different from*

48. Letter dated November 26, 1830, in *Register of Pennsylvania*, ed. Samuel Hazard, vol. 7 (March 12, 1831), p. 162.

49. Eli J. Bontreger, "Amish Church Observes 400th Anniversary this Year," *Middlebury Independent*, June 8, 1936, p. 7. For a modern Amish view of Ammann, see David Luthy, "The Amish Division of 1693," *Family Life*, October 1971, pp. 18–20.

50. The natural history of dissident movements has been the concern of a number of social scientists. See Rex D. Hopper, "The Revolutionary Process: A Frame of Reference for the Study of Revolutionary Movements," in Ralph H. Turner and Lewis M. Killian, *Collective Behavior* (Englewood Cliffs, N.J.: Prentice-Hall, 1957), pp. 310–19. A more recent study is that of Ron E. Roberts and Robert M. Kloss, *Social Movements* (St. Louis: C. V. Mosby, 1974).

51. Sociologically defined, the sect is a movement of religious protest which tends toward perfectionism and exclusiveness from the dominant institutions of society. See the excellent treatment by Bryan Wilson, *Religious Sects* (New York: McGraw-Hill, 1970). For the distinction between "church" and "sect" as sociological types, see the classical work of Ernst Troeltsch, *The Social Teachings of the Christian*

that of the parent group in order to break off relations with it. Emergent beliefs tend to be selected on the basis of their difference from the parental group. They are essentially negative doctrines that state what the movement is against. Ammann succeeded in making *Meidung* a major issue that precipitated a cleavage.

The articulation of differences in belief by an enthusiastic leader claiming divine authority is an early condition necessary for the emergence of a sect. Beliefs are always articulated by persons who manifest leadership abilities. There is evidence that Ammann was both highly articulate and aggressive. Though Ammann had two other preachers with him on his tour of investigation, he was the main spokesman and relied upon his own inspiration rather than on authority shared by others who were with him.

A sense of urgency is vocalized by an authoritarian person who imposes negative sanction on opposing persons or groups. An appeal to patience and cautious deliberation made no sense to Ammann. In his view, the church was slipping farther and farther into worldliness, and could be salvaged only by immediate action. The founder of a movement acts on the basis of personal, charismatic authority, and not on authority delegated by the group. Ammann could not follow a middle course and he would not respond to those who fell on their knees to beg for patience.

The goals of a sect must be specific rather than general if they are to gain acceptance. Ammann's goals were specific and literal rather than general and philosophical. Most social movements are based on both kinds of motivation, but concrete goals are a vital ingredient in the initial stages of forming a movement. Broadly defined goals give room for personal interpretation, but specific goals demand uncompromising conformity. Ammann's specific and attainable goals defined a new order.

A sect must establish cultural separatism by invoking symbolic, material, and ideological differences from those of the parental group. The symbols of separation in Ammann's group took the form of different styles of dress, grooming, and physical appearance. For Jacob Ammann, doctrinal matters had to take on visible and explicit, not just "spiritual," character. *Meidung* was to be practiced not only at the communion table, or in spiritual matters, but in all areas of daily living and interaction. Nonconformity to the world meant not only a difference in thought and in the heart but also an outward material

---

Churches (New York: Macmillan, 1931). Such structural analyses are essential but are of limited value in explaining motivation and vision and how the subculture creates its own cosmos.

separation as characterized by Ammann's emphasis on the avoidance of "worldly" hair, beard, and dress styles. The example of Jesus washing the feet of His followers was to be taken not only spiritually but literally.

In the course of their natural history, the Amish have proved similar to other social movements in four ways: (1) they attempted to change or keep from changing certain beliefs or practices among existing groups; (2) they appealed to the people as a means of achieving their goals and thereby distributed responsibility among followers and leaders according to the vision or skill of the dominant leader, which resulted in (3) a geographical scope that transcended the local community and (4) persistence through time.[52] The Amish achieved all these features.

The persistence of custom, its slow response to change, is a distinctive feature of the Amish people. The pervasiveness with which the Amish literally adhere to their traditional religious practices is carried over into the social and economic aspects of their lives. Sociologists call this slow pace of change cultural inertia, cultural lag, or formalism. Through it we can observe how Amish society has remained relatively stable while the dominant society has changed radically.

52. C. Wendell King, *Social Movements in the United States* (New York: Random House, 1956), pp. 25–27.

CHAPTER 3

To America

ℳ

THE AMISH CAME to America as part of a much larger movement of Palatine German-speaking people, including the Mennonites and other religious groups. The Amish of today derive from two peak immigration periods, one in the eighteenth century (1727–1770) and the other in the nineteenth (1815–1860) (see Figure 3). Before the Amish became a separate body in 1693, several groups of Mennonites from the Netherlands and northern Germany had already found their way to Pennsylvania. The first permanent settlement of Mennonites was founded in 1683 in Germantown, which is today a municipal division of Philadelphia.

THE TORMENT IN EUROPE

The Anabaptist groups in Europe had encountered severe persecution, and conditions arose that forced numerous migrations. Those of Swiss background migrated primarily to southern Germany, France, and Pennsylvania, but small groups also went to Holland, Prussia, and Polish Russia. The Anabaptists were highly valued within the German Empire as skillful and productive farmers, but they were not given legal religious status. They were completely dependent on the good will of lesser rulers for a peaceful existence.

The lands north of Switzerland along the Rhine were sought by the Swiss Mennonites as a place of refuge prior to 1620. Today this area is known as Alsace in France, and Rhineland-Pfalz (the Palatinate) and Baden in Germany. Between 1671 and 1711 several hundred Swiss Anabaptists left the canton of Bern to find homes in Alsace and the Palatinate. Although the Amish were largely of Swiss origin, many of them lived in Alsace or the Palatinate before crossing the Atlantic.

A secret police force of "Anabaptist hunters" was organized to spy, locate, and arrest Anabaptists for their nonconformist beliefs. A Commission for Anabaptist Matters was formed by the Swiss government (and sanctioned by the Reformed church) to confiscate the property of the Anabaptists, enforce the mandates, determine the length of prison sentences, and decide who should be banished. Finding an Anabaptist leader yielded a higher reward than finding a member or sympathizer. Children of Anabaptist parents were declared illegitimate because the parents had not been married by a Reformed minister, and were therefore disallowed the inheritance of their parents' estates. The expenses of imprisonment, the work of spying and arresting, and the rewards for the secret police were all paid for through the sale of the property confiscated from the Anabaptists. Considered a threat to the land because they refused to serve in the military, take oaths, or baptize their infants, the Anabaptists were punished for their nonconformity in a variety of ways. Some were imprisoned, others were sent to Italy as galley slaves. Men were taken to the border, branded with hot irons, and threatened with death if they returned, but in spite of the threats, they kept coming back to their wives, children, and relatives.

Although some Palatine lords provided farming opportunities for the Anabaptists, the area was politically unstable. Located as it was in the very heart of Europe, between France and many German states, the Palatinate was the battlefield for the major wars of the seventeenth century. During the Thirty Years' War (1618–1648) the armies of both Catholic and Protestant forces played havoc with the lives and possessions of the people in this area. The Treaty of Westphalia (1648) provided that each prince was to determine the religion of his people. But the religions were restricted to Catholic, Lutheran, or Reformed. This resulted in further chaos, for the Palatinate was fragmented into small principalities, and populations that were Protestant were required to become Catholic and vice versa.[1] Those people who refused

---

1. Karl Scherer, Director of Heimatstelle Pfalz, a provincial archives of the Palatinate, states that within an eighty-square-mile area there were forty-four different sovereign ministates, each having its own laws, administration, monetary system, and units of measures and weights. In addition, he says, "there had been for about a hundred years continuous religious quarrels." Address to the Pennsylvania German Society, May 4, 1974, published in "The Fatherland of the Pennsylvania Dutch," *Mennonite Research Journal* 15 (July 1974): 25.

membership in the approved religions—and they included the Anabaptists, Huguenots, and Walloons—were called "sectarians" and were
driven from the country. Catholic princes turned against Protestants,
and both Catholic and Protestant forces turned against the sectarians.

The devastation of war, plunder, and fire was followed by famine
and pestilence. People ate roots, grass, and leaves. Some even resorted
to cannibalism. The gallows and graveyards were guarded. The bodies
of children were not safe from their mothers. Once flourishing farms
and vineyards were now raided by hordes of hungry people. In the
War of the Palatinate (1688–1697) Louis XIV ordered his generals
to devastate the area once again. These conditions precipitated the
great Palatinate emigration to America in the first half of the eighteenth century. The emigration movement encompassed many people
of every known faith in the region. Most numerous were the Lutherans
and Reformed, but there were Catholics, Schwenkfelders, and a variety
of mystics, as well as groups of Mennonites and Amish. All these groups
spoke the Palatinate dialect known today as Pennsylvania German or
Pennsylvania Dutch. Related to these refugees in faith and culture
were the Dunkards and Moravians, who also came to Pennsylvania in
the eighteenth century.

Mennonite emigration began in 1709, a year that was unusually cold
and severe throughout Europe, but the largest migrations of Swiss
Mennonites to America took place betwen 1717 and 1732, when an
estimated three thousand left the Palatinate to come to Pennsylvania.[2]
Many Palatines came to London expecting help from the British to
cross the Atlantic. Queen Anne had for several years been trying to
obtain colonists for unoccupied possessions in America, and had even
sent agents to the Palatinate for this purpose. William Penn had
traveled up and down the Rhine inviting oppressed peoples to come
to Pennsylvania. The Society of Friends in London helped some of
the immigrants to pay for their passage, and the Mennonites in the

2. For an understanding of Mennonite and Amish emigration, see C. Henry
Smith, *The Mennonite Immigration to Pennsylvania*, vol. 28 (Norristown, Pa.:
Pennsylvania German Society, 1929); and idem, *The Mennonites of America*
(Goshen, Ind.: By the author, 1909). For a general history of Swiss emigration, see
A. B. Faust, "Swiss Emigration to the American Colonies in the Eighteenth Cen-
tury," *American Historical Review* 12 (October 1916): 21–41. The latter was also
published in A. B. Faust and G. M. Brumbaugh, *Lists of Swiss Emigrants in the
Eighteenth Century to the American Colonies*, 2 vols. in 1 (1920; reprint ed.,
Baltimore: Genealogical Publishing Co., 1968). For an exhaustive bibliography on
Pennsylvania German emigration, see Emil Meynen, *Bibliography on German
Settlements in Colonial North America, Especially on the Pennsylvania Germans
and Their Descendants, 1683–1933* (Leipzig: Otto Harrassowitz, 1937).

Netherlands organized the Commission for Foreign Needs to aid their Swiss brothers with a variety of problems.

By 1699 the prisons in Bern were full and the Swiss authorities had to take action, either to deport the Anabaptists or to permit them to emigrate. European governments generally looked upon emigration with disapproval in the eighteenth century.[3] To leave one's fatherland was considered a sin equivalent to desertion and a shirking of one's duties. Martin Luther's translation of the Psalms (37:3) commanded the young to remain in the land of their forefathers and make an honest living.[4] Those who departed were considered an undesirable class of people. Moreover, Switzerland feared the loss of its population through emigration as much as it feared such loss by war or pestilence because one of the country's primary sources of income came from furnishing the powerful nations of Europe with young soldiers. For a price, these mercenary soldiers were provided by the wealthy Swiss noblemen to the warring countries of Europe. Soldiers from Switzerland fought on all the major battlefields of Europe, serving on both sides of a conflict.[5] To permit a liberal emigration policy would have provoked the powerful nobles, and granting military exemption to the Anabaptists would have instigated rebellion of the common people against the autocratic military system, a system widely disliked.

At about this time a scheme to deport undesirables was promoted by two merchants who organized a marine company called the Ritter Company. The Bern government became interested in the matter. Here was an opportunity to rid itself of two classes of people, the paupers (the homeless *Landsassen*), who were squatters but not citizens, and the Anabaptists.[6] In 1709 the Ritter Company was secured to take a boatload of Anabaptists and paupers to the Carolinas in America. When the vessel reached the Netherlands, the Dutch government (influenced by Dutch Mennonites) refused to grant passage to a vessel carrying passengers who were being deported against their will. The passengers were set free and guards were prevented from harming their prisoners. The Anabaptists visited their Mennonite brothers in the

3. Faust and Brumbaugh, *Lists of Swiss Emigrants*, p. 5.
4. Ibid., p. 4. Psalms 37:3 (RSV) reads: "Trust in the Lord and do good; so you will dwell in the land, and enjoy security." Luther's translation of the latter phrase is in the imperative: "Bleib im Lande und nähre dich redlich . . ." ("Stay in the land of thy forefathers, and earn an honest living therein"). The *Züricher* and *Froshauer* Bible (1535), widely read by Anabaptists, reads: "So wirdst du im Land wohen [wohnen] und es wirt dich wailich [wahrlich] neeren [nähren]" ("So you will dwell in the land, and enjoy an honest living").
5. Faust and Brumbaugh, *Lists of Swiss Emigrants*, p. 7.
6. Ibid., p. 2.

Netherlands and then most returned to the Palatinate. The captain, who had been promised 45 thaler for each Anabaptist he deported to America, was left without money or friends. Three of the Anabaptists went to Amsterdam and gave a full report of their experiences to the Mennonite Commission for Foreign Needs. One of these was Benedicht Brechbühl, a minister and elder from Trachselwald who later became a leader in the Mennonite emigration to Pennsylvania.

EIGHTEENTH-CENTURY EMIGRATION

Meanwhile, negotiations continued between the Dutch government and Bern over the plight of the Bernese Anabaptists. After many discussions it was agreed that emigration rather than forced deportation was the solution. The question was, emigration to where? King Wilhelm I of Prussia invited all the Swiss Anabaptists to his country, and it was also suggested that the Anabaptists settle the swamp areas of the Bernese territory. Finally, Bern agreed to allow the Anabaptists to go to the Netherlands and choose a destination from there. Meanwhile, the Dutch began to collect money for the emigration and to plead with the Bernese government to grant certain conditions: (1) to permit the Anabaptists to choose whether they wanted to migrate to Holland or to Prussia; (2) to declare a general amnesty so that the Anabaptists could come out in the open and sell their goods before leaving; (3) to appoint someone to care for possessions not sold before leaving; (4) to release all Anabaptists in prison; (5) to allow those who were married to non-Anabaptists to take their spouses and children with them; and (6) to exempt the Anabaptists from the ordinary departure tax. Most of the conditions were granted. However, released prisoners were to pay for their stay in prison, and those who were not steadfastly Anabaptist were to pay the 10 percent departure tax.

Five boats were prepared by the Ritter Company. The day of departure was set for July 13, 1711, but there were still other complications. Some did not want to leave their homeland; Hans Gerber, who did not want to leave, was sentenced as a slave to the Venetian galleys.[7] The Ammann and Reist factions did not want to travel together on the same vessel. Since the number of Anabaptist emigrants did not reach the expected total of 500, other passengers (paupers) were taken along. After a stay of four days in Basel, four boats sailed down the Rhine. A description of the sadness that came over the group is pro-

---

7. Ernst Müller, *Geschichte der Bernischen Täufer* (Frauenfeld, Switz., 1895), p. 300.

vided by Ernst Müller.[8] It appears that in spite of the cruel persecution, few of them wanted to leave. Many were suspicious of plans and promises made by the government. At various points along the Rhine, dozens of passengers got off the boat to join their brethren in Alsace and in the Palatinate. Later some of them found their way back to Switzerland. The majority of the Anabaptists who arrived in Amsterdam were of the Amish faction. Most of the Reist group had left the boats at various points on their journey.[9] A large warehouse provided temporary shelter for the group in Amsterdam. The citizens of Amsterdam came to see the emigrants, and collection boxes were set up to receive voluntary contributions for the refugees.

Before an investigative delegation of Anabaptists had returned from a tour of Prussia, the emigrants were taken to several Dutch Mennonite communities. There they were taken into the homes of the Old Flemish and Waterlander Mennonite groups. Preferring Holland to Prussia, the leaders of the emigrant group soon began to earn a livelihood as farm workers and dairymen. The Amish formed congregations at Groningen, Sappemeer, and Kampen. The small Reist group went to Harlingen, and declaring that it was difficult to fellowship with the Amish, returned to the Palatinate in 1713. The approximately three hundred Amish who settled in Holland maintained a small cultural island for almost a century, but eventually they acquired a Dutch language and their congregations merged with the Mennonites of the Netherlands. After 1720 the Amish in Holland split into the "Old" and "New" Swiss.[10] From visits and reports written by Hans Nafziger of the Palatinate in 1781, much has been learned about their disintegration before they were assimilated into Dutch life in the Netherlands.[11] There is no evidence that any of the Amish who came to the Netherlands in 1709 ever reached America.

Just when the first Amish came to America remains unknown. There is a possibility that some may have arrived with the Swiss Mennonites in 1710 when they bought from William Penn ten thousand acres of land comprising an area in Lancaster County known as Pequea (pronounced *peck-way*) Colony, but documentation is lacking. However, the area is heavily populated by the Amish today. Some Amish indi-

---

8. Ibid., p. 304.

9. Ibid.

10. The cause of the division was a house, called the "large monastery," the preacher Hans Anken had purchased. Its architecture offended some as being too ostentatious. See *Mennonite Encyclopedia*, s.v. "Anken, Hans."

11. Published in John D. Hochstetler, ed., *Ein alter Brief* (Elkhart, Ind., 1916). For an English account, see "An Amish Church Discipline of 1781," *Mennonite Quarterly Review* 4 (April 1930): 150–48.

viduals likely arrived in America between 1717 and 1736.[12] Then, as now, the Amish did not formalize the movement of their members, and as a persecuted group they did not keep formal records. Families were not prevented by church rules from moving if they wished. The Amish as a whole were very reluctant to leave their native Switzerland, a fact which is borne out by a careful study of the sources. It may well be that the first to come to America were those who were least dedicated and most opportunistic.

Arriving in Philadelphia on October 2, 1727, the ship *Adventure* had on its passenger list several typical Amish names.[13] Ten years later, on October 8, 1737, the ship *Charming Nancy* brought numerous families whose residence and genealogy can be established as Amish. As the first "Amish ship," it brought enough Amish to make an assembly or congregation possible. In this group were Jacob Beiler, Christian Burki, Hans Gerber, Christian Hershberger, Christian Kurtz, Jacob Mueller, Hans Schantz, and Hans Zimmerman.[14] Others who likely were Amish were listed as Erb, Garber, Hertzler, Kauffman, Lehman,

12. The tradition that the first Amish arrived in America in 1714 (a widow Barbara Yoder, whose husband had died at sea, and nine children, according to C. Henry Smith, *The Mennonite Immigration to Pennsylvania*, p. 225) is not borne out by recent genealogical and historical research. The "widow Barbara" story has been verified by genealogist Hugh Gingerich, but he claims she was an immigrant of 1742.

Immigration records between 1717 and 1736 contain names typical of the Amish, either of those in Europe before the immigration or of those in America, but it is virtually impossible to prove that they were Amish. For a discussion of these names, see C. Henry Smith, *The Mennonites of America*, pp. 154, 210; and idem, *The Mennonite Immigration to Pennsylvania*, p. 155. The task of identifying Amish immigrants has been facilitated by the publication of ships' passenger lists. The heavy influx of Germans into Pennsylvania alarmed the Engilsh, so in 1727 the Provincial Council required all vessels to submit a list of passengers. A declaration of allegiance to the King of Great Britain also was required of passengers. These lists date from September 21, 1727, and continue to the Revolutionary War. See Ralph B. Strassburger and William J. Hinke, *Pennsylvania German Pioneers*, 3 vols. (Norristown, Pa.: Pennsylvania German Society, 1934); and I. D. Rupp, *Foreign Immigrants to Pennsylvania, 1727–1776* (Philadelphia, Pa.: Leary, 1898).

13. Strassburger and Hinke, *Pioneers*, pp. 15–16. These names were Beydler (Beiler), Kurtz, Leman (Lehman), Mayer, Miller, Pitscha (Peachey), Riesser, Snyder, Stutzman, and Swartz. Names typical of the European Amish were Bowman, Hess, and Histand. Arrival dates of other persons with Amish-like names were Peter and Ulrich Zug (Zook), September 27, 1727; Johannes Lap, Johannes Reichenbach, and Johannes Slabach, September 29, 1733; and Jacob Hostedler, Johannes Lohrentz, Peter Rupp, and Melchior Detweiler, September 1, 1736. When Amish-like names appear on ship lists in clusters, they are thought almost certainly to have been Amish. When such names appear infrequently among less typically Amish names, their affiliation is considered more doubtful.

14. Strassburger and Hinke, *Pioneers*, ship list 49A, pp. 188–91.

Lichty, and Mast. The period of heaviest immigration appears to have been 1737–1754. By 1770, with the dawn of the Revolutionary War, Amish immigration had almost ceased, and few new immigrants came until the nineteenth century.

During the colonial period the Amish formed several settlements in Berks, Chester, and Lancaster counties (see Figure 3). Through the use of land records, tax lists, wills, and the alms books of the Amish, it is possible to ascertain the location of the early communities.[15] Most were named after a watershed or valley.

The Northkill settlement was situated in what later became known as Tilden, Upper Bern, Centre, and Penn townships in Berks County, and is presently west of Hamburg between the towns of Shartlesville and Centre Point. Berks County had just been opened for settlers the year before the Amish arrived, which may help to explain why they chose this area. As the largest of several Amish settlements in the country, it may have accommodated from 150 to 200 persons. In the same year of their settlement, however, several families (Erb, Gerber, Kurtz, Tschantz) went to Lancaster County. An Amish cemetery and a historic marker on the old residence of Bishop Jacob Hertzler, an immigrant of 1749, are still maintained.[16]

The Tulpehocken Valley settlement, in what is now Heidelberg and North Heidelberg townships, was occupied by Amish families from about 1764. A few families lived west of the town of Womelsdorf. A small cemetery is located on the farm that was occupied by John Kurtz, the deacon.

A third settlement, Maiden Creek Valley, was located near the mouth of Maiden Creek and the Schuylkill River in Maiden Creek Township. A small cemetery is located near Leesport. Amish families were scattered southward along the Schuylkill River to Shillington in the borough of Reading. Whether Maiden Creek, and those families living around Reading, constituted more than one district is not clear.

15. Documentation for the early settlements was gleaned by the author from the work of Grant M. Stoltzfus, "History of the First Amish Mennonite Communities in America" (M.A. thesis, University of Pittsburgh, 1954), published with the same title in the *Mennonite Quarterly Review* 28 (October 1954): 235–62. Additional help from Amish persons who have mapped the early Amish homesteads is gratefully acknowledged. See the continued series by Joseph F. Beiler, "Our Fatherland in America," in *The Diary* (Gordonville, Pa.), beginning in 1972, and another by Amos L. Fisher, "To Recall a Few Memories of the Past."

16. Immigrant Jacob Hertzler has long been considered the first Amish bishop in America. This appears doubtful, however, in view of the many Amish who arrived in 1737 and who depended upon the services of a bishop for performing marriages and conducting communion. For a history of the Hertzler descendants, see Silas Hertzler, *The Hertzler-Hertzler Family History* (Goshen, Ind.: By the author, 1952).

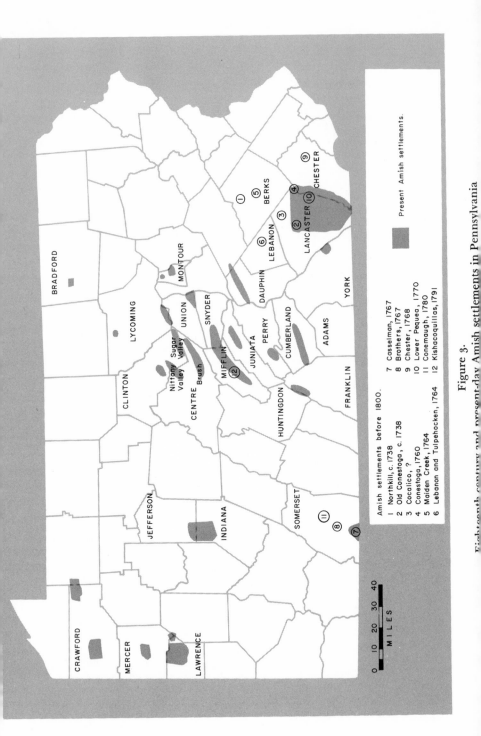

Amish settlements before 1800.

1 Northkill, c. 1738
2 Old Conestoga, c. 1738
3 Cocalico, ?
4 Conestoga, 1760
5 Maiden Creek, 1764
6 Lebanon and Tulpehocken, 1764

7 Casselman, 1767
8 Brothers, 1767
9 Chester, 1768
10 Lower Pequea, 1770
11 Conemaugh, 1780
12 Kishacoquillas, 1791

Present Amish settlements.

Figure 3.
Eighteenth century and present-day Amish settlements in Pennsylvania

The Conestoga Valley settlement, between Churchtown and Elverson, spans the corners of Chester, Berks, and Lancaster counties. From 1760 this region was occupied by families from the Northkill settlement who bought land from Welsh settlers. The region has been continuously occupied by the Amish since that time.

The Chester Valley settlement, located in Whiteland Township, Chester County, near Malvern, was founded by the Zook, Lapp, and Kauffman families in 1768 and continued until 1834. A cemetery and the ruins of an Amish meeting house remain near Malvern.[17]

Lancaster County, the location of the most densely populated Amish community in Pennsylvania today, contained three separate settlements in the eighteenth century. "Old" or "West Conestoga," mentioned in Amish writings and believed to have been occupied by some Amish as early as the founding of the Northkill settlement,[18] is located in Manheim and Upper Leacock townships. According to some accounts, there was also a Cocalico settlement, concentrated in East and West Cocalico townships and the nearby townships of Brecknock and Clay. This area is north of Ephrata and would have been near the Tulpehocken Amish in Berks County. The Amish may have settled here as early as 1742. In later years this area was occupied by Mennonite families. The "Lower Pequea" settlement around Whitehorse, Compass, and Honeybrook (largely in Salisbury Township) grew as the Berks County group declined before the close of the eighteenth century.

In addition to these communities, there is evidence from land records that many Amish families settled in Lebanon County in an area extending from the Tulpehocken community all the way to Dauphin County. The strong proselyting influence from other religious groups appears to have eventually destroyed the Amish in this area.

PROBLEMS OF THE EARLY COMMUNITIES

The early settlements were small, disbursed, and isolated from each other. Primarily agriculturalists, farm laborers, and tenants, most Amish emigrants had little means. There were, however, Amish people who bought land soon after they arrived. In Europe some had invested their resources in livestock-raising and in the improvement of their living houses. Some may have had savings until they were forced by war to leave.

17. See Maurice A. Mook, "An Early Amish Colony in Chester County," *Mennonite Historical Bulletin* 16 (July 1955). For photographs of the tombstones, see *Christian Living*, October 1956, p. 20.

18. Joseph F. Beiler, "Eighteenth Century Amish in Lancaster County," Mennonite Research Journal 17 (October 1976): 37.

Prior to the American War of Independence there were at least eight small settlements in Pennsylvania. The Amish probably came first to Lancaster County, but seeing that it was already settled by Mennonites, sought land in adjoining Berks County. They were soon faced with problems: assaults by the Indians, proselyting from other religious groups, and internal difficulties. Some Amish who were unable to pay for their passage came to America as redemptioners. Upon landing in Philadelphia, their services were auctioned to the highest bidder as payment for their passage from Europe. Canvassers, ship captains, and innkeepers tended to take advantage of simple and trusting emigrants. The traffic in redemptioners was profitable, and ship captains were prone to entice persons, including children, onto their vessels and to sell their services once they reached America. In this manner, Amishman Melchior Plank and his wife were brought to America. Philip Lantz, a boy of five, was kidnapped by a captain, brought to Baltimore, and indentured to Peter Yordy of Lancaster County.[19] Whether Yordy sought the services of the young man as a form of brotherly service is not known. According to tradition, Lewis Riehl (b. 1746), a boy of eight, was coaxed onto a boat and brought to America. Following a period of inhuman servitude in Philadelphia, he was attracted to "Germans" he saw on the street one day. They were Amish people. He later joined them.[20]

Little is known about the journeys of the Amish to America because few eighteenth-century diaries have been preserved. One fragment of a diary written by Hans Jacob Kauffman, a passenger on the *Charming Nancy* (arriving October 8, 1737), speaks of tragedy:

The 28th of June while in Rotterdam getting ready to start my Zernbli died and was buried in Rotterdam. The 29th we got under sail and enjoyed only 1½ days of favorable wind. The 7th day of July, early in the morning, died Hans Zimmerman's son-in-law.

We landed in England the 8th of July remaining 9 days in port during which 5 children died. Went under sail the 17th of July. The 21 of July my own Lisbetli died. Several days before Michael's Georgli had died.

On the 29th of July three children died. On the first of August my Hansli died and Tuesday previous 5 children died. On the 3rd of August contrary winds beset the vessel from the first to the 7th of the month three more children died. On the 8th of August Shambien's (?) Lizzie died and on the

19. C. Henry Smith, *Mennonites of America*, p. 172.

20. "Pioneer Life of Our Ancestors" (mimeographed history by descendants and relatives of the Riehl families of Pennsylvania, n.d., 6 pp.). For the literature on redemptioners and indentured servants see Meynen, *Bibliography on German Settlements in Colonial North America*, pp. 83–84.

An artist's conception of the ship *Charming
Nancy*, which brought the first major
group of Amish to America in 1737

9th died Hans Zimmerman's Jacobi. On the 19th Christian Burgli's child
died. Passed a ship on the 21st. A favorable wind sprang up. On the 28th
Hans Gasi's (?) wife died. Passed a ship 13th of September.

Landed in Philadelphia on the 18th and my wife and I left the ship on
the 19th. A child was born to us on the 20th—died—wife recovered. A
voyage of 83 days.[21]

The journey was a frightful ordeal according to Gottlieb Mittelberger, a Württemberger who came to America in 1750 and returned
to Germany four years later.[22] He speaks of thirty-six different customs
houses between Heilbronn and Holland, each involving long delays
and additional expense. In Rotterdam, he observed that people were
"packed into the big boats as closely as herring." He describes the
stench of fumes, dysentery, vomiting, and scurvy. Filthy food and water

21. See S. Duane Kauffman, "Early Amish Translations Support Amish History,"
The Budget, February 22, 1978, p. 11; and "Miscellaneous Amish Mennonite Docu-
ments," *Pennsylvania Mennonite Heritage* 2 (July 1979): 12–16. The diary was
found among papers of the late Dr. D. Heber Plank, who had translated it into
English. Other diaries include those of Daniel Gingerich, an emigrant from
Waldeck, Germany; see David Luthy, "Sailing to America, 1833," *Family Life*,
March 1974, pp. 14–18; Jacob Swartzendruber, *An Account of the Voyage from
Germany to America* (N.p.: By the author, 1937); and Delbert Gratz, *Bernese
Anabaptists* (Goshen, Ind.: Mennonite Historical Society), pp. 147–50.

22. Gottlieb Mittelberger, *Journey to Pennsylvania* (Cambridge: Harvard University Press, 1960), pp. 7–12.

were a major source of misery, together with lice, disease, and severe storms. Overcrowding gave way to stealing, cheating, cursing, and bitter arguments between children and parents, husbands and wives. On arrival in America, those who could pay for their journey were released first. Those who lacked the money to pay, including the sick, were held on board until their future labor was auctioned to the highest bidder.

On the whole, Pennsylvania's Quaker government maintained peaceful relations with the Indians until about 1755. Under pressure from the British citizenry, a chain of forts was established along the Blue Mountains, Pennsylvania's frontier during the French and Indian War. The Jacob Hochstetler family was one target of the numerous Indian attacks on settlers in the Northkill area. On the evening of September 19, 1757, after the family had retired, there was a disturbance. One of the boys opened the door and was shot in the leg. He quickly reached for the rifle but his father objected, stating that it was against their principles to take human life. The house was set afire by the Indians, and when the family escaped through the cellar window, the mother, a son, and a daughter were scalped. Jacob and his sons Joseph and Christian were taken captive. After several years of living with the Indians they managed to return.[23] The encounter with the Indians, it has long been believed, was responsible for the decline of this Amish settlement. There likely were other reasons for the movement of families out of Berks County, however, such as the influence from proselyting groups.

The Amish families were neighbors to other immigrants of other religions, including German Reformed, French-speaking Huguenots, and various pietistic sects, especially Dunkards. As a result many Amish families joined the Dunkard or Church of the Brethren religion. The Methodist revival movement that swept through Pennsylvania attracted the Amish and some became leaders in that denomination.[24] An Amish minister, Abram Draksel (Troxell) of Lebanon County, was silenced for making "too much of the doctrine of regeneration" and became a

23. For an account of the attack, see Harvey Hostetler, *The Descendants of Jacob Hochstetler* (Elgin, Ill.: Brethren Publishing House, 1912), pp. 29–45. Peter Glick, an immigrant of September 15, 1748, came to Berks County with a large family, but all except a son John died when their house was burned by Indians. The Glick families trace their lineage to John, who escaped the Indians by hiding in a hollow tree.

24. Grant Stoltzfus, "History of the First Amish Mennonite Communities in America," p. 254. See also C. Z. Mast and Robert E. Simpson, *Annals of the Conestoga Valley* (Elverson Pa.: By the authors, 1942), p. 88; and Joseph F. Beiler, "Revolutionary War Records," *The Diary*, March 1971, p. 71.

leader in the revival movement.[25] When the young began marrying non-Amish, the most devout of the Amish leaders began to regroup. By 1767 the Amish had begun three settlements in Somerset County in southwestern Pennsylvania.[26] Mifflin County had attracted families from most of the early small communities by 1791. The Stoltzfus family, immigrants of 1766, settled in Berks County but soon moved to the Conestoga Valley.[27]

To the Amish community the Revolutionary War was more disruptive than the assaults of the Indians. Amish genealogist Joseph F. Beiler writes: ". . . most of our initial ancestor families in America have not raised more than one son to remain in the old. faith. Some have not kept any sons in the church, some have kept a few. . . . After the war there was a steady flow of Amish converts to the Tunkers or Brethren, German Baptists and even to the Lutherans as well as the Moravians."[28] Before the Revolution, Beiler states, not one family pedigree showed that all the children had remained with the Amish church.

Had the early Amish settlers not relocated in order to solve their problems, such as finding adequate and productive land, stability and unanimity in church discipline, and leaders who were committed to Amish principles, it is doubtful that they would have survived at all. The early settlements are illustrative not of failure but of the trial-and-error process integral to ongoing community-building.

During the War of Independence from Great Britain, the Amish and Mennonites retained the principle of nonresistance. Their opposition to taking the oath of allegiance and joining the militia was interpreted by patriots as an alignment with the British. The Amish, unlike the Quakers, generally paid the war tax but disclaimed any responsibility for its use.[29] In refusing to take the Oath of Renuncia-

25. C. Brane, "Landmark History of United Brethren in Pennsylvania," *The Pennsylvania German* 4 (July 1903): 326.

26. The three settlements were (1) Conemaugh, including Johnstown, Pa., named after Amishman Joseph Schantz (see Maurice A. Mook, "The Amishman Who Founded a City," *Christian Living*, July 1955, pp. 4–7); (2) Brothers Valley (also called Glades), near Somerset, Pa.; and (3) Casselman, centered near Meyersdale and Elklick, Pa. The backgrounds of these settlements are discussed by Sanford G. Shelter, *Two Centuries of Struggle and Growth* (Scottdale, Pa.: Herald Press, 1963). See also Ivan J. Miller, "The Amish Community at Grantsville," *Tableland Trails* 2 (Summer 1956): 91–94.

27. See Wilmer D. Swope, *The Genealogical History of the Stoltzfus Family in America, 1717–1972* (Seymour, Mo.: Edgewood Press, 1972).

28. Joseph F. Beiler, "Revolutionary War Records," p. 71.

29. Wilbur J. Bender, "Pacifism among the Mennonites, Amish Mennonites, and

tion and Allegiance they were told that they would be disqualified from serving on juries, suing at law, holding public office, or buying and selling land. The Amish, along with the Mennonites and Quakers, refused the oath not only on religious grounds but also because they had promised allegiance to the Crown and feared perjuring themselves.[30] Several Amish people were charged with treason and were held in jail at Reading, Pennsylvania.[31]

The first communities were made up of clusters of families, most of whom were related by kinship ties. There was no overall or master plan of settlement. In fact, individualism and strong family autonomy seem to have had greater reign than church control. The behavior of some Amish was inconsistent with the tradition of the Amish as we know it today. Some married non-Amish neighbors, the color of their wagon tops was not yet uniform, and in Chester County the Amish built a meeting house. The long, intense voyages across the ocean may have resulted in alliances and friendships with persons who were not Amish. For many years a single bishop, traveling by foot and horseback, performed marriages and offered communion to scattered clusters of families. The Lancaster Amish settlement was not divided until 1843, nearly a hundred years after the first Amish families arrived in America. With the growth of settlements, the Amish ordained resident bishops, and thus church control began to be exercised over family and kinship rule. A new identity began to emerge as Amish were distinguished from non-Amish, and with this major trend, both religious and secular controversies began to plague the Amish people.[32] Families began to move to other settlements or regroup on the basis of a stricter or milder discipline.

Schwenkfelders of Pennsylvania to 1783, Part II," *Mennonite Quarterly Review* 1 (October 1927): 26, 46 n. 127.

30. It appears that the Amish petitioned the Provincial Assembly for exemption from the oath in securing naturalization. The Provincial Council passed a bill on November 11, 1742, naturalizing Protestants not of the Quaker faith (*Pennsylvania Archives*, p. 626). A copy of the petition appears in *Register of Pennsylvania*, ed. Samuel Hazard, vol. 7 (1831), p. 151; it was submitted for publication by Redmond Conyngham, who stated that it was written for the Amish by Emanuel Zimmerman and was submitted to William Penn on May 20, 1718. The date may have been in error, as C. Henry Smith writes in *The Mennonite Immigration to Pennsylvania*, p. 232 n. 35.

31. Richard K. MacMaster, Samuel L. Horst, and Robert F. Ulle, *Conscience in Crisis: Mennonites and Other Peace Churches in America, 1739–1789* (Scottdale, Pa.: Herald Press, 1979), chap. 7.

32. The trend toward church over family control was noted by James E. Landing, "Amish Settlement in North America: a Geographic Brief," *Bulletin of the Illinois Geographical Society* 12 (December 1970): 65–69.

NINETEENTH-CENTURY EMIGRATION

The second wave of emigration to North America from Alsace, Lorraine, Bavaria, Waldeck, Hesse-Darmstadt, and the Palatinate began in 1816 and continued until 1860, with a few latecomers arriving in 1880.[33] These settlers formed communities in Butler, Stark, Wayne, and Fulton counties in Ohio; Adams, Allen, and Daviess counties in Indiana; Woodford and Tazewell counties in Illinois; Henry and Washington counties in Iowa; Lewis County, New York; Somerset County, Maryland; and Waterloo and Perth counties in Ontario. Altogether there were possibly three thousand Amish Mennonite immigrants during the nineteenth century, in contrast to an estimated five hundred in the eighteenth century.[34]

Precipitating this migration were the unsettling conditions in Europe, the French Revolution (1789–1799), followed by the Napoleonic Wars until 1815, and various economic hardships. The European Amish learned that the Amish in America were not being molested but were prospering.

Most of the Amish immigrants of this period formed contacts with Amish groups upon their arrival in America. However, most never affiliated with the descendants of immigrants of the pre-Revolutionary period. The nineteenth-century immigrants found the American Amish more traditional than themselves. Several regional conferences were founded by the nineteenth-century immigrants, and many of their congregations later merged with the Mennonite Church.[35]

Today Old Order Amish descendants of the nineteenth-century immigrants live in Adams, Allen, and Daviess counties, Indiana, and in Perth County, Ontario. Although these groups maintain fellowship with the early Pennsylvania churches, they also perpetuate unique and distinguishing material cultural traits. The Amish of Adams County, Indiana, who came from Switzerland and from Montbéliard, speak a Swiss dialect. Families here still sing Swiss yodels that were common in Switzerland in the nineteenth century. The family names of those

33. No better description of the emigration of this period exists than that of C. Henry Smith, *The Mennonites of America*, pp. 275–92.

34. The estimate of five hundred is based on the ship lists and the first tax assessments in Berks County. Married family heads who appeared on the ship lists (from 1737 to 1749) and who also appeared on the first tax lists (1754) numbered approximately 102. Estimated at five persons per household, the total population would have been about five hundred. Estimated with the assistance of Joseph F. Beiler, 1978.

35. *Mennonite Encyclopedia*, s.v. "Amish Mennonites." See also Jean Séguy, *Les Assemblées anabaptistes-mennonites de France* (The Hague: Mouton, 1977).

who emigrated to North America during this period are distinct from those who came in the eighteenth century.

The Ontario Amish community began with the coming of Christian Nafziger of Bavaria. He landed in New Orleans in 1822 and after going to Lancaster County in Pennsylvania, was directed to Ontario. Here he secured a large tract of land for his congregation, which was still in Bavaria.[36]

The Amish port of entry in the eighteenth century had usually been Philadelphia. In the nineteenth century many of the Amish came to New Orleans and Baltimore in order to take advantage of low-cost transportation. When French ships came to New Orleans to obtain large amounts of cotton, they brought with them many German-speaking people who were eager to come to the United States.[37] The Germans continued their voyage up the Mississippi River. When the Germans began to trade with the United States they came to Baltimore for tobacco cargo, and they, too, sought out passengers for their westbound voyages.

THE FATE OF THE EUROPEAN AMISH

Today there are no Amish congregations in Europe that have retained the name and practices of the original group. The group's descendants in Europe have reunited with the Mennonites or have otherwise lost their Amish identity.[38] Some of the families and churches are aware of their Amish background, but it is only in North America that the name and distinctive practices of the Amish have survived.

The Amish in Europe were scattered and were unable to live in compact settlements because of economic and social factors such as the scarcity of land and the general intolerance for Anabaptists. Individuals and families who were either exiles or fugitives from the countries where they had been persecuted accepted asylum wherever they were tolerated. In Europe the Amish lived in Switzerland, Alsace, France, Germany, Holland, Bavaria, Galicia (Poland), and Volhynia (Russia). Geographic distance made association between families extremely difficult. Worship services, held in their own farm homes, took place monthly or every two weeks, but always at different places. Those who

36. Orlando Gingerich, *The Amish of Canada* (Waterloo, Ont.: Conrad Press, 1972).

37. Barbara K. Greenleaf, *America Fever: The Story of American Immigration* (New York: The New American Library, 1974), p. 57.

38. For assimilation in Europe, see *Mennonite Encyclopedia*, s.v. "Amish Mennonites." See also John A. Hostetler, "Old World Extinction and New World Survival of the Amish," *Rural Sociology* 20 (September/October 1955): 212–19.

lived within a short distance could attend the services, but they found it possible to come only once or twice annually. Under such conditions the scattered Amish families associated more with local non-Amish persons than with people of their own affiliation. The Amish who became renters or managers of large estates employed many laborers whose families also lived on the estate. The laborers, who were usually of a different religious affiliation, lived side by side with Amish families on the same estate. The Amish made no attempt to gain converts other than their own offspring.

With the passing of long years of suppression, the descendants of the Anabaptists changed their goals from reforms to ways and means of physical survival. It was under these conditions that they learned the disciplines of mutual aid, intensive agriculture, thrift, and toil, qualities for which they were later sought by emperors and princes to transform wastelands into productive soil. Thus the Swiss Brethren, including the Amish, became "the quiet people of the land" and formed agrarian cultural islands.

In Switzerland there were two settlements of Amish, one in the Emme Valley and one in the Lake Thun area. The Amish founded two other congregations, La Chaux-de-Fonds and Neuchâtel (Neuenburg), when there was a general emigration from the canton of Bern to the bishopric of Basel in the eighteenth century. There were still two Amish congregations in Switzerland as late as 1810, but they have since gradually lost their distinctiveness. In 1886 these groups still practiced foot washing, but by about 1900 they no longer called themselves Amish. They affiliated with the Swiss Mennonite Conference. The present Mennonite congregation in Basel (Basel-Holeestrasse) dates from 1777 and is of Amish background.

In southern Germany, Amish families lived in scattered places, but especially in the vicinity of Kaiserslautern. An Amish group from Alsace also settled at Essingen, near Landau. The Amish never developed large communities in the Palatinate, but emigrated in large numbers from the Palatinate to other points in Germany and to North America. In 1730 a group settled in middle Germany in the Hesse-Cassel region at Wittgenstein (later Waldeck), and in 1800 some settled in the Lahn Valley near Marburg. Small groups found their way to the vicinity of Neuwied and the Eiffel region. The groups from middle Germany, known as Hessian Amish, left for North America, and by 1900 all traces of the Amish had vanished from that area. A group from Hesse settled in Butler County, Ohio, beginning in 1817. The Waldeck and Marburg groups came to Somerset County, Pennsylvania, and Garrett County, Maryland.

Another group of Amish from the Palatinate, along with others from Alsace and Lorraine, moved to Bavaria near the towns of Ingolstadt, Regensburg, and Munich. Descendants of the Amish still live at Regensburg. The Amish who settled in Bavaria overcame many of the prejudices against them through diligent work and agricultural inventiveness. Because they were excluded from village life, they became tenants on large estates. Here they had more opportunity to experiment with farming methods than did the peasants with their few plots of ground and their deeply regimented economic routine. Their marginal nonconformity and marginal acceptance motivated them to work harder and produce more than non-Amish tenants, and this gave them the incentive to adopt new methods. Some of the descendants of the Bavarian Amish are today superior farm managers. Their distinct Amish organization was lost before the advent of the present century, but a few practices, such as foot washing, the wearing of the cap by women, and congregational autonomy, persisted longer.

In 1791 small groups of Anabaptists from the Palatinate and from Montbéliard, France, emigrated to Galicia (Poland) and to Volhynia (Russia), having been attracted to these areas by liberal offers from progressive noblemen who sought their agricultural talents.[39] They were few in number, and through intermarriage and close association with the Swiss Mennonites they lost most of their Amish consciousness before emigrating to Moundridge, Kansas, and Freeman, South Dakota, in 1874.

In the Palatinate, the Amish congregation that maintained distinctive practices the longest, including the use of lay preachers, strict shunning, foot washing, and the wearing of beards and hooks and eyes, was Ixheim, near Zweibrücken. Some of the older members practiced foot washing until 1932, but hooks and eyes were discarded before 1880. The congregation also served scattered families in the Saar. The Ixheim Amish were long called *Häftler* (hookers), while the nearby Ernstweiler Mennonite members were known as *Knöpfler* (buttoners), but consciousness of their differences largely disappeared in the twentieth century. The two churches were officially merged in 1937 and the Ixheim meeting house still stands as a private dwelling.[40]

In Alsace and its neighboring principality Lorraine, there are about three thousand Mennonites today who are descendants of the Amish. The Amish were formally expelled from the valley of Markirch in 1712. The natives complained that they did not have to bear arms.

39. *Mennonite Encyclopedia*, s.v. "Volhynia." See also Martin H. Schrag, *European History of the Swiss Mennonites from Volhynia* (North Newton, Kans.: Mennonite Press, 1974).

40. *Mennonite Encyclopedia*, s.v. "Ixheim."

Amish of Alsace and Bavaria. *Upper left*: Bishop Peter Hochstetler (1814–1885), born in Alsace, died in Bavaria. *Upper right*: Maria (Hage) Hochstetler, wife of Peter Hochstetler, in work garments. *Lower left*: Magdelena (Roggy) Güngerich (1815–1879), wife of Johannes Güngerich (1808–1886). *Lower right*: George Guth (1811–1897), deacon at Ixheim Amish Church, Zweibrücken.

A large farm estate in Altkirch occupied
by descendants of the Amish

The industry, thrift, and prosperity of the Amish Mennonites was related to the vigorous protest the natives made to authorities. King Louis XIV gave orders that only the Lutheran and Reformed religions were to be tolerated, and the Anabaptists were ordered to leave without exception. Many migrated to Montbéliard, Lorraine, Zweibrücken, and the German Palatinate. The Amish organized a strong community in the small province of Montbéliard,[41] where they lived on farms, many of which belonged to Duke Leopold-Eberhard. In spite of the displeasure of the native population, the duke gave them full protection, granting them exemption from the swearing of oaths, as well as permission to have their own cemetery and their own schools. Following the French Revolution, many of the Anabaptists in this area were able to become landowners.

41. Jean Séguy explains the background of this expulsion (*Les Assemblées*, pp. 133–37). See also Gratz, *Bernese Anabaptists*, p. 87. The *Gemeindebuch*, or church record book, from 1750 remains the property of the Mennonite congregation at Montbéliard.

The Amish Mennonites developed special farming techniques in France. Their industry and prosperity, together with their practice of magical healing, led to the notion among the French people that they had powerful secrets or gifts others did not have.[42] Their honesty, thrift, hard work, and productive capabilities made them all the more desirable to the landed nobility.

If all the Amish had remained in Europe, it is doubtful they would have survived at all as a cultural group. When they came to America in the eighteenth century, they found conditions favorable for growth and development. Land was available in unlimited quantities. They could live adjacent to one another on family farms and maintain relatively self-sufficient and closely knit communities. Under these conditions an integrated folk culture could develop and maintain an identity. Thus the Amish survived in the New World, emerging as distinctive, small, homogeneous, and self-governing communities.

42. Séguy, *Les Assemblées*, pp. 509–15.

Part II

Stability and Fulfillment

CHAPTER 4

The Amish Charter

THE AMISH have lived in America for approximately two and one-half centuries. During this time span they have formed unique communities, communities that differ from those in their European homelands. With privileges of landownership in America and freedom to move about at will, they have been virtually unrestricted in the develpment of their ideals. The Amish communities of today have syncretized many traditional elements of their material culture with elements in the New World.

We turn now to the organizing principles that support Amish community life. From the viewpoint of the Amish people themselves, we will describe the major elements in their world view and their view of themselves. The fundamental values and common ends recognized by the people and accepted by them have been designated as the charter.[1] The charter encompasses basic beliefs and a body of tradition and wisdom that guide the members in their daily lives.

The Amish view of reality is conditioned by a dualistic world view.[2] They view themselves as a Christian community suspended in

1. Bronislaw Malinowski, *A Scientific Theory of Culture* (Chapel Hill: University of North Carolina Press, 1944), pp. 48, 162. In a little community like the Amish one, the charter need not be reduced to writing to be effective.

2. For an elaboration of the Anabaptist "Doctrine of the Two Worlds," see Robert Friedman, *The Theology of Anabaptism* (Scottdale, Pa.: Herald Press, 1973), pp. 36–48.

a tension-field between obedience to God and those who have rejected God in their disobedience. Purity and goodness are in conflict with impurity and evil. The Amish view, however, differs from classic dualism, in which matter is set in opposition to spirit. The Creation account, as revealed in Genesis, encompassing a garden with animals, plants, and marine life, is viewed as good and for the benefit of mankind. The Amish are suspended between pride and humility (*Demut und Hochmut*), stewardship and greed, submission and disobedience. The Amish sanction marriage, family, and children, and a disciplined life in a disciplined brotherhood. The Amish rejected the European monastic system, which emphasized celibacy and a disciplined life expressed in a hierarchy. Monastics renounced personal property, although the wealth of the community was lavishly and symbolically expressed in great cathedrals and in elaborate altars. The Amish view personal property, expressed in farms and family dwellings, as a form of stewardship, but they carefully avoid any ostentatious display of wealth. The fruits of their labor are used to perpetuate community life through sharing, hospitality, stewardship, and underwriting the cost of an expanding population.

The rejection of worldly structures and the creation of their own cosmos is manifest in all phases of the Amish charter. The following description of the Amish charter will focus on *Gemeinde* as a redemptive community, separation from the world, the vow of baptism, *Ordnung* and tradition, excommunication and social avoidance, and closeness to nature.

GEMEINDE AS A REDEMPTIVE COMMUNITY

Amish fraternity is based upon the understanding of the church as a redemptive community. To express this corporateness they use the German term *Gemeinde* or the shorter dialect version pronounced *Gemee*. This concept expresses all the connotations of church, congregation, and community. The true church, they believe, had its origin in God's plan, and after the end of time the church will coexist with God through eternity. The true church is to be distinguished from the "fallen church."[3] Like numerous other Christian groups, the Amish hold that at some point in Christian history the established church became corrupt, ineffectual, and displeasing to God.

The church of God is composed of those who "have truly repented, and rightly believed; who are rightly baptized . . . and incorporated

---

3. Franklin H. Littell, *The Origins of Sectarian Protestantism* (New York: Macmillan, 1964), p. 55.

into the communion of the saints on earth."[4] The true church is "a chosen generation, a royal priesthood, an holy nation," and "a congregation of the righteous."[5] The church of God is separate and completely different from the "blind, perverted world."[6] Furthermore, the church is "known by her evangelical faith, doctrine, love, and godly conversation; also by her pure walk and practice, and her observances of the true ordinances of Christ."[7] The church must be "pure, unspotted and without blemish" (Eph. 5:27),[8] capable of enforcing disciplinary measures to insure purity of life and separation from the world. These definitions and conceptions of the church are ideals, the recognized purposes toward which the members strive. Community-building is central to the redemptive process; salvation is not an individualistic effort to be practiced when convenient or in keeping with one's personal definition. The aim of the Amish is to incarnate the teachings of Jesus into a voluntary social order.

SEPARATION FROM THE WORLD

The individual Amish member is admonished to keep himself "unspotted from the world" and separate from the desires, intent, and goals of the worldly person. Amish preaching and teaching draw upon passages from the Bible that emphasize the necessity of separation from the world. Two passages, perhaps the most often quoted, epitomize for the Amishman the message of the Bible. The first is: "Be not conformed to this world, but be ye transformed by the renewing of your mind that ye may prove what is that good and acceptable and perfect will of God" (Rom. 12:2). To the Amish, this means among other things that one should not dress and behave like the world. The second is: "Be ye not unequally yoked together with unbelievers; for what fellowship hath righteousness with unrighteousness? What communion hath light with darkness?" (II Cor. 6:14). This doctrine forbids the Amishman from marrying a non-Amish person or entering into a business partnership with an outsider. It is applied generally to all social contacts that involve intimate connections with persons outside the ceremonial community. This literal

4. *The Dordrecht Confession*, art. 8.
5. Ibid.
6. Dietrich Philip, *Enchiridion or Hand Book* (Aylmer, Ont.: Pathway Publishers, 1966), p. 86. This work by a sixteenth-century Anabaptist represents a comprehensive scriptural interpretation of the meaning of being Christian and the meaning of the redemptive process as understood by the Anabaptists.
7. *The Dordrecht Confession*, art. 8.
8. King James Version.

emphasis upon separateness explains the Amish view of themselves as a "chosen people" or "a peculiar peole."[9]

The principle of separation conditions and controls the Amishman's contact with the outside world; it colors his entire view of reality and being. By the precepts of Christ, the Amish are forbidden to take part in violence and war. In time of war they are conscientious objectors, basing their stand on biblical texts such as "My kingdom is not of this world: if my kingdom were of this world, then would my servants fight" (John 18:36).[10] The Amish have no rationale for self-defense or for defending their possessions. Like many early Anabaptists they are "defenseless Christians." Hostility is met without retaliation. The Amish farmer who is in conflict with the world around him is admonished by his bishop to follow the example of Isaac: after the warring Philistines had stopped up all the wells of his father, Abraham, Isaac moved to new lands and dug new wells (Gen. 26:15–18). This advice is taken literally, so that in the face of hostility, the Amish move to new locations without defending their rights.

Both the Amish and the Mennonites practice adult rather than infant baptism, nonresistance and the refusal to bear arms, the refusal to take oaths, and both generally refrain from holding public office. Religion is a total way of life, not a compartmentalized activity. The Amish today differ from the the main body of Mennonites in the extent to which external changes have affected the groups. Most Mennonites are more willing to accept changes and to incorporate them into their religious values.[11] Most are technologically modern, and they generally accept higher education. Furthermore, during the nineteenth century they founded their own institutions of higher education.

The Amish show little interest in improving the world that is outside their immediate environment. They profess to be "strangers and pilgrims" in the present world. The Amish interpretation of salvation differs in emphasis from that of modern fundamentalism. Belief in predestination is taboo, as is the idea of assurance of salva-

---

9. This concept was present in the Old Testament in the case of the Jews (Exod. 19:5; Deut. 14:2), and the Amish tend to apply the concept to themselves using New Testament passages I Pet. 2:9 and Titus 2:14. Max Weber observed that the notion of the "chosen people" comes naturally with ethnic solidarity and is a means of status differentiation ("Ethnic Groups," in *Theories of Society*, ed. Talcott Parsons, 2 vols. [Glencoe, Ill. The Free Press, 1961], 1: 305).

10. The teaching of nonresistance implies not only refusal to bear arms but an exemplary life that is not revengeful. See *Dordrecht Confession*, art. 14.

11. Excepted are the Old Order Mennonites, some of whom, like the Amish, use horses for farming and transportation.

ion. A knowledge of salvation is complete only after the individual hears the welcome words at the last judgment, "Come, ye blessed of my Father, inherit the kingdom prepared for you from the foundation of the world" (Matt. 25:34). Furthermore, the commands of obedience and self-denial are given more emphasis than is the teaching on "grace through faith alone." To assert that "I know I am saved" would be obnoxious because it smacks of pride and boasting. Humility (*Demut*) is highly prized but pride (*Hochmut*) is abhorred. Among the highly traditional Amish, Christ becomes a *Wegweiser*, "One who shows the way," and not merely one who has atoned for the sins of mankind.

Amish preaching and moral instruction emphasize self-denial and obedience to the teaching of the Word of God, which is equated with the rules of the church. Long passages from Old Testament are retold, primarily the crucial events in the lives of Abraham, Isaac, Jacob, Joseph, and Moses. The escape of the Israelites from Egyptian bondage and Moses's giving of the law are sermon themes. The choice put before the congregation is to obey or die. To disobey the church is to die. To obey the church and strive for "full fellowship"—i.e., complete harmony with the order of the church—is to have *lebendige Hoffnung*, a living hope of salvation. Thus an Amish person puts his faith in God, obeys the order of the church, and patiently hopes for the best.

Although separation from the world is a basic tenet of the Amish charter, the Amish are not highly ethnocentric in their relationships with the outside world. They accept other people as they are, without attempting to judge or convert them to the Amish way of life. But for those who are born into the Amish society, the sanctions for belonging are deeply rooted.

THE VOW OF BAPTISM

Membership in the Amish church-community is attained by becoming an adult and voluntarily choosing instruction and baptism. Baptism signifies repentence, total commitment to the believing church-community, and admission to adulthood. This vow embodies the spiritual meaning of becoming an Amish person, an acceptance of absolute values, and a conscious belief in religious and ethical ends entirely for their own sake, quite independent of any external rewards. This orientation to *Wertrational*,[12] or absolute values, makes

12. Max Weber, *The Theory of Social and Economic Organization*, trans. A. M. Henderson and Talcott Parsons (Glencoe, Ill.: The Free Press, 1947), p. 165.

In summer, worship services are often held in barns
rather than in houses. Here members
gather for a funeral.

certain unconditional demands on the individual. Members are required to put into practice what is required by duty, honor, personal loyalty, and religious calling, regardless of the sacrifice.

When young people reach late adolescence, they naturally think about becoming members of the church. In their sermons, ministers challenge young people to consider baptism. Parents are naturally concerned that young people take this step. In most cases, persistent parental urging is not necessary, since it is normal for young people to follow the role expectation of their peers. No young person can be married in the Amish church without first being baptized in the faith.

After the spring communion, a class of instruction is held for all who wish to join the church. This is known as *die Gemee nooch geh*, or literally, "to follow the church." The applicants meet with the ministers on Sunday morning at worship service, but separately. The Confession of Faith (Dordrecht) is used as a basis for instruction. The ministers very simply acquaint the applicants for baptism with the incidents in the Bible that suggest the right relationship with God and the right attitudes toward the community. After six or eight periods of biweekly instruction, roughly from May to August, a day is set for the baptismal service. The consent of the members is obtained to receive the applicants into fellowship. Baptism occurs prior to the fall *Ordnungsgemee* ("preparatory service"), which is followed by *Grossgemee* ("communion"). Great emphasis is placed upon the difficulty of walking the "straight and narrow way." The applicants are told that it is better not to make a vow than to make a vow and later break it; on the Saturday prior to baptism they are asked to meet with the ministers and there they are given the opportunity to "turn back" if they so desire. The young men are asked to promise that they will accept the duties of a minister should the lot ever fall to them. The following account of a preaching and baptismal service will serve to illustrate both the nature of the individual commitment and its community context:

It is a beautiful September morning. The sun shines brightly into the faces of the audience through large, swinging, red barn doors. The huge doors are propped open with sticks on the barn's sloping banks. The rows of benches on the barn floor are almost filled—men on one side and women on the other—except for two rows in the middle. To the right, behind the women, alfalfa bales are stacked high. A curtain of binder canvas is tacked along the side to prevent the stubble from scratching the women's backs and to improve the barn's appearance. To the left is a long granary, on the side of which the men have hung their large-brimmed black hats.

As the *Vorsinger* ("song leader") begins to sing the first song, the ministers, bishops, and deacons retire to a room in the house for consultation and to meet with the baptismal applicants for the last time. Here they will also agree on the order of the service for the day.

Between hymns there is a deep silence in the audience. The aroma of the haymow and the sounds of the birds and insects penetrate the consciousness of the audience. One can hear the horses munching hay below. While waiting for the next hymn to begin, the farm owner notices that it is too warm, and with some difficulty opens a second barn door on the side where the women are seated. The ventilation taken care of, he returns to his seat.

Several hymns are sung and the applicants for baptism—on this occasion six girls aged eighteen and upward—file up the barn bank and take their seats in the center section near the minister's bench. Both young and old intently watch the six young women who are ready to make their vows to God and the church, to say "no" to the world and "yes" to Jesus Christ and his *Gemein* here on earth. Each sits with bowed head, as though in deep meditation and prayer for the lifelong vow about to be taken. None dare to risk a glimpse at the audience or to gaze about, for it is a solemn occasion. Their clothing is strictly uniform: black organdy caps, black dresses, white organdy capes, long white organdy aprons, black stockings, and black oxfords. The fabric of the dresses and the color of ribbon bows at the left shoulder, faintly showing through the organdy capes, are the only evidence of personal taste.

The ministers now enter, quietly removing their hats. All seven, including several visiting deacons and bishops for this special service, offer handshakes to those nearby as they slowly make their way to the ministers' bench. They take their seats. The one who will make the *Anfang* ("opening address") sits at the head of the bench; the bishop who will give the longer message sits next in line. As soon as the ministers are seated the assembly stops singing.

Sitting silently in anticipation, the audience listens to two sermons. Two hours of intense waiting finally give way to the climax of the day as the bishop turns to the applicants with a personal admonition. The deacon leaves the service and returns with a small pail of water and a tin cup. The bishop reminds the applicants that the vow they are about to make will be made not to the ministers or to the church but to God. He requests the applicants to kneel if it is still their desire to become members of the body of Christ. All six kneel. The bishop asks a few simple questions[13] and each gives an affirmative answer.

After the applicants respond to the preliminary questions, the bishop asks the assembly to rise for prayer. He reads one of the simple prayers from *Die Ernsthafte Christenpflicht*, a prayer book of the Swiss Anabaptists.

The assembly is seated, but the applicants continue to kneel. The bishop, a deacon, and the deacon's wife proceed with the baptism. The three stand at the head of the line while the deacon's wife unties the ribbon of the first applicant's cap and removes the cap from her head. The bishop then lays his hands on the girl's head and says: *Auf deinen Glauben den du bekennt hast vor Gott und viele Zeugen wirst du getauft in Namen des Vaters, des Sohnes und des Heiligen Geistes, Amen* ("Upon your faith, which you have confessed before God and these many witnesses, you are baptized in the name of the Father, the Son, and the Holy Spirit, Amen"). The deacon pours water into the bishop's hands, cupped above the young woman's head, and it drips down over her hair and face.

Overhead, the pigeons flap their wings and fly from one end of the

---

13. The method of baptism is pouring, not immersion. Two sets of baptismal questions appear in *Handbook für Prediger* (Arthur, Ill.: L. A. Miller, 1950). An English translation appears in Harvey J. Miller, "Proceedings of Amish Ministers Conferences, 1826–1831," *Mennonite Quarterly Review* 33 (April 1959): 141.

barn to the other. A gentle breeze from the open door of the straw shed stirs up a cloud of fine particles of chaff and dust. An airplane roars in the distance.

When the rite of baptism is completed, the bishop takes the hand of each kneeling applicant in turn and greets her: *In Namen des Herrn und die Gemein wird dir die Hand geboten, so steh auf* ("In the name of the Lord and the Church, we extend to you the hand of fellowship, rise up"). The applicant stands up and the bishop then gives her hand to the assisting wife, who greets the new member with the Holy Kiss. All applicants remain standing until the last one is greeted, and then the bishop asks them to be seated. A few tears are brushed aside as they retie their covering (cap) strings. They will now be considered members of the church and will enjoy full privileges as members of the *Gemein.*

The bishop takes his former speaking position and admonishes the congregation to be helpful to the new members. He instructs those just baptized to be faithful to the church and to the ministry. To illustrate the importance of obedience, he retells the story of the idolatry committed by the children of Israel while Moses was up on the mountain praying, comparing Israel to the young people who throw parties and engage in other sinful activities while parents are away from home. He concludes the long sermon with the reading of Romans 6. Other ministers are invited to give testimony to his sermon, and three of the remaining six give brief statements of approval. After four hours the service ends in the usual way: everyone kneels for prayer, a short benediction is given, and a hymn is sung.

The text of the Amish vow is not significantly different from that required by Christian churches generally. What is significant is the promise to abide by implied rules not explicitly stated in the vow. By inference or otherwise, the strict Amish churches include in the vow the promise to help maintain the *Regel und Ordnung* ("rules and order") and the promise not to depart from them in life or death. "That's the way we have it in our church," explains one bishop. "It seems to me that every person should stay in church where he is baptized. He should never leave that group if he once makes a vow."[14] A more moderate view of the vow requires commitment to the true church of Jesus Christ, but does not imply a lifetime commitment to the particular rules and regulations of a given district. For instance, the late Bishop John B. Peachey said, "It is not right

14. John B. Renno of Mifflin County, Pa., in a personal interview.

to make the young people promise to stay with the *Ordnung* for life,
but rather with the teachings of the Bible."[15]

The difference in these two views can become very important in
case of excommunication. Social avoidance is implied in the former
but not in the latter. As a young man considering baptism in the
Amish church, I remember the above two opposing views being
expressed by two ministers. I did not want to take a vow I could
not keep, nor take a vow that implied social avoidance in case I could
not live by Amish standards. Consequently, on the day my chums
began their instruction for baptism, I drove my horse and buggy
to the nearby Mennonite church.

ORDNUNG AND TRADITION

The process of social ordering is embodied in the *Ordnung* (in the
dialect pronounced *Ott-ning*). These regulations represent the consensus of the leaders and the endorsement of the members at a special
meeting (*Ordnungsgemee*) held semiannually, before communion
Sunday, and are considered necessary for the welfare of the church-
community. All members know the *Ordnung* of their congregation,
which generally remains oral and unwritten. Most rules are taken
for granted, and it is primarily borderline issues that call for discussion at the *Ordnungsgemee*.

Two kinds of regulations must be distinguished—those made at
special conferences in history from the sixteenth century onward, and
the contemporary *Ordnung* of each church district. The former rules
have been printed,[16] but most contemporary rules governing the
district have not. The older rules clarify the basic principles of
separation, nonresistance, apostasy, and exclusion. The contemporary
Ordnung guides members in the application and practice of the
principles.

The *Ordnung* clarifies what is considered worldly and sinful, for
to be worldly is to be lost. Some of the rules have direct biblical support; others do not. Regulations that cannot be directly supported

15. John B. Peachey of Mifflin County, Pa., in a personal interview.
16. For published disciplines, see Harold S. Bender, "Some Early American
Amish Mennonite Disciplines," *Mennonite Quarterly Review* 8 (April 1934), which
covers the conferences of 1809, 1837, and 1865. For the conferences of 1779 and
1781, see ibid. 4 (April 1930) and 11 (April 1937); for "An Amish Bishop's Conference Epistle of 1865," see ibid. 20 (July 1946). See also *Christlicher Ordnung or
Christian Discipline* (Aylmer, Ont.: Pathway Publishers, 1966), and Miller, "Proceedings of Amish Ministers Conferences, 1826–1831." Other published tracts and
manuscripts are known to exist.

by biblical references are justified by arguing that to do otherwise would be worldly.[17] The old way (*das alt Gebrauch*) is the better way. A father who tried living in a newly formed Amish settlement "without the rigid traditions, where everything was figured out according to the Bible (or the understanding of the Bible)," found that "it didn't work." Following this experience he said, "I have a healthy respect for the traditions in the larger communities."

To be separate from the world is to be different from the world. Being different is more important, within limits, than specific ways of being different. The Amish, for example, feel some affinity to other Anabaptist groups (viz., Hutterite and Old Colony Mennonites) that differ from them in specific ways, but that maintain separation from the world. The strong commitment to the principle of separation from the world also helps to explain why the Amish are not disturbed by slightly different rules in other Amish communities.

The congregation must agree on *how* to be different from the world, for the body of Christ must be "of one mind." Twice each year the members must express their unity before communion. This unanimous expression of unity implies satisfaction with the *Ordnung*, peace among all the members, and peace with God. Unless there is a group expression of unity, the Lord's Supper is not held.

The rules of the Amish church cover the whole range of human behavior. In a society where keeping the world out is a primary goal, there are many taboos, and customs become symbolic, although they vary from one community to another. The most universal Amish norms in the United States and Canada are: no high-line electricity, telephones, central heating systems in homes; no automobiles; no tractors with pneumatic tires; beards are for all married men, but moustaches are not allowed. Required are long hair (covering part of the ear for men, uncut for women), hooks and eyes on dress coats, and the use of horses for farming. No formal education beyond the elementary grades is a rule of life, but there are infrequent exceptions to this rule.

Besides a means of separation, the *Ordnung* provides a communal means of managing the natural human tendency toward self-exaltation (*Hochmut*) and manipulative power. Through individual submission (*Gelassenheit*) to the community's will, members are able to contribute to a network of community relationships. Tendencies viewed as disruptive and dangerous—such as self-seeking, personal power, wealth,

17. For insights on the Amish practice of separation, I am grateful to Gertrude Enders Huntington, "Dove at the Window: A Study of an Old Order Amish Community in Ohio" (Ph.D. diss. Yale University, 1956), pp. 109–18.

and status—are channeled into a social order of love and brother-hood. Order and tidiness characterize the physical Amish community. Witness the well-tended gardens and fields, the well-kept buildings and lawns, and the laundry hanging out on the line in rows according to size and color.[18]

A contemporary Amish minister says of the *Ordnung*: "A respected *Ordnung* generates peace, love, contentment, equality and unity. It creates a desire for togetherness and fellowship. It binds marriages, it strengthens family ties to live together, to work together, to worship together and to commune secluded from the world." Concerning those who disobey, he explains: "We will always have members that, when they fall prey to sin, will blame the *Ordnung*. A rebelling member will label it 'a man-made law with no scriptural base.' We have a minority who resist the *Ordnung*. Obedience is a close associate to *Ordnung* for it is a symbol informing us whether the member loves the church or if he does not. One is either in the church or on the outside. There is no happy medium. In spite of an outsider's view that *Ordnung* is a law, a bondage of suppression, the person who has learned to live within a respectful church *Ordnung* appreciates its value. It gives freedom of heart, peace of mind, and a clear conscience. Such a person has actually more freedom, more liberty, and more privilege than those who would be bound to the outside."[19]

EXCLUSION: EXCOMMUNICATION
AND SOCIAL AVOIDANCE

In keeping with Anabaptist practice, to assure the purity and un-blemished character of the church the wicked and the obdurate mem-bers must be excluded from the group. According to Menno Simons, who vigorously taught that exclusion must apply to all without respect to persons, three classes of persons must be expelled from the believers' church: those who live in open sin, those who cause divisions, and those who teach a false doctrine.[20]

The German term *Bann* means excommunication. Social avoidance

18. I am indebted to Sandra Cronk for insights on the relationship of communal control of manipulative power through the ritual process ("Gelassenheit: The Rites of the Redemptive Process in Old Order Amish and Old Order Mennonite Com-munities" [Ph.D. diss., University of Chicago, School of Divinity, 1977], pp. 14–21). The emergence of an "Old Order" type in America on the basis of a search for *Gelassenheit* is a useful concept. There are some problems, however, in explain-ing the Ammann-Reist division with the *Gelassenheit* model.

19. Comments by Joseph Beiler, Lancaster County, Pa.

20. *The Complete Writings of Menno Simons* (Scottdale, Pa.: Herald Press, 1956), p. 94.

(*Meidung*), also called shunning, is the practice of restricting member associations with persons who have been excommunicated. The biblical instruction is that one neither "eat" with such a person nor "keep company" (I Cor. 5:11). The term *avoidance* is taken from Romans 16:17, where the apostle instructs the believer to "avoid" those who work against the peace of the church. The believer is advised in II John 10 neither to "receive into the house" nor to greet a person who advocates anything but a true doctrine.

In the sixteenth century social avoidance was exercised by the Anabaptists against fanatical groups such as the Munsterites, Baden-burgers, and Davidians.[21] Jacob Ammann introduced the practice to the Swiss churches, and as explained in Chapter 2, the result was the Amish division. The Amish today practice *Meidung* as taught by Ammann. According to Matthew 18:15-17, excommunication from membership is exercised after the offender has been properly warned and remains unwilling to desist from his transgression, divisive teaching, or rebellion. The ordained leaders attempt to be loyal to every instruction of the Word, to avoid offending the weak believers, and to cause the sinner to examine himself and repent. According to Matthew 18:18, the church of Christ has the authority to "bind" and to "loose" and to exercise the "keys of the Kingdom."

The affect of shunning on the life of the individual is illustrated in the life of a young man whom we shall fictitiously name Joseph. Joseph grew up in a very strict Amish home under the influence of parents who were known for their orthodoxy. He was baptized at the age of twenty. Three years after his baptism Joseph was excommunicated and shunned. Charges laid against him included the following: he had attended a revival meeting, associated with excommunicated persons, bought an automobile, and began to attend a Mennonite church.

Joseph was excommunicated in the presence of the assembled congregation after a series of warnings. At home, the young man could no longer eat at the family table. He ate at a separate table with the young children who were not church members. Joseph was urged by parents and ministers to mend his ways, to make good his baptismal promise. Several times he attended preaching services with his family. Since members may not accept services, goods, or favors from excommunicated members, he could not take his sisters to church, even if he used a buggy instead of his offensive automobile, but they could drive a buggy and take him along. It was not long until Joseph accepted employment with a non-Amish person and began using his automobile for transportation to and from home. When shunned friends came to his home for conversation, Joseph's parents met them at the gate and turned them away. It was not long until his father and mother asked him to leave home. He explained: "I had to move away from home or my parents could not take communion. My parents were afraid that younger persons in the family would be led astray. They didn't exactly chase me off the place, but I was no longer welcome at home."

Persons who acknowledge their sins and wish to make amends are received back into the fellowship usually within two or three weeks. For minor offenses, such as flaunting the dress codes or exchanging hostile words with another person, the offender makes a formal apology to the church. For major offenses such as adultery, fornication, or teaching heresy, the offenders must confess their error while kneeling, and are only then restored into the church by the welcome hand of the bishop.

Among Amish communities today, differing views on shunning have led to numerous divisions. The moderate interpretation, taken by many of the "milder" groups, holds that moral transgressors should be excommunicated and shunned, but if the offender is restored to some other congregation or branch of the pacifist Anabaptist faith, then shunning should be discontinued. But this, according to the adherents of "strict" shunning, is a departure from Ammann's teaching. In speaking of a former Amish member who joined the Mennonites, a bishop explained: "The only way for us to lift the ban is for him to make peace with the Old Order church, going back and living his promise made on his knees before God and the church."[22] According to this view, an excommunicated person must be shunned for life unless he restores his previous relationship with the group. By shunning him in all social relations, the community gives him a status that minimizes the threat to other members of the community. This perpetuation of the controversy undoubtedly helps the Old Order group to remain distinct and socially intact.

The Amish make no effort to evangelize or proselyte the outsider. It is their primary concern to keep their own baptized members from slipping into the outer world, or into other religious groups. With greater mobility and ease of travel and communication, Amish solidarity is threatened. Members who may wish to have automobiles, radios, or the usual comforts of modern living face the threat of being excommunicated and shunned. Thus the ban is used as an instrument

22. John B. Renno, letter of October 19, 1950.

Farming is a moral directive and is generally a meaningful experience
for the entire family. This farm is located
in Holmes County, Ohio.

of discipline not only for the drunkard or the adulterer but for the
person who transgresses the *Ordnung*. It is a powerful instrument for
preventing involvement in outside loyalties.

CLOSENESS TO NATURE

The Amish have a strong affinity for the soil and for nature. Working with the soil was not one of the original issues that gave rise to
the Anabaptist movement or the Amish group, but was a basic value
acquired during the process of survival. As persecuted people, the
Amish found it possible to survive in the hinterlands, and there they
developed unique skills for crop production and livestock-raising.[23]

23. For the ingenious agrarian development of the Anabaptist groups in Europe,
see especially Ernst Correll, *Das schweizerische Täufermennonitentum* (Tübingen:
Mohr, 1925); and Jean Séguy, *Les Assemblées anabaptistes-mennonites de France*
(The Hague: Mouton, 1977).

Harvesting wheat in the traditional way. Farming requires
commitment and cooperation among family members.

In America the Amish perpetuated the skills they had acquired in
the valleys of Switzerland, France, and Germany.

The physical world is considered good, and in itself is not cor-
rupting or evil. Its beauty is apparent in the universe, in the orderliness of the seasons, the heavens, in the world of living plants as well
as in the many species of animals, and in the forces of living and
dying. It is not uncommon to see an Amish family visiting the zoo
in a large metropolitan area. Animals are considered part of the
Creation, and those not found on Amish farms are of great interest.

The charter of Amish life requires members to limit their occupation to farming or closely associated activities such as operating a
saw mill, carpentry, or masonry. The Amishman feels contact with
the material world through the working of his muscles and the aching

of his limbs. In the little Amish community, toil is proper and good, religion provides meaning, and the bonds of family and church provide human satisfaction and love. In Europe the Amish lived in rural areas, always in close association with the soil, so their communities were largely agrarian in character. It is in America that they have found it necessary to make occupational regulations for protection from the influence of urbanism.

The preference for rural living is reflected in attitudes and in informal interactions rather than in an explicit dogma. For the Amish, God is manifest more in closeness to nature, in the soil and the weather, and among plants and animals than in the man-made city. Hard work, thrift, and mutual aid find sanction in the Bible. The city, by contrast, is held to be the center of leisure, of nonproductive spending, and often of wickedness. The Christian life is best maintained away from the cities. God created Adam and Eve to "replenish the earth, and subdue it; and have dominion over the fish of the sea, and over the fowl of the air, and over every living thing that moveth upon the earth" (Gen. 1:28). In the same way, man's highest calling in the universe today is to care for the things of creation. One Amishman said, "The Lord told Adam to replenish the earth and to rule over the animals and the land—you can't do that in cities." Another said, "While the Lord's blessings were given to the people who remained in the country, sickness and ruination befell Sodom. Shows, dances, parties, and other temptations ruin even the good people who now live in cities. Families are small in cities; in the city you never know where your wife is, and city women can't cook. People go hungry in the cities but you will never starve if you work hard in the country."[24]

The Amish have generally prospered on the land more often than their neighbors. Lancaster County, Pennsylvania—a center of Amish life—has long been distinguished as the garden spot of the nation. The product of an intensive kind of farming on relatively small holdings, it reflects long experience with agricultural practices of the Old World and a philosophy of work and thrift. Some Pennsylvania landowners occupy farms that were acquired directly from William Penn or his land agent. As farms have been handed down from father to son, so have the experiences and the wisdom associated with the care of livestock and farming. The Amish attribute their material success in farming to divine blessing.

24. Quotation is from Walter M. Kollmorgen, *Culture of a Contemporary Community: The Old Order Amish of Lancaster County, Pennsylvania*, Rural Life Studies no. 4 (Washington, D.C.: U.S. Department of Agriculture, 1942), p. 23.

The main objective of their farming, as Walter Kollmorgen has pointed out, "is to accumulate sufficient means to buy enough land to keep all the children on farms. To this end the Amish work hard, produce abundantly, and save extensively."[25] Farming is a subject of Amish conversation and their concern for it is reflected in their publications. Topics customarily covered in *The Budget*, a weekly newspaper, are the weather, seeding, planting activity, and harvest. In springtime we read that "farmers were busy in the fields last week." "Some are sowing wheat." "Wheat and alfalfa fields look nice." In summer we read that "farmers are busy threshing oats and picking tomatoes." "People are starting to make hay and are picking strawberries." "The women are picking wild berries and putting up peas." "Most of the beans are harvested and some people are beginning to pick corn." During the winter months reporters normally comment about livestock, sales, farm accidents, and construction work. The farm provides a space in which the family can function independently of the larger society. A farm of sufficient size may include several dwellings, a diversity of enterprises, and meaningful work for all family members.

The Amish charter is strongly supported by the myths and beliefs of the society. In this context, the beliefs perform a conservative function in maintaining the social order. Acting as a charter, the beliefs justify the norms of Amish society. When supported by beliefs, deeds, and a living faith, the Amish charter performs an integrative function in keeping the society together.

25. Ibid., p. 30.

CHAPTER 5

The Community

AMISH COMMUNITIES may be found in various geographic locations but not as discrete villages, counties, or compounds. In any region where there are Amish farmers, their families live on either side of the highway, around small rural towns, and they are interspersed among "English" farm families. The Amish are not a social class or a caste, a commune or a monastic order, but a religious community constituting a subculture in America. As a corporate group in the United States and Canada, the Old Order Amish celebrate communion and break bread together; they represent a community of "one mind," one discipline, and "one body." The Amish community attempts to be "in the world, but not of the world" (John 17:16).

SETTLEMENT PATTERNS

The Amish have developed a unique community structure in America. In addition to the household, which is comprised of the married couple and their offspring, the community consists of the *settlement*, a *church district* or districts, and the *affiliation*. These terms characterize the basic social groupings.

A *settlement* consists of Amish families living in a contiguous relationship, that is, households that are in proximity to one another. A settlement may be small, consisting of a few families and their or-

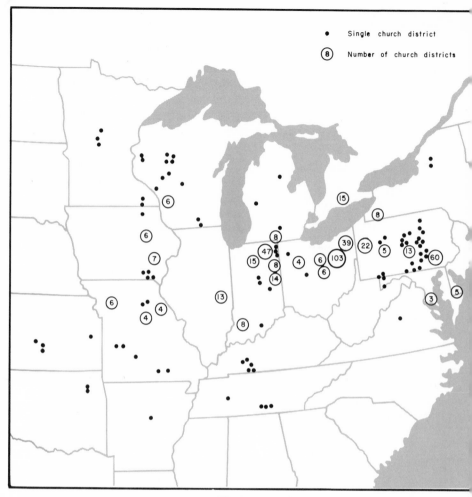

Figure 4.
Location of Amish church districts,
United States and Canada

dained leaders, or it may embrace several counties. The largest
settlement of Amish is located in Holmes and several adjoining
counties in Ohio. The two next largest are Lancaster County and
vicinity in Pennsylvania and Elkhart and Lagrange counties and
vicinity in Indiana. No specific limits are imposed upon the size of
a settlement. The location and density of the settlements in the
United States are indicated in Figure 4.

The *church district* is a congregation, a ceremonial unit encompassing a specific geographic area within a settlement. The size of
the church district is determined by the number of people who can

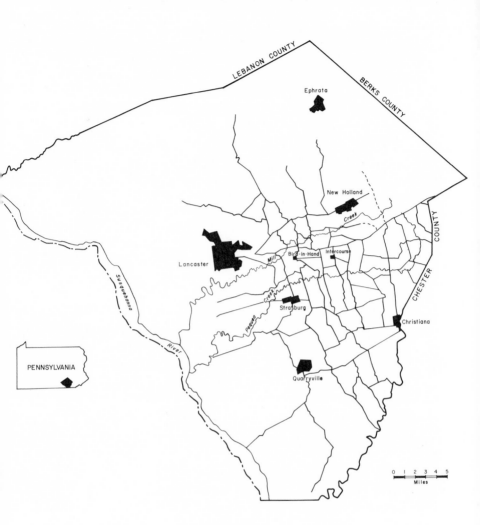

Figure 5.
Amish church districts, Lancaster County,
Pennsylvania

be accommodated for the preaching service in one farm dwelling. The
church district is a self-governing body with ceremonial and institutional functions reinforced by the preaching service. Baptisms, marriages, ordinations, and funerals are functions of the district. The
boundaries of the church districts are agreed upon by the leaders
and members, and they constitute such guidelines as roads, creeks,
cable wires, or small mountain ranges. Districts on the fringes of the
settlement are not assigned physical boundaries but encompass all the
Amish households in that general area. The curved and oblong shapes
of the Lancaster districts contrast sharply with the Elkhart and La-

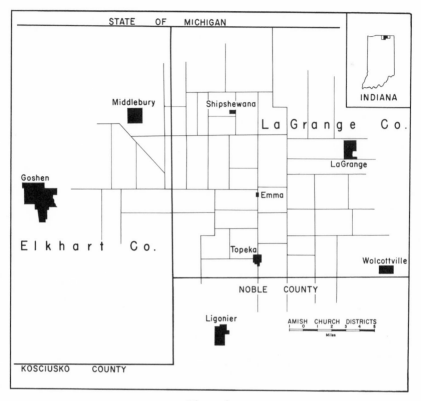

Figure 6.
Amish church districts, Elkhart
and Lagrange counties, Indiana

grange settlement in Indiana, where the districts are measured by square miles. (Compare Figures 5 and 6.) In the Lancaster settlement each district encompasses an area of about four square miles. In Indiana, where farms are larger, the districts average about six square miles in total area. Amish members and their children are obliged to attend the preaching services in the church districts in which they reside.

The church district is the "home church" for all the members who live within its borders and who observe communion together. A member can be disciplined only by his own church district, not by an outside authority. Likewise, a member who is disciplined has no recourse outside his home district. Members may attend other church district services on "off" Sundays when there is no service in their home district. Young people may date and marry persons in other districts. The Old Order districts attempt to keep their discipline fairly uniform. The ordained leaders themselves attempt to maintain uniformity, and for the sake of "peace" and of being an example, they often adhere to regulations more strictly than do lay members.

Through its kinship and many informal contacts, the district is an integral part of the wider settlement. The older settlements, for example, that have spawned new communities experience a high degree of informal association. Amish families have relatives in various settlements or in neighboring districts. The frequent visiting back and forth not only between relatives but also among friends makes a formal relationship between districts unnecessary. Some of the important life rituals, including weddings and funerals, reach across church district boundaries, as do economic and social activities such as barn-raisings and mutual aid.

An *affiliation* is a group of church districts that have a common discipline and that commune together. In other words, it is an exclusive ceremonial group. A clear separation is maintained between the Amish church and the world. But what about other groups that have broken away from the Old Order discipline, or churches that are altogether worldly? The Old Order Amish tend to classify groups according to their degree of worldliness, from "low" to "high" church. A low church (the most simple and humble) is one that observes strict discipline, teaches separation from the world, and practices social avoidance. A high church is one that has relaxed its discipline. Between the extremes many affiliations are recognized. The degree of interaction with other groups is governed by the social distance between them. Districts that are generally said to be of one mind are "in fellowship" with one another. They reciprocate with one another in maintaining discipline, so that if a member is excommunicated in his home district, the other districts will respect the action and will practice social avoidance.

Affiliations arise most frequently from liberal-progressive interpretations of the discipline. The various Amish affiliations have their analogues in the numerous subdivisions within most Protestant denominations. Because minor symbolic traits distinguish one affiliation from another, differences in affiliation among the Amish are not apparent to the outsider. All the large Amish settlements have several affiliations. In Lancaster County there are the Old Order Amish and two more progressive groups known as the "Beachy Amish" and "New Amish." The Beachy Amish permit the ownership of automobiles, the use of a meeting house for preaching services, and the use of English in ceremonial functions. The New Amish began when a group of families wished to relax the restrictions on the use of telephones, electricity, and tractor-driven farm machinery. They formed a separate affiliation in 1966. In Ohio and Indiana there are several affiliations of Amish in the same settlement with the Old Order Amish. The different affiliations add to the complexity of community organization, for the geographic boundaries of each affiliation overlap the boundary lines of other affiliations. Old Order Amish, who do not associate ceremonially with other Amish groups, simply say, "They are not in fellowship with us." Full fellowship means, in addition to common agreement in discipline and communing together, that ordained persons are permitted to preach during exchange visits.

In addition to the varied Amish affiliations within a single region, there are often different groups of Mennonites in the larger settlements. The Mennonites also have a spectrum of liberal-to-orthodox groupings ranging from the horse-and-buggy Old Order Mennonites, who speak the dialect, dress, and farm like the Amish, to those who are indistinguishable from "worldly" people. Their separate subdivisions include the Wisler, Stauffer, Wenger, Burkholder, and "Black Bumper" Mennonites. All these orthodox-type Mennonite groups, together with still others such as the Reformed Mennonite, Old Order River Brethren, Church of the Brethren (Dunkards), and Old Colony Mennonites, are affiliations apart from the Old Order Amish but in some instances exist in the same region.

GROWTH AND EXPANSION

The Amish themselves do not keep precise records of their membership beyond the number of families in a district and the number of children in school.[1] The names of the districts and their ordained leaders are published annually in *The New American Almanac* at Baltic, Ohio, by an Amish bookseller. The number of original Amish immigrants remains unknown. The 1890 U.S. *Census of Religious Bodies* reported twenty-two Old Order Amish congregations with 2,038 baptized adult members in nine states.

1. The Amish distaste for keeping an exact membership count is based upon the ill-advised example of King David, who, after "numbering the people" against the wishes of Jehovah, suffered a disastrous pestilence (II Sam. 24). Although the Amish may indirectly benefit from the work of non-Amish investigators who conduct demographic studies (namely, for medical genetic purposes), they lay no claim to the consequences. For many years (from 1905 to 1967) the *Mennonite Yearbook* reported memberships of the Old Order Amish. Five periods of Amish settlement are discussed by W. K. Crowley in "Old Order Amish Settlement: Diffusion and Growth," *Annals of the Association of American Geographers* 68 (June 1978): 249–64.

Table 1

Old Order Amish church districts and population by decade

Year	Total number of districts	Estimated population	Districts in vicinity of		
			Lancaster County	Holmes County	Elkhart County
1890	22	3,700	5	6	4
1900	32	5,300	6	7	6
1910	57	9,500	9	8	8
1920	83	14,000	11	13	10
1930	110	18,500	12	16	12
1940	154	25,800	18	24	18
1950	197	33,000	25	40	25
1960	258	43,300	38	49	29
1970	343	57,600	47	70	37
1979	526	85,783	60	103	47

Sources: Mennonite Yearbook (Scottdale, Pa.), 1905–1967; The New American Almanac (Baltic, Ohio), 1930–1979; U.S., Census of Religious Bodies, 1890; and Amish informants.

The Amish population has grown steadily since 1890 (Table 1). Each decade the population has increased from 30 to 48 percent. The total population is estimated as accurately as possible from published sources and informants. There are generally more children (non-baptized persons) than baptized persons in a district. The districts vary in size, but each group is kept small by horse-and-buggy transportation and by the number of people who can gather for worship in either the farmhouse or barn. The three largest settlements average about 35 households per district. The largest settlement (in Ohio) averages 86 baptized members and 113 nonmembers in a district, or a total of 199 persons per district.[2] (For every 100 baptized persons, there are at this rate 131 unbaptized persons [or children] in the Amish population.)

The present population by state (and province) is shown in Table 2. The total population is estimated at 85,783, with Amish settlements existing in twenty states and one Canadian province. There have been many attempts to form communities in the Great Plains, and in such faraway states as New Mexico, Mississippi, and North Dakota, as well as in Mexico, Paraguay, and Honduras, but those families have

2. Harold E. Cross, "Genetic Studies in an Amish Isolate" (Ph.D. diss., The Johns Hopkins University, 1967), p. 42.

Table 2

Location and characteristics of the Old Order Amish by state and province

Location	Estimated population	Number of districts	Number of settlements	Date of settlement
Ohio	29,137	160	14	1808
Pennsylvania	22,570	125	25	1737
Indiana	16,628	99	12	1839
Missouri	2,560	22	9	1947[a]
Iowa	2,280	18	5	1846
Wisconsin	2,280	18	8	1925
Ontario	2,040	15	9	1824
Illinois	1,690	13	1	1864
Michigan	1,290	11	6	1900[a]
New York	1,120	10	3	1949
Maryland	970	5	2	1850
Delaware	775	5	1	1915
Minnesota	610	5	5	1972
Kentucky	550	5	3	1958
Tennessee	410	5	3	1944
Kansas	520	4	3	1883
Oklahoma	180	2	1	1892
Florida	40	1	1	1927
Montana	60	1	1	1970[a]
Arkansas	55	1	1	1976[a]
Virginia	18	1	1	1942[a]
Totals	85,783	526	115	

Sources: *The New American Almanac, 1979* (Baltic, Ohio); Amish directories; and correspondence with Amish informants. Estimates are based on mean district size within each settlement.

[a] Date of present settlement, not of extinct, earlier settlement.

either returned to the large "mother" communities or have associated with more modernized affiliations.[3] Approximately 75 percent of the Amish are located in three states: Ohio, Pennsylvania, and Indiana. Also indicated in Table 2 are the dates of settlement in each of the states (or province) and the approximate number of settlements. With the formation of many new settlements in recent years, we may expect the number to vacillate within each of the states.

3. For a discussion of settlements on the Great Plains, see John A. Hostetler, "The Old Order Amish on the Great Plains: A Study in Cultural Vulnerability," in *Ethnicity on the Great Plains,* ed. Fred Luebke (Lincoln: University of Nebraska Press, forthcoming).

POPULATION CHARACTERISTICS

The Amish have large families, a low rate of infant mortality, increasing longevity, and prohibitions against birth control. Thus they have experienced a much greater net population gain in recent years than have non-Amish people. In an intensive study of the Amish population, several Amish population growth patterns have been ascertained.[4] The highlights of these findings, with comparisons to the population of the United States and the Hutterites (the fastest-growing U.S. subpopulation on record), are discussed in the following sections.

Age at marriage. The median age at first marriage for Amish women is just under twenty-two years.[5] The median age for men at first marriage is slightly more than twenty-three years. Amish women marry at about the same age as other women in the United States. The age difference between husband and wife for the U.S. population as a whole is about 2.5 years. Among the Amish the age difference is about 1.5 years.

There are differences between the three largest regions—Pennsylvania, Ohio, and Indiana. Amish women in Pennsylvania marry at a slightly younger age than do those in Ohio or Indiana, where their age at marriage is very similar. Amish men tend to marry later in Ohio and Indiana than they do in Pennsylvania.

Not only are there variations between the three largest Amish settlements but there have been variations during the past forty years as well. Amish women today tend to marry at a younger age in Pennsylvania and Ohio than they did forty years ago. Only in Indiana do they marry at a slightly older age than they did in previous years. Amish men in Indiana get married at about the same age as they did forty years ago.

4. John A. Hostetler et al., "Fertility Patterns in an American Isolate Subculture," Final Report of National Institutes of Health Grant (NICHHD) No. HD-08137-01A1, 1977. For a substantial publication based on this report, see Julia A. Eriksen et al., "Fertility Patterns and Trends among the Old Order Amish," *Population Studies* 33 (July 1979). The study is one of several projects resulting from collaboration between Victor A. McKusick and his associates at The Johns Hopkins University School of Medicine and the author. The demographic aspects of the study incorporate the three largest settlements of the Old Order Amish in the United States, one each in Pennsylvania, Ohio, and Indiana.

5. These findings support those of earlier investigators, but this study for the first time measures fertility trends over time. Earlier works include Harold E. Cross and Victor A. McKusick, "Amish Demography," *Social Biology* 17 (June 1970): 83–101; and "Pockets of High Fertility in the United States," *Population Bulletin* 24 (December 1968).

Family Size. The average number of live births per Amish couple is seven. The Ohio Amish have the lowest average number of live births, while the Pennsylvania and Indiana Amish groups have the highest (Table 3). Since the Ohio Amish marry at a slightly older age, one would expect the number of live births among them to be smaller. Over a span of forty years, Amish family size has increased. The influence of modern medicine and better health care would seem to account for this trend. The percentage of childless couples has declined over the forty-year period, particularly in Pennsylvania and Ohio. As medicine has improved, infecundity has declined generally among the Amish as it has among all American women. It is not surprising that the rate of childlessness for the Amish is lower than that for the United States as a whole (4.4 percent compared to 7.5 percent),

Table 3
Trends in family size in the three largest Old Order Amish settlements

Births	Pennsylvania (Lancaster County and vicinity)	Ohio (Holmes County and vicinity)	Indiana (Elkhart County and vicinity)	Total
Number of live births (mean)				
Pre-1899	7.1	6.3	6.7	6.6
1899–1908	8.2	6.2	7.0	6.8
1909–1918	6.9	6.4	6.7	6.6
1919–1928	7.2	6.8	7.2	7.0
Percentage of childless couples				
Pre-1899	7.6	7.8	4.3	6.6
1899–1908	2.8	6.7	3.2	5.0
1909–1918	6.6	5.1	5.2	5.5
1919–1928	2.9	5.3	5.2	4.4
1929–1938	0.9	3.1	3.9	2.6
Percentage of couples with ten or more children				
Pre-1899	28.7	21.0	21.8	22.7
1899–1908	33.5	14.7	25.6	21.2
1909–1918	25.2	19.1	16.7	20.0
1919–1928	25.7	19.4	24.5	21.8

Note: Includes first marriages only; number of live births is for women married before the age of forty-five.

since among the Amish there is no divorce and children are wanted. Hutterites have an even lower rate, 2.9 percent.[6] The consistently high growth trend among the Amish is indicated by the proportion of couples who have ten or more children: 21.8 percent. The percentage is higher in Pennsylvania than in Ohio or Indiana, probably in part because of the younger age of women at marriage in Pennsylvania. This rate is still only half that reported for Hutterites, 48.2 percent.[7]

The Marriage Season. Among the Amish, as in many agrarian societies, it has been the custom to marry after the crops are harvested. The marriage involves a two-day period of preparation and festivity for both sets of relatives, to say nothing of the longer period of preparation on the part of the bride's family. Weddings are accommodated into the community's schedule most suitably after the summer's work is over, from October to December.

The preferred months for marriages are November and December. The tendency to marry in these two months is most marked in Pennsylvania. Here 92 percent of all marriages occur during these months as contrasted to 41 percent in Ohio and 34 percent in Indiana. Marriages in Ohio and Indiana also take place in January, February, and March. Second marriages or remarriages often occur during the "off season" because they do not require the same degree of community involvement and festivity as do first marriages.

By observing the marriage calendar over time, one can see that the Pennsylvania Amish have consistently concentrated their marriages in November and December. Marriages in Indiana have occurred consistently in January, February, and March. Marriages in Ohio have declined in number in January but have tended to spread into March, April, and May.

Variations between Communities. Reasons for the differences among the three largest settlements (Ohio, Pennsylvania, and Indiana) with respect to age at marriage, family size, and marriage season are not obvious without some knowledge of the customs of each community. These differences can be explained in part by economic and cultural factors. The Ohio and Indiana Amish have much in common. Penn-

6. Joseph W. Eaton and Albert J. Mayer, *Man's Capacity to Reproduce: The Demography of a Unique Population* (Glencoe, Ill.: The Free Press, 1954), p. 31, where the figure is erroneously given as 3.4.

7. Ibid. Amish persons having the largest number of living descendants have been noted. Moses Borkholder of Indiana (d. 1933) had 554 living descendants. Eli S. Miller of Delaware (d. 1977) had 494.

sylvania stands out consistently as distinct from the Midwestern settlements. The Pennsylvania Amish have a long tradition of living on highly productive soils. They also have smaller acreages than the Midwestern Amish, but they farm more intensively. Work organization and the motivations for work may be other factors associated with family size. The Lancaster County Amish people, it is recognized, are more aggressive and work with greater rigor than the Midwestern Amish. Their horses, for example, reflect better breeding and trot faster than those in other Amish communities. Motivation for high economic productivity may not have a direct relationship to family size, but there appears to be an indirect one.

The discipline that limits the kind of modernization in the three communities is different. Although the three are in "full fellowship" with one another, and visiting officials may preach in the others' communities, the *Ordnung* that restricts farm technology is different in each region. The Lancaster churches have allowed some technological concessions, thereby permitting their young, aggressive farmers to stay on the farm. Power-driven farm implements are permitted if they are horse drawn. Dairy barns are equipped with milking machines, bulk tanks, and diesel-powered cooling systems. Incentives for hard work and motivation for staying on the farm appear to be maintained in this manner. The Midwestern Amish communities have relaxed some restrictions that symbolize greater individual convenience, such as the use of bicycles and store-bought clothes, but have been firm in opposing farm technology, which would yield greater profits and motivation for staying on the farm. In some Ohio regions where the districts have not permitted milking machines and improvement of farm technology, the younger men have given up farming. Instead, they have become carpenters, construction workers, or employees in small factories. Although they are still Amish members, the social structure and character of the Amish community have changed.

Population Growth and the Loss of Members. There is no indication that the Old Order Amish are reducing their growth rate by birth control. There has, in fact, been a slight increase in the rate of population growth over the past seventy years. The land area occupied by the Amish in Lancaster County, Pennsylvania, in 1940 was 150 square miles, compared to approximately 525 square miles in 1980 (see Figure 7). The number of church districts has increased dramatically (see Table 1). There were six districts in 1900, twenty-five in 1950, and sixty in 1979. The slow growth rate from 1910 to 1930 is accounted for by the formation of a division in 1911 that is today known as the Weavertown Amish Mennonite church.

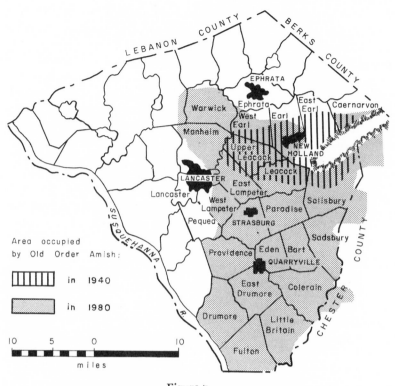

Figure 7.
Area occupied by the Amish in Lancaster County,
Pennsylvania, 1940 and 1980

What is the extent of membership loss and what influence does it have on population growth? In a comparative study of Old Order Amish and former Amish family size, it was found that the number of children born per former Amish family was significantly reduced.[8] For example, the average number of live births among Old Order Amish (using the birth cohort for 1900–1909) was 7.2, but among former Amish who had Amish parents it was 4.0, and among former Amish whose parents were not Amish, 3.9. We have evidence, therefore, that leaving the Amish is coupled with a reduction in family size. To be Old Order Amish is to have a large family.

What proportion of the children born to Amish parents do not remain with the Amish church? With genealogical records and the

8. Eugene P. Ericksen, Julia Ericksen, and John A. Hostetler, "The Cultivation of the Soil as a Moral Directive," *Rural Sociology*, in press.

help of Amish informants this information was computed for Lancaster County, Pennsylvania. The overall rate of loss to the Old Order from 1880 to 1939 was 22.4 percent (Table 4). There is considerable variation, however, when ten-year birth cohorts are examined. The rate of loss was high prior to 1880, had declined by 1919, and rose again by 1939. It is impossible to compute a comparable loss rate for the current period because persons born since 1939 have not yet completed their families. The land pressures in recent years, it appears, are making an impact, but not to the extent that a high rate of population increase is impossible.

The decision to remain or leave the Amish church is related to the economic problems of setting up a farm or Amish business. Leaving often occurs after marriage and at the beginning of the child-bearing stage. Buying land for the adult children, or loaning them money or collateral, visiting them frequently—in short, aiding them in a variety of socially supportive ways—is recognized by the parents of married children as an important obligation. In a study of dropouts it was found that instead of occurring at random, they were clustered in certain families. Generally, the fathers of sons who left the Amish were themselves not earning money from farming. Where the fathers were physically disabled, the children frequently did not learn farming and thus did not remain Amish.

Other Unique Characteristics. Several unusual features of the Amish population have been revealed in studies of genetic diseases among the

Table 4

Proportion of Old Order Amish offspring who are not members of the Old Order Amish church, Lancaster County, Pennsylvania

Birth cohort	Number of cases	Percentage not Amish
Pre-1880	612	28.1
1880–1899	599	19.5
1900–1909	400	22.0
1910–1919	645	17.9
1920–1929	917	21.7
1930–1939	450	23.7
Total	3,623	22.4

Note: The percentages are based on the number of offspring who were born Old Order during specified periods but who are not members of the Old Order Amish. The percentages do not indicate the trend for the present population or for those born after 1939. I wish to thank Eugene P. Erickson for assistance in compiling these data.

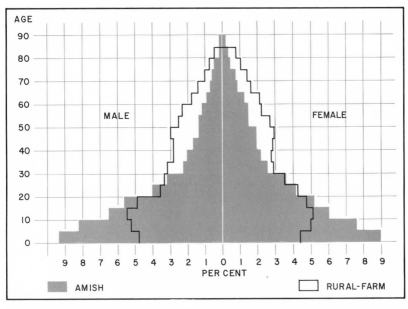

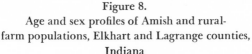

Figure 8.
Age and sex profiles of Amish and rural-
farm populations, Elkhart and Lagrange counties,
Indiana

Amish.[9] The Amish have the highest twinning rate of any known
population (15.3 per 1,000 live births among the Ohio Amish families,
21.1 among the Indiana Amish). The natural rate of population
increase per year for the Ohio settlement has been computed to be
3.019 percent, or a doubling of the population every twenty-three
years.[10]

As seen in Figure 8, the age and sex composition of the Amish
population is strikingly different from that of the rural-farm population of the rest of the United States.[11] The differences reflect the

9. Victor A. McKusick, *Medical Genetic Studies of the Amish: Selected Papers,
Assembled, with Commentary* (Baltimore: The Johns Hopkins University Press,
1978); see especially chap. B1, "Amish Demography," by Harold E. Cross and
Victor A. McKusick (pp. 29–47).

10. The reported rate for Hutterites is 4.1265, or a doubling every sixteen years;
see Eaton and Mayer, *Man's Capacity to Reproduce*, p. 44.

11. Based on the U.S. Census of 1970 and the *Indiana Amish Directory* (1970).
Adapted from and published with the permission of Richard F. Hamman, "Pat-
terns of Mortality in the Old Order Amish" (Ph.D. diss., The Johns Hopkins
University, 1979).

social and cultural patterns of Amish life. A comparison of Amish to non-Amish rural-farm populations shows that the Amish population has only half the proportion of people over the age of sixty-five that the non-Amish population has, and that for persons under twenty years of age, the Amish proportion is double that of the rural-farm population. The age distribution of a society has important economic and social consequences. As long as the Amish population over the age of sixty-five remains relatively small, the financial problems at retirement are less acute than in the general population. Although the Amish are opposed to receiving Social Security payments from the government, the difference in age structure is a sound reason why benefits payments are more critical to the general population in America than to the Amish. The profile for the Amish does not reflect a low birth rate during the Depression, just before the sudden increase in the birth rate of 1940, as does the profile for the non-Amish population.

LEADERSHIP

Among the Amish—who have rejected coercive powers as worldly, and who cultivate humility, obedience, and simplicity—the selection of leaders is a delicate process. One who is chosen to lead must not seek either authority or power, but in reality he is placed in a position where he must exercise both. In selecting candidates for office, members look for humility and evidence of good farm and family management. Any forwardness or idiosyncratic tendencies are quickly detected. An Amishman would never prepare himself for the vocation of preacher, nor would he announce that he felt called of God to prepare for the ministry, as members of evangelical groups do. Attending a seminary would be a sure sign of worldliness and reason for excommunication, for it would indicate a loss of humility and the development of ego. The Amish method of using nominations for election and selection by lot helps to prevent manipulative power and personal ambition. Authority is widely distributed among all members so that no single leader or subgroup will have all the power. Leaders are expected to help the community in the redemptive process but never to stand in the way. We will return to the method of selecting leaders after their functions have been described.

The organization of the Amish community is focused in the church district. The elected officials are called *Diener* (literally, "servants", and each district has three kinds. Traditionally they are the *Voelliger-Diener* ("minister with full powers" or "bishop"; *Diener zum Buch* ("minister of the book" or "preacher"; and *Armen-Diener* ("minister to the poor" or "deacon"). These three positions in the dialect are *Vellicherdiener, Breddicher,* and *Armediener.* Each district ideally has one bishop, two ministers (also called preachers), and one deacon.

The bishop is the leader of the congregation and its chief authority. He administers the rites of communion, baptism, marriage, and excommunication, and reinstates "backsliders" to membership in the church. He supervises the choice of ministers by lot and performs ordination services. He announces disciplinary action against violators of the church *Ordnung.* The bishop is responsible for obtaining "the voice" or vote of the church in decision-making processes where such unanimity is required. The bishop also takes his turn at preaching *es schwere Deel* "the main sermon" at regular meetings for worship. Upon his ordination, the bishop is given the following lifetime charge:

(1) So in the name of the Lord and of the church the complete ministry or bishop's office is entrusted to you (2) that you shall declare the Lord's bitter suffering and death and observe the breaking of bread and wine (3) and if there are people who wish to unite with the church then you shall teach them the Christian faith and baptize them (4) and, with the counsel of the church, you shall punish the disobedient and sinners and when they manifest repentence and conversion you shall receive them again with the counsel of the church (5) and when there are brethren and sisters in the church who wish to marry you shall unite them according to the godly ordinance (6) and you shall also ordain ministers with full authority [i.e., bishops] whenever it is necessary and requested in the church (7) and when you become old and weak you are to ordain a man after you in your place (8) and may the Lord strengthen you with his holy and good spirit through Jesus Christ Amen.[12]

In addition to the bishop there are typically two preachers in every district who are expected to preach when their turn comes. The bishop and preachers must be able to stand before the congregation, without notes or the aid of books, and admonish the people in the ways of God. On those Sundays when there is no preaching in his own district, an ordained person may, if he wishes, visit other districts. Very frequently visiting preachers are called to preach if they are "in full fellowship" with the host district. Preachers also assist the bishop in distributing the wine and bread at the communion service, held twice each year. Upon ordination, the preacher is given the following

12. The passage is a translation from German sources; see John Umble, "Amish Ordination Charges," *Mennonite Quarterly Review* 13 (October 1939): 236.

charge: "So in the name of the Lord and of the church the ministry to the book is committed to you that you shall preach [expound the Word], read, and pray with the church, help protect good and help punish evil."[13]

A deacon is given the following charge at the time of his ordination:

So in the name of the Lord and of the church the ministry to the poor is committed to you that you shall care for widows and orphans and receive alms and give them out with the counsel of the church and if there are brethren and sisters who wish to enter the marriage state then you shall serve them according to the godly order and read the scriptures for the ministers when it is requested and shall serve with water in the baptismal ceremony if you are requested to do so.[14]

The deacon assists regularly in the worship service by reading a chapter from the Bible. The reading is usually prefaced by voluntary admonitions on his part. As his title (*Armen-Diener*) implies, he is charged with looking after any needy members or widows by disbursing funds collected for that purpose. At the special service for baptism he pours the water into the cupped hands of the bishop over the applicant's head. He looks after the cups, bread, and wine for the communion service and keeps the chalice filled during the service. He assists in the foot-washing service, which accompanies the communion, by preparing the pails of water and the towels. He becomes a kind of housekeeper working behind the scenes on ceremonial occasions. Two other important functions are assigned to the deacon: he is often sent by the bishop to secure information about transgressors, and he conveys messages of excommunication. As an adjuster of difficulties between members, he has the most difficult task of the three ordained officials. This distasteful task is perhaps offset by the more pleasant function of the *Schtecklimann*, or "go-between," in the arrangements for marriage. When a couple wishes to be married, the deacon is so informed by the prospective bridegroom. The deacon then inquires whether the bride's parents approve. *Wann nix im Weg schteht* ("if nothing stands in the way"), he informs the bishop, who announces the intended marriage to the congregation about two Sundays before the wedding.

In some instances, a bishop must supervise two or three districts. This is usually considered a temporary arrangement until the additional district becomes large enough to warrant its own bishop or

13. Ibid., p. 237.
14. Ibid.

until the right person is found for the position. A bishop generally may not move from one district to another if dissatisfaction has been expressed within his district. Preachers and deacons are perhaps freer to do so, but in any event, not without prior consultation with the districts involved. The ordained positions of bishop, preacher, and deacon are appointments for life unless persons holding them are "silenced" for misbehavior or transgression.

Each church district is a small, face-to-face human group, a self-government unit. There is no central organization or conference to interpret policy for the local group. The bishop is the chief authority figure within his district. In large settlements of Amish, however, there is informal consultation among the different bishops in the area. In Lancaster County the ordained officials meet for consultation before communion in the spring and fall. At these meetings questions of discipline or causes for disunity also are dealt with. The oldest bishop generally is the one who calls these ministers' meetings and presides at them.

Each district conducts its own business and deliberations following the preaching service after nonmembers, including children, have been dismissed. The decision-making processes are of the patriarchal-democratic type. While a bishop may exercise considerable power in making a decision, he is subject to *der Rat der Gemein* ("the counsel or vote of the church"). For example, a member is excommunicated and put under the ban only by the vote of the baptized members, men and women. He is reinstated by vote. The deacon assists poor members only when authorized by the vote of the congregation. Although the ideal of congregational rule is maintained, the ordained persons usually bring a suggested course of action to the assembly for a vote. The ordained persons meet for the *Abrot* ("ministers' council") at every preaching service. This regular meeting provides occasion for any of the ministers to discuss circumstances that they feel should be brought to the attention of all. Any matter brought before the congregation must first be discussed by the ministers. Furthermore, a plan of procedure must be agreed upon by all the ministers before the problem can be brought before the members' meeting.

The selection of leaders is a serious occasion and is marked by an orderly sequence of communal rites.[15] As stated earlier, the individual

15. An insightful treatment of the ideal patterns of Old Order leadership is that of Sandra Lee Cronk, "Gelassenheit: The Rites of the Redemptive Process in Old Order Amish and Old Order Mennonite Communities" (Ph.D. diss., University of Chicago, 1977), esp. pp. 77–92. Amish practices and exceptions to the rule are discussed by David Luthy in "A Survey of Amish Ordination Customs," *Family Life* (March 1975): 13–17.

does not determine whether God is calling him to a position. Instead, the "voice" of the church, followed by the lot, constitutes the call. Admonitions to lowliness of mind are assured, but there is no provision for training or education, and no pay. All candidates are selected from within the district; no outsider is ever brought into the congregation and ordained to be bishop, preacher, or deacon. A bishop is selected from among the ordained preachers. Once chosen by lot, it would be a bad omen for him to refuse the calling. For most preachers it is a traumatic experience. A few have suffered mental relapses. In speaking of the newly ordained, a preacher's wife observed that "it makes them sickly, for as long as five years sometimes."

In anticipation of an ordination the congregation is urged to examine its corporate life. If there is a feeling of unity among the members, the signs are right for an ordination. If there is a spirit of friction or misunderstanding, an ordination may be delayed. Once an ordination is considered appropriate, the bishop will announce the proposal and set a two-week period for serious deliberation and prayer, usually prior to the biannual preparatory service (*Attningsgmee*). All members must agree to an ordination.

Most bishops try to have the ordination service on the day of communion. Since communion is a high point of the group's spirituality, the selection and installation of a leader is fitting for this time. Following the communion service the assembly remains for the ordination. The presiding bishop reminds all of the seriousness of the occasion and reads a Biblical passage dealing with the qualifications of the ministry (I Tim. 3). He may comment on the qualifications but will likely not mention what is taken for granted, that the nominee for the office must be married and must be a man. The ordained men go to an adjoining room. All the members file past a door (or window) that is slightly open, and whisper the name of a person qualified for the office to the deacon. The deacon relays the name to the bishop, who writes down the name and keeps an accounting of the votes. In order to be a candidate, a person must receive at least two votes. In some districts three votes are required. Those who support the rule of three votes hold that trickery can be eliminated. (A husband and wife or two persons cannot plot to nominate a certain person out of spite.) Members, including husbands and wives, are not to discuss among themselves whom they will nominate. The ministry does not make nominations.

In the event that only one person receives all the votes, that person will be ordained without using the lot. There have been as many as sixteen names in the lot, but typically there may be from four to eight nominations. Once nominated, a person may not withdraw his name for any reason. In Lancaster County, Pennsylvania, candidates for bishop must have children who are members of the Amish church, or at least one child must be a member, and all the children must be in good Amish standing. One consequence of this rule is that there are no young bishops. Among the Swiss settlements of Adams and Allen counties in Indiana, only two nominees for minister, those with the most votes, are placed in the lot.

Using the lot as a method of selection is based upon the example of the apostles in selecting a successor to Judas (Acts 1:23–26). The instrument used in the lot, a small piece of paper, frequently contains a Bible verse. Two verses used are: "The lot is cast into the lap; but the whole disposing thereof is of the Lord" (Prov. 16:33). "And they prayed and said Thou, Lord which knowest the hearts of all men, show whether of these two thou hast chosen" (Acts 1:24). The piece of paper is placed in a hymnbook. Additional hymnbooks are selected to equal the number of candidates. The books are rearranged and placed on a table or bench. Following a prayer by kneeling, the candidates are asked to select a book. The bishop then examines the books until he finds the one containing the lot. When he finds the book containing the slip of paper, he repeats the man's name so all can hear.

The man "struck" by the lot is asked to stand for the charge placed upon him by the bishop. If it is a bishop who is chosen, he is asked to kneel and the hands of two presiding bishops are placed on his head as the charge is given. The bishop greets the newly ordained man with a handshake and the Holy Kiss. Noticeable at these services are sobbing and weeping, a ritual mourning, expressing deep sympathy for the heavy burden placed on the chosen servant. All the members are enjoined to encourage and pray for the newly ordained brother as the assembly is dismissed. Even though the community might view the man chosen as less qualified than another nominee, the members are satisfied with the result because the choice was God's.

PATTERNS OF INTERACTION

As indicated earlier, the charter requires that a definite line of separateness be maintained between the Amish church and the world. Complete geographic isolation is neither sought after nor considered desirable. There are necessary and preferred patterns of interaction. Interaction patterns are governed by the way in which the Amish

classify groups according to their shades of worldliness. Thus interaction with other Amish, with Mennonite and related groups, or with
other religious groups is different from interaction with the world. In
his home district the individual member is surrounded by a series
of "fences" or lines of separation which must be learned and observed
with great discretion. Since the interaction within the Amish community was discussed earlier, we will consider here the social and
economic aspects that require interaction with the world.[16]

Separation from the world has some practical consequences. By
keeping the clock either slower or faster than worldly time, the Amish
effectively stay out of step with the world. When daylight-saving time
first went into effect, the Amish resisted it, saying "the world is
changing too fast anyway." Thus, when the world changes to daylight-
saving time, the Amish keep "slow" time. When the world changes
to standard time, the Amish set their clocks a half-hour ahead. Not
only is this puzzling to the outsider, but it introduces an ambiguous
element between the Amish community and the rest of the world.
Whether practiced consciously or unconsciously, it is an effective
means of insulating the Amish from the activity and structures of
the world. In keeping appointments with an Amish person the outsider must make sure whether the appointment is for "slow" or "fast"
time. Within the Amish community the time frame is understood, but
when interacting with the outside world the Amishman abides by
worldly time.

The Amish community is knit together by community patterns of
consumption, employment, and the sharing of capital and mutual
aid. In order to survive, the Amish must have a strong economic
base, and this base must attract and hold the children. Many of the
farms today are not completely self-sufficient, and additional income
is necessary. The family members are the labor force. An Amish boy
will work on his father's farm until he is trained. After this he may
hire out to relatives, or if he works outside the Amish community, in
construction work or in a small factory, he will typically work with
other Amish persons. After the age of twenty-one, his earnings are
his own, and he will save money for a down payment on a farm.

Amish girls tend to hire out at a younger age than boys, and a girl
will typically live with the Amish family she works for. Her earnings
are returned to the family. The family will then return some to her
for spending money and clothes, spend some for family needs, and

16. For insights on interaction patterns, I am indebted to Gertrude E. Huntington, "Dove at the Window: A Study of Old Order Amish Community in Ohio"
(Ph.D. diss., Yale University, 1956), pp. 230–396.

save some for her until she reaches the age of twenty-one. An Amish girl will occasionally work for an English family or in a small business, frequently as domestic help or as a cleaner, and in a capacity where she will not meet the public. Working away from home is usually enjoyed, and being a hired girl is considered part of growing up.

There is a certain amount of neighboring with rural people who are not Amish. An English neighbor may invite the Amish housewife to a kitchenware "party." She may or may not accept. The Amish will assist English neighbors with harvest or in an emergency when they are not likely to visit socially. Attending movies, farm conventions, banquets, or fairs is off limits, but parents and children will often plan a trip to the city to visit the zoo; since the animals are creations of God, they may be seen and enjoyed. The visiting schedule of the Amish is always full, and most complain that they are behind in their visiting, so that there is no time left to visit with the English people.

The Amish do not send representatives to interchurch gatherings or conferences. Individuals may contribute to various non-Amish causes such as the local volunteer fire company or send contributions to agencies for the relief of human suffering, but they do not meet with other churches to discuss common problems or programs of action.

Almost every Amish family knows and interacts with English friends on a long-standing basis. These meetings occur at random. They are cherished by the Amish as well as by the English. Because the interaction is so infrequent, and the physical distance between them so great, the rule of separation is not violated. A German-speaking tourist, for example, halted an Amish carriage and asked for directions. The German-speaking couple was invited to the Amish home and later visited the Amish preaching service. The tourist was a physician from New York City and supplied the couple with medical advice and prescriptions. The two couples enjoyed each other's company over a period of fifteen years.

The Amish turn to the outside world for markets for their farm products. All their grain and hay is fed to livestock. They are sensitive to price fluctuations and follow market reports carefully. They produce far more than they can consume or sell to other Amish people, and their major income is from dairy, livestock, and other products sold to outside markets. They will ship their produce to a distant place if the market is better there.

They buy staple foods such as sugar, salt, and flour and other groceries in village stores. They will not buy canned goods, for many Amish families preserve up to 500 quarts of fruit, meat, and vegetables yearly. Some Amish will buy yard goods and other items regularly from mail-order catalogs and from salesmen who come to their door. Various farm magazines subscribed to by the husband may influence dairy or poultry production and ways of marketing, but they have little influence on the home. Needless conveniences, luxuries, and fancy clothing bear the stigma of worldliness.

CHAPTER 6

Agriculture and Subsistence

🌿

SOIL HAS for the Amish a spiritual significance. As in the Hebrew account of Creation, the Amish hold that man's first duty is to dress the garden. That is, he is to till it, manage it, presumably for pleasure and fulfillment (Gen. 2:15). Second, man is to keep the garden, protecting it from harm through the use of his labor and oversight. Ownership is God's (Ps. 24, "the earth is the Lord's . . ."), while man's function is looking after it in behalf of God. The parables in the New Testament also indicate to the Amish that man is the steward of an absentee landlord. His stewardship is continuous, ending in a day of reckoning when man will be called to give an account.

This view of land implies not only sustenance but to a certain extent pleasantness, attractiveness, and orderliness. Man has limited dominion. He has power over animals and vegetation, but land also must receive proper toil, nourishment, and rest. If treated violently or exploited selfishly, it will yield poorly, leaving mankind in poverty. The Amish view contrasts sharply with the so-called western world view, which sees man's role as an exploiter of nature for his own advancement and progress. To damage the earth is to disregard one's offspring.

The primary occupation in Amish society is farming, and if farming is not possible, then occupations of a rural or semirural character are preferred. The Amishman does not farm to make money. On the contrary, he works and saves so that he can farm and support himself and his family with minimum interference from the world. The advice

117

of Menno Simons in the sixteenth century expresses the sentiments of the Amish people today: "Rent a farm, milk cows, learn a trade if possible, do manual labor as did Paul, and all that which you then fall short of will doubtlessly be given and provided you by pious brethren."[1]

This description of Amish agriculture will focus on three elements: agricultural skills in the Amish tradition, the differences in resources and soil productivity among Amish settlements (especially between Lancaster County, Pennsylvania, and the other settlements), and farm management strategy within the bounds of Amish values. The involvement in nonfarming enterprises will conclude the chapter.

THE EUROPEAN AGRICULTURAL HERITAGE

Distinctive Amish and Mennonite agricultural practices began when the Anabaptists were disfranchised politically in their homelands and were forced to devise new farming methods in previously unproductive regions and climates. In the seventeenth century they practiced rotation of crops, the stable feeling of cattle, meadow irrigation, used natural fertilizers, and raised clover and alfalfa as a means of restoring soil fertility.[2] Instead of "mining the soil" and moving away when fertility declined, they devised ways of restoring productivity.

Model Farmers. The Anabaptists' reputation for skilled farming was established as a result of their success in Alsace. Soon after the Amish were expelled from the valleys of Markirch (Sainte Marie-aux-Mines) in 1712, the local rulers wrote to the French authorities complaining about the economic setback caused by the expulsion. The Anabaptists, they said, "apply themselves with extraordinary care to agriculture, an occupation for which they have admirable knowledge."[3] They transformed "sterile and dry lands" into "tillable lands and the most beautiful pastures of the province," the report said. The Anabaptist farmers cleared land, created meadows and pastures, and combined farming with cattle-raising. In addition, what the princes liked was that they paid their taxes "with utmost exactness and without compulsion."[4]

---

1. Menno Simons, *The Complete Writings of Menno Simons* (Scottdale, Pa.: Herald Press, 1956), p. 451.
2. Ernst Correll, *Das schweizerische Täufermennonitentum* (Tübingen: Mohr, 1925), p. 101.
3. Jean Séguy, "Religion and Agricultural Success: The Vocational Life of the French Anabaptists from the Seventeenth to the Nineteenth Centuries," trans. Michael Shank, *Mennonite Quarterly Review* 47 (July 1973): 182.
4. Ibid.

Contemporary observers claimed they could identify Anabaptist farms by taking a look at the cultivated hills and fields. This favorable image of the Anabaptist farmer persisted well into the nineteenth century.

Having been denied the ownership of land, the Anabaptists combined animal husbandry with intensive cultivation on the farms they rented. The family occupied a farm, and the entire household worked there. Married children sometimes lived with the family in anticipation of renting the farm. The parents would retire early and help their children financially, spending their later years assisting the young couple to take over. In this manner all the generations of a farming family were integrated by agricultural labor. Improvement of the soil and the dwellings was made feasible by long-term leases. The principles of family occupancy, family entrepreneurship, continuity, and motivation for labor were combined in the management of the farms.

Tenants in Europe, Owners in America. In Europe the Amish acquired the skills of clearing the land and methodically improving the soil by using manure from their herds and by using mineral fertilizers. Deposits of gypsum were mined and processed in kilns for spreading on the land. A three-year system of crop rotation typically consisted of (1) wheat; (2) rye, barley, and clover; and (3) potatoes, carrots, and turnips. Livestock farming was one of the most distinctive features of Anabaptist farmers. Additional pastures were rented, some in the high mountains of the Jura and Vosges ranges. The Bernese Anabaptists are credited with introducing many varieties of clover to France and Germany, as well as with cross-breeding new strains of cattle. Milk provided a good income, and in the eighteenth century the Anabaptists were renowned for making cheese. In the nineteenth century, Jacques Klopfenstein, a successful Amish-Mennonite farmer of Belfort, was awarded a gold medal by the Agricultural Society in France for his outstanding achievements as a model farmer. He was also the founder of an almanac, *The Anabaptist Farmer by Experience.*[5] The tradition of good farming took shape in Europe.

The Amish who came to Pennsylvania showed a strong preference for family-sized holdings on soils that were suited to relatively intensive kinds of cultivation. Furthermore, they wanted to combine agriculture with a preferred way of life, and not farm primarily for commercial

---

5. Séguy, *Les Assemblées anabaptistes-mennonites de France* (The Hague: Mouton, 1977), pp. 503–7. See also John H. Yoder, "Mennonites in a French Almanac," *Mennonite Life* 7 (July 1952): 104; and Ernst Correll, "Master Farmers in France," ibid. 6 (July 1951): 61. Klopfenstein's almanac was issued from 1812 to 1821.

The Anabaptist farmer (cover
of an Alsatian almanac, 1841)

gain. The Amish, like other Germans, sought limestone soils, which
they believed to be superior. The Amish presence on nearly all the
limestone soils in southeastern Pennsylvania today is due not to the
original land selection but to a process of resettlement. Although
the Amish located on large acreages, ranging from 100 to 400 acres at
the outset, they gradually reduced their holdings to what could be
managed with family labor. Plantations or large-scale farms did not
interest them.

The agricultural practices of the two major immigrant groups of
the colonial period—the English-speaking Scotch-Irish and the Swiss-
Germans—were very different.[6] The Scotch-Irish were more mobile,
"forever changing," and were inclined to move to cheaper land.[7] The
Swiss-Germans, who settled in communities, soon made the land valuable. Pennsylvania's famous physician and citizen Benjamin Rush
observed that the German farms were "easily distinguishable from

6. For a discussion of the different traditions, see Richard H. Shryock, "British
versus German Traditions in Colonial Agriculture," *Mississippi Valley Historical
Review* 26 (June 1939): 39–54.

7. Walter M. Kollmorgen, "The Pennsylvania German Farmer," in *The Pennsylvania German*, ed. Ralph Wood (Princeton: Princeton University Press, 1942),
p. 33.

those of others, by good fences, the extent of orchard, the fertility of soil, productiveness of the fields, and luxuriance of the meadows."[8] This observation is still apt today, for the Amish have maintained these characteristics, as can be seen when driving through the Amish farmlands. Moreover the Germans (and Amish) tended to secure the farms of the Scotch-Irish after they had moved and to improve and restore the depleted land.[9]

SOIL PRODUCTIVITY AND MANAGEMENT

In the upkeep of the soil, equipment, and buildings, and of themselves as well-groomed persons, there is diversity among Amish communities. The public image of the Amish as "picturesque Americans," or as "a solid culture that produces happiness as well as abundance," appears to be based upon the Lancaster group. No Amish communities excel this group in outward appearance: newly painted farm buildings, abundant gardens, and tidy children. Other settlements that reflect fine farm upkeep are those in Somerset and Mifflin counties in Pennsylvania. Settlements in the Midwest vary a great deal from farm to farm and from one settlement to another.

Lancaster County, Pennsylvania, is the oldest continuously occupied farming area of the Amish in the United States. The soils in Lancaster and Chester counties in Pennsylvania are considered among the most productive in the United States, indeed in the world.[10] There is a long-established belief among Pennsylvania Germans that limestone soils are superior to other types of soil. Many Amish today prefer limestone, believing that the soil has greater depth and will hold moisture better than other soil types. It appears that eighteenth-century settlers found native limestone and alluvial bottom lands superior in fertility. Through experience, however, it has been found that high productivity does not depend on limestone soils. Soil types that were earlier considered inferior are today as productive as limestone lands.[11] The

8. Benjamin Rush, *An Account of the Manners of the German Inhabitants of Pennsylvania, Written in 1789*, with notes added by I. Daniel Rupp (Philadelphia: Samuel P. Town, 1875), pp. 11–12.

9. According to Fletcher there were many farms with depleted soil in Pennsylvania by 1730. See S. W. Fletcher, *Pennsylvania Agriculture and Country Life, 1640–1840* (Harrisburg: Pennsylvania Historical and Museum Commission, 1950), p. 124.

10. James T. Lemon, *The Best Poor Man's Country: A Geographical Study of Early Southeastern Pennsylvania* (Baltimore: The Johns Hopkins Press, 1972), pp. 39–40.

11. Ibid.

Newly cut grain on an Amish farm in Lancaster
County, Pennsylvania

application of humus and fertilizers in recent years, and the uniform
climate and vegetation pattern over a long period of time, have reduced the differences in fertility among soil types. Wheat, one of the
most profitable crops in the eighteenth century in Lancaster County,
has been largely replaced by corn.

Diversity Preferred. Amish farmers today, as in earlier periods, prefer
general farming or a diversity of crops. They do not raise one crop to
the exclusion of other crops, nor do they cultivate a single crop for
cash income. The Amish raise corn, oats, rye, a variety of hay crops
for feeding, and a great number of vegetables for home consumption.
Where possible, their farms incorporate woodlands and pasture lands.
They maintain a careful plan of crop rotation, usually a three- or
four-year system including a corn, grain (oats, wheat, or barley), and
hay crop, often alfalfa or clover. An abundance of animal manure,
crop rotation (especially the use of a clover or hay crop), and lime
and commercial fertilizers are used to maintain soil fertility and
conservation.

The Amish farm typically maintains livestock of various kinds—

horses, dairy cattle, beef cattle, hogs, poultry, and sheep. Orchards earlier occupied an important place on most farms. A diversified vegetable garden and the production of milk and cheese, fruit, cereals, and meat have aided the Amish in maintaining a high degree of self-sufficiency. Farming is a means whereby the Amishman has maintained himself and members of his family on the land while supporting the religious community of which he is a part.

Land Pressure. With the passing of each decade and the invention of new machines, farm management has not been easy. Population pressure has forced the Amish to have smaller farms, to engage in specialized farm enterprises, and to carefully assess the influence of technology on their community life. These changes are accentuated in Lancaster County, Pennsylvania, where land prices have skyrocketed.[12] In 1850, farms in the county averaged 92.1 acres. The average size declined to 62.7 acres by 1954 but increased to 84 acres by 1978. Today Amish farms range from 30 to 120 acres. The Amish subdivided their farms in order to keep the young generation on the farm and they also bought farms from the non-Amish as they became available. When land prices fluctuated in the Midwest, the Amish in the East remained calm and were not inclined to speculate with their homesteads. As the Lancaster Amish community expanded, land prices in the center of the community rose consistently.[13] One reason for this is that the Amish (and other plain people) prefer to live together in reasonable proximity, and their horse-and-buggy mode of travel limits the distance they wish to travel from their own kin.

Diminishing farm size and the high price of land, together with price fluctuations during critical periods (in times of war and depression), have forced the Amish into more intensive land use. The result is an increase in specialized farming, raising crops for cash (e.g., tobacco, potatoes, tomatoes, peas), and the production of fluid milk and poultry. The Amish in Lancaster County prepare their seedbeds more intensively than do the Amish in the Midwest. With the rapid adoption of herbicides there has been a great reduction in cultivation for the purpose of weeding.

12. For historical data on Amish agriculture, I am indebted to Walter M. Kollmorgen, *Culture of a Contemporary Community: The Old Order Amish of Lancaster County, Pennsylvania,* Rural Life Studies no. 4. (Washington, D.C.: U.S. Department of Agriculture, 1942), pp. 23–55. See also Ira D. Landis, "Mennonite Agriculture in Colonial Lancaster County, Pennsylvania," *Mennonite Quarterly Review* 19 (October): 254–72.

13. Prices in the center ranged from $300 to $400 per acre and on the margin about $200 in 1938. The highest price paid for farmland in 1978 was $6,400 per acre for 47.5 acres.

Cash Crops. It appears that the Amish in Lancaster County started raising tobacco soon after the tobacco industry was established there, probably about 1838.[14] They, along with a group in Saint Mary's County, Maryland, are the only Amish in the nation who grow tobacco. In 1929, 85 percent of the Amish farmers in Leacock Township, Lancaster County, grew tobacco. It is estimated that about one-third of the Amish farmers raise tobacco today. A good crop will yield 2,000 pounds per acre. Tobacco has helped to maintain the high land values. In more recent years whole milk and tomatoes have replaced tobacco as the main source of cash income. When a new silo is built, it frequently signifies a change from tobacco to milk production. Agricultural reports show a striking correlation between the areas occupied by the Amish (and Mennonites) and the regions where tobacco is grown. Experts do not regard the Lancaster County soil as superior to adjacent lands for raising tobacco. The explanation for this correlation is that the Amish have the necessary labor and realize substantial returns. In winter, when there is little other farm work, stripping tobacco is a way to keep the family occupied with a good income-producing activity.

Raising potatoes is a potential source of cash income but is difficult for the Amish. Although potatoes grow well and yield from 400 to 450 bushels per acre in Pennsylvania, raising potatoes requires special machinery and heavy labor input and presents marketing problems. Large wholesale outlets will not bother with growers who have small acreages. Harvesting, processing, and delivering potatoes requires speed, and farmers without a telephone have a poor chance of competing with the automated market.

Amish in the Cornbelt. The Midwestern Amish communities have larger acreages than do the Lancaster County Amish.[15] They too have been compelled to develop more intensive land use and specialized farming. The Indiana Amish supplemented their income with mint

14. Fletcher, *Pennsylvania Agriculture*, p. 165. For additional discussions, see J. Winfield Fretz, "The Growth and Use of Tobacco among Mennonites," *Proceedings of the Seventh Annual Conference on Mennonite Cultural Problems* (1949), pp. 87–100; and idem, "Plain People Grow Big Tobacco," *Farm Quarterly*, Autumn 1951, p. 60.

15. Average acreage of the Nappanee, Indiana, Amish farms is reported to be 104, and for the non-Amish in the same region 261 acres. See Alice Rechlin, "The Utilization of Space by the Nappanee, Indiana, Old Order Amish: A Minority Group Study" (Ph.D. diss., University of Michigan, 1970), p. 89. In Illinois the acreage differences are greater: Amish, 85; non-Amish, 500. See John A. Dukeman, "Way of Life of Illinois Amish-Mennonite Community and Its Effects on Agriculture and Banking in Central Illinois" (The Stonier Graduate School of Banking, Rutgers—the State University, New Brunswick, N.J., 1972), p. 43.

farming until it was no longer profitable.[16] The presence of Amish in the center of a rich corn- and soybean-producing area in central Illinois brings into focus the values of the Amish farmers in contrast to highly mechanized farmers. Here the economic costs of remaining Amish become obvious. In central Illinois, one man with modern machinery and a small amount of part-time help can operate a 600-acre farm. Because of high labor costs he does not raise livestock. The Amish farmer, who has on the average 85 acres, concentrates on livestock production, and raises a diversity of crops, does not fit into this intensive, single-crop income-producing activity. A banker who compared the financial trends of the Amish with those of commercial grain farmers concluded that the Amishman is "reaching a serious financial crisis which can be traced to his way of life."[17] He pointed out that over a ten year period the non-Amish farmer had increased his net worth 48 percent over the Amish farmer, and predicted that with continued large families, the Amishman's plight "cannot improve, and will gradually worsen."[18] From an economic point of view, commercial grain production calls for large units, competitiveness, high production, low labor costs, and access to large amounts of capital and management expertise. Some economists would argue that the Amish are "holding back the economy of the area" and therefore are a liability to the economic growth of the region.[19]

Although the Amish may be reproved for holding down their income potential by refusing to increase the scale of their operations, they cannot uniformly be held accountable for low unit yields. When the Amish were urged by a U.S. government spokesman following World War II to use tractors to produce "more grain for starving peoples of the world," Amish bishops issued a firm response. They asserted that they were growing more food with horse power than their neighbors were with tractors. Every member of their group had already plowed every square inch of his farm (by April), they said, while the neighbors with tractors were just starting to plow. "Our hearts go out to hungry

16. For further reading, see James E. Landing, "An Analysis of the Decline of the Commercial Mint Industry in Indiana" (M.A. thesis, Pennsylvania State University, 1963); and Melvin Gingerich, "Mint Farming in Northern Indiana," *Mennonite Life* 4 (October 1949): 40–41, 46.

17. Dukeman, "Way of Life of Illinois Amish-Mennonite Community," p. 52.

18. Ibid. These views are those of a banker and appear to lack solid supporting data. The Amish realize many noneconomic values.

19. Ibid., p. 57. It is reasoned that if the Amish (in Illinois) would produce on their 20,000 acres at the same rate as the non-Amish farmers, the economy would rise. "This would also put more funds in the area for the banks to loan which would in turn increase the GNP of the area" (ibid., pp. 57–58).

Natural sources of energy. *Left*: Water wheel in a meadow stream generates power for the family farm. *Right*: A single water wheel provides power for five nearby farms.

people wherever they are," they stated, and plowing and planting take place "right under the fences."[20]

Moderate Energy Demands. Crop yields vary among Amish communities. One study reports that for some farm enterprises the Amish use less energy than the other farmers to achieve the same yields.[21] It also appears that Amish farmers have more moderate yields than fully mechanized farmers. In Illinois the Amish corn yield ranges from 70 to 130 bushels per acre in contrast to mechanized farmers, who report 150–170 bushels.[22] The Illinois Amish do not use commercial fertilizer, use much less nitrogen, and maintain wider rows in the field than do non-Amish farmers.

20. The spokesman was Clyde A. Zehner, Chairman of the Pennsylvania Agricultural Adjustment Administration; see *New York Times*, April 28, 1946, p. 12. Before "factories in the field" made some average county figures so high, average farm incomes in counties where large proportions of "plain people" lived were the highest in the nation, according to Charles P. Loomis, former Senior Social Scientist, U.S. Department of Agriculture.

21. W. A. Johnson, Victor Stoltzfus, and Peter Craumer, "Energy Conservation in Amish Agriculture," *Science*, October 28, 1977, pp. 373–78. The study appears to be inconclusive, but the variations among Amish communities are impressive. In this study energy is defined as "the amount of food energy produced per unit of energy spent to produce it."

22. Victor Stoltzfus of Eastern Illinois University, Charleston, provided the data on yields.

The Amish are moderate consumers of fossil energy. They make limited demands, using natural power resources to support their way of life. In many communities the Amish use windmills. In Lancaster County they harness streams in their meadows by constructing water wheels. In other regions the water supply is piped from a reservoir in the mountains. The Amish purchase less fuel, fertilizer, feed, and equipment than do commercial farmers. To buy an automobile, one Amishman said, would mean milking five more cows. One wonders how many more cows it would take to maintain and operate an automobile and a farm truck or to furnish the farm dwellings with electrical appliances. While the Amish have worked out a satisfactory way of life with simple technology and have avoided major financial crises, their experience can scarcely serve as a model for wide application in the modern world. Farmers of today would not appreciate the constraints of manual labor and the austere consumption pattern.

When tractors were first introduced on American farms, the Amish rejected them with the comments, "They don't make manure" and "They ruin the land." Most outsiders accepted the comment as a harmless rationalization, and yet no in-depth study has ever been made of the conservation factor in Amish horse-powered farming as contrasted to tractor farming. Even with horse power, the Amish with few exceptions are first to have their fields plowed and seeded. Tractor farmers have greater convenience, more choice as to when they will till the land, and can get the job done faster than the Amish. Tractors, Amish farmers say, compact the land, which results in reduced yields. Amish farmers who have bought land from the non-Amish have noted that the soil begins to work easier after the third year. The land also begins to drain better, so it is ready for plowing earlier in the spring. Plant roots penetrate the soil better and crops survive better during periods of drought where the soil structure has not been destroyed by compacting. The Amish are more systematic than commercial farmers in getting waste plant material back into the soil.

Amish farmers must make a concerted effort to maintain adequate horse power for field and road. Normally a farm operator will have six draft horses and one or two light horses for road transportation. In every large Amish settlement there are several horse dealers, both Amish and non-Amish, who either raise or deal in horses. Amish farmers make it a point to attend auction sales to transact business. Those who do not buy or sell will nevertheless attend in order to keep abreast of trends, prices, and the thinking of their respected peers. The joking, storytelling, intense sharing, and comradeship among those who buy and deal in horses is a coveted experience. Belgian and Percheron horses are common breeds among the Amish.

Each spring Amish farmers assess the adequacy
of their horse power for the agricultural season.

Young horses are shipped from the Western states to the eastern regions, but the Amish also maintain breeding stock. Many farmers in Lancaster County prefer mule power for field work, believing that mules eat less and have greater endurance. Such preferences appear to vary among farmers, as others consider mules to be more obstinate than horses. In Ohio, raising mules was forbidden by an Amish Ministers' Conference in 1865 on the grounds that it was "improper to mix the creatures of God such as a horse and donkey by which mules arise, because the Lord God did not create such in the beginning."[23]

Modernization and Amish Rules. Many Amish dairy herds produce well, but according to experts the Amish are not the highest producers. The names of many Amish farmers do not appear on the published

23. Harold S. Bender, "Some Early American Amish Mennonite Disciplines," *Mennonite Quarterly Review* 8 (April 1934): 97.

lists of producers, because they do not wish "to be advertised." Although they may have pure-bred herds that produce well, and may use artificial insemination, the Amish are not permitted to have registered livestock. Members are discouraged from belonging to dairy herd associations. Not only would membership "draw too much attention from the world," but there are more informal reasons. Excessive record-keeping and "paper work" is one deterrent. The kind of manipulation required for competitive production appears unethical to the Amish.

The Amish have made some adaptations to modernization, but they will not allow technology and convenience to run away with their family and community. The Old Order Amish try to maintain a balance between the discipline of the Amish community and modernization. The more the rules are believed to be incompatible with survival, the greater the likelihood of a high rate of membership loss or the breakup of the community. Lay leaders know the costs of being Amish, and the sacrifices of maintaining the simple life and loyalty to the church-community. Those who are unwilling to make the sacrifices will accommodate, and most large settlements have several progressive Amish (Mennonite) churches with which former Amish members affiliate. The pressures for greater economic gain imply more modernized machines, and these impulses are felt by the bishops. Bishops moderate the sentiments for and against change and may propose a course of action, but not all, as outsiders think, dictate the rules. Should disagreement occur among the ministers on how much modernization should be permitted, a new settlement may be formed. The most orthodox groups will typically disallow hay bailers, bulk tanks, and milking machines.

During the past twenty years the Amish have introduced many changes in their farming practices.[24] The agitation for tractors that was keenly felt twenty years ago has subsided. Today, the Amish say, farms in Lancaster County, Pennsylvania, are too small for tractors. Improved production also has relieved the pressure for tractor farming. With better seed and greater productivity, corn cribs are too small, even though the acreage is only half that of years ago. The traditional method of crop rotation has changed. Today corn is grown on the same soil in successive years. Crops are planted in contoured terraces to conserve the soil and moisture, a practice scorned by the Amish as "book farming" thirty years ago.

24. Gideon L. Fisher, *Farm Life and Its Changes* (Gordonville, Pa.: Pequea Publishing Co., 1978). In this book a Lancaster County Amish farmer discusses changes in farming over a period of a century or more.

In Midwestern settlements, where tractors with steel wheels are allowed for field work, Amish farmers are faced with additional problems. Local laws forbid vehicles with lugs on asphalt- or oil-surfaced roads. Several Iowa Amish attempted to solve this problem by outfitting their tractors with pneumatic tires. They were excommunicated and soon formed a Beachy Amish congregation. The Old Order Amish kept their tractors off the surfaced roads or secured detachable rims that covered the steel lugs.

Although the Lancaster County Amish have often been considered very conservative and a trusted source of authority in religious matters by other Amish communities, they have also been the most innovative in economic affairs. They have been more exposed to industrial life and are keenly aware of the pressures of worldly economic competition. Ordained leaders from all the districts in Lancaster County meet twice annually to discuss the welfare of the community. Many divisions have undoubtedly been avoided by this moderation of some of the more delicate pressures felt by the separate districts. Lancaster County Amish farmers are permitted to have milking machines and bulk milk tanks operated by diesel engines, but pipes connecting the milkers to the bulk tank are not accepted.[25] These adaptations allow farmers to realize a stable income from selling whole milk. Also permitted are gasoline-driven motors on horse-drawn farm implements. Amish repair shops will buy old tractor equipment, adapt it for horse-drawn use, and mount a gasoline motor on the chassis for operating a hay mower, rake, crimper, baler, corn picker, and stalk shredder. Although self-propelled grain combines are used by the Kansas Amish, the Pennsylvania Amish have not adopted any combines.

Whether the Lancaster Amish can have it both ways (conservative in doctrine and enterprising in farm management) may be an open question. In the past this appears to have been the case. When the Midwestern churches needed ministerial advice in doctrinal matters, they called upon the Lancaster Amish. The Lancaster Amish often felt that the Midwesterners were too lax in shunning. The Midwestern Amish chided the Easterners for raising tobacco and for their modern farm machinery. Presently the Lancaster Amish are seldom called upon in matters pertaining to arbitration, for their bulk tanks and farm practices symbolize for the very conservative Western Amish a credibility gap.

---

25. A period of experimentation with bulk milk tanks, cooled by diesel and air power, resulted in their adoption in Illinois in 1972 when the bishops informally agreed not to oppose or endorse the innovation. See Victor Stoltzfus, "Amish Agriculture: Adaptive Strategies for Economic Survival of Community Life," *Rural Sociology* 38 (Summer 1973): 196–206.

Mules are preferred by many Amish in Pennsylvania,
for they are capable of enduring hot weather
and are believed to eat less than horses do.

Amish communities that have firmly opposed milking machines and the modernization that is required if one is to sell fluid milk have probably declined in their economic capabilities as well as in their ability to provide an incentive for the young men to remain on valuable farms. In Geauga and Trumbull counties in Ohio, the young who saw no prospect of securing a farm started working in local factories in large numbers. Many Amish farmers who cannot meet the standards for selling fluid milk sell their milk at a reduced price to cheese factories. The cheese industry is well developed in certain Amish communities.

One difficulty encountered with the commercialization of the farm has been the traditional observance of Sunday as a holy day. Believing that Sunday is a day on which there should be no business transactions, the Amish have consistently refused to allow their milk to be picked up by trucks on Sunday. Most firms agree to pick up the Sunday milk on Monday morning if proper cooling and storage are assured. Even so, milk companies in most instances will not take on producers unless they agree to sell milk seven days per week. This has often resulted in a serious problem for the Amish. They have sought other

Gardens and roadside markets, common in most
Amish communities, help supplement
the family income.

ways to solve the problem, some by separating the milk and selling
cream, and some by taking an inferior price. The adoption of bulk
tanks and cooling systems has alleviated this problem in communities
where they are permitted. Government subsidy checks, whether for
milk or other parity purposes, are refused on the grounds that money
not earned in honest toil cannot be accepted in good faith. Some feel
that the acceptance of such checks would lead to complications and
perhaps binding obligations to the government.

Saving for a Farm. The Amish save their money to buy additional
farms for their sons and daughters, and they spend much on the upkeep and improvement of their farm dwellings. Many forms of assistance are given to young married couples who are struggling to establish themselves as farmers. Lending money at a low interest rate to
fellow members is common. Land is nearly always kept in the family.
Although Amish inheritance practices differ little from those of other
people, a son is more likely to get the home farm than is a daughter,
and a younger son is more likely to get the family farm than is an

older son. The aging parents usually reserve the privilege of domicile on the farm as long as they live.

Many farm households receive a modest income from selling their products at roadside stands. Often the sales go to regular or favorite customers. A sign at the end of the lane announces goods and produce for sale: potatoes, violets, lawn chairs, dry goods, honey, lumber, brooms, home-baked bread, greenhouse plants, and vegetables in season. For many years the Moses Stoltzfus family sold ice cream cones on their farm. When the sign at the end of the lane brought too many customers, it was removed, but the flow of traffic scarcely diminished. The farm also became a distribution center for Amish-made rugs, quilts, hand-painted dishes, and other handicrafts. This practice, however, is hardly typical of Amish farms.

Traditionally, a young Amishman who climbed the agricultural ladder in Lancaster County began as a laborer or farm hand on an Amish farm, then became a one-third-share tenant, then a one-half-share tenant, next a cash tenant, and finally a farm owner.[26] This has changed somewhat because fewer farms are available. It is now possible to go from laborer to owner very quickly when a farm does become available. Amish boys do not go to high school and therefore may begin as farm hands at the age of sixteen. Their accumulated savings are invested in livestock or machinery. Renting usually precedes buying a farm. Amish boys who receive considerable assistance from their parents will obtain a farm in their own name a few years after they are married. Securing enough land for farming has been a continuous problem in most Amish communities. With many non-Amish youth leaving the rural community for the city, however, there has been a tendency for the Amish to buy the "English" farms as they become available. The Amish have also founded new settlements when land has become difficult to obtain in the older settlements.

Moderation and Austerity as a Life Style. The Amish make a reasonable living with horse-drawn implements and limited acreages. At the same time, they refuse to accept direct cash subsidies from the government for any reason. How do they manage? Artificial income would introduce dangers for them in several respects. They fear the moral consequences of accepting government aid, which is for them an erosion of conscience and motivation. This rejection is also related to their desire to avoid the spiral of rising income, rising costs, and an even higher standard of living. Having achieved a certain plateau of

---

26. Based on the Kollmorgen study with revisions; see Kollmorgen, *Old Order Amish of Lancaster County*, pp. 42–45.

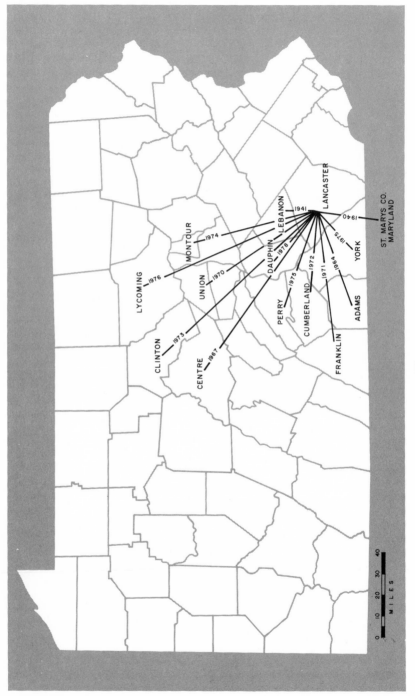

Figure 9.

living, the Amish do not want to be forced to live on a higher standard than what they feel comfortable with. In a recent election year when presidential candidates were promising a higher standard of living, an Amish patriarch remarked: "Striving for such a high standard of living is nothing more than the worship of the golden calf." The Amish simply want to avoid unrealistic inflation of their income-producing capacity.

Moderation and contentment are only part of the secret of survival. Making a reasonable living also involves knowing how to teach children to work and to enjoy the positive aspects of family labor in various contexts—among members of the farm family, within the extended family and religious community, and between the generations. Stable social traditions support this type of resource, which the Amish are quick to point out "cannot be bought with money." Fertile soil with proper intensive cultivation, good seeds, and adequate fertilizer is an important asset. Even after all these techniques are used, barnyard manure still makes a difference in getting the highest possible yields.

Given their high rate of population growth and the limited supply of land in their larger settlements, the Amish face three basic choices. One is to establish new settlements where farming can be realized, but where the land is less productive than that in the larger settlement. The response of the Lancaster settlement in forming new settlements elsewhere in the state has been dramatic since 1967 (see Figure 9).[27] A second alternative is to find nonagricultural occupations while maintaining the Amish pattern of living. This is not easy, and many recognize that it is not a satisfactory solution. A third alternative is to continue to subdivide existing acreages and farm the land more intensively. This might mean expanding dairy and poultry enterprises, but at the cost of buying rather than growing most of the feed. Some Amish sons have persuaded their fathers to sell them small plots of ground on which they have built mechanized poultry or hog barns. This arrangement permits the father to be at home with his children, a necessary element in Amish family life. Those who buy farms at a high price and pay a high interest rate (from $20,000 to $40,000 per year) also find it necessary to construct mechanized hog, poultry, and dairy barns to assure an adequate overall income. All these alternatives are developing in the larger settlements. Some farms are beginning to appear like agrifactories, and the traditional image of a peaceful, quiet countryside is disappearing.

27. For a history of this development, see Rachel K. Stoltzfus et al., *History and Directory of the Old Order Amish of Brush, Nittany, and Sugar Valleys in Centre and Clinton Counties, Pennsylvania* (Gordonville, Pa.: Pequea Publishers, 1979).

WORK AND SEASONAL ACTIVITIES

Generally speaking, the Amish set high standards of work for themselves. Work patterns take on the characteristics of ritual. Communities will differ, however, in the tempo of work and in motivation. Few Amishmen will hire an outsider to do farm work. Outsiders, they say, "do not know enough and they don't work hard enough." When Amish boys were drafted as conscientious objectors during wartime, the Amish said, "If we must hire outsiders, who want to work short hours and do things in a slipshod way, we'll all go broke."[28]

The Work Day. The day begins between four and five o'clock in the morning with milking and other chores. Depending on the number of adults and the number of cows, this daily chore may take from one to two hours. Breakfast may be served at five-thirty during the busy season of the year. During plowing, seeding, and harvest, field work receives the major amount of attention. In the wintertime, feeding the livestock and hauling manure are the most important tasks. The noon meal is served in some areas as early as eleven o'clock. After a short rest period the teams again go into the fields. Supper is served between four and five o'clock. The daily chores of feeding and milking must then be done, if not by the working men, by the women, who often help out during the busy season. This permits the men to go back to the fields and work until dark. Bedtime comes at nine o'clock or a little later.

The Amish workweek ends abruptly on Saturday evening. Outside of the busy season, Saturday is reserved for stable-cleaning and preparing for Sunday. Only the animals and the essential routine chores are taken care of on Sunday, which is a day of rest. On Sunday the major activity is the preaching service, except on alternate Sundays, when visiting is common.

The Yearly Work Cycle. Not only are the agricultural activities of sowing and reaping reflected in the annual calendar, but so too are leisure activities and customs, which tend to become associated with the different seasons of the year. Such seasonal activities vary from one settlement to another. The account that follows is based upon the yearly cycle of the Lancaster County, Pennsylvania, Amish and with the exception of the raising and harvesting of tobacco, would apply generally in other areas.[29]

28. Kollmorgen, *The Old Order Amish of Lancaster County*, p. 43.
29. Ibid., pp. 45–46.

In January the few farmers who have not finished stripping their tobacco complete this work. If steers are being fed, they receive considerable attention at this time so that they will be ready for market whenever prices seem favorable. January, like December, is a popular month for the slaughtering of meat animals. If the winter is mild, apple trees may be trimmed. Frequently visiting is done during this month.

Harnesses are mended and greased in February. If there is little frost in the ground, the farmer begins to plow. During February and March, when the curtain is about to rise on the farming season, farmers who wish to retire or to restrict their operations hold farm sales. Items offered for sale are usually confined to farm machinery, stock, harnesses, household items, and stored grains and feeds, but the farm itself may also be sold. These sales are not only business occasions but also important social events, providing men, women, and children with an excellent opportunity for visiting. School teachers find it expedient to dismiss youngsters when sales take place in the neighborhood. Many sales are attended during March even if there is no need to buy anything.

Manure is hauled during the winter months when the ground is frozen and dry. When the ground is in the right condition, the fields are plowed. Clover or alfalfa seed is sown in the wheat field. Liming requires the attention of some farmers during March. Tobacco beds are sterilized with steam, and some vegetables are planted in the garden.

Potatoes are planted as early in April as possible. Tobacco seed is sown in the sterilized tobacco bed. Farmers who raise oats seed the crop during this month. The ground is well prepared for corn planting. The garden receives much attention and is prepared with manure from the barn.

Corn is generally planted during the last week in April or early in May. Toward the end of May, the young tobacco plants are transplanted into the field. More vegetables are planted in the garden. If the growing season begins early, the cultivation of corn and potatoes is begun in the last part of May.

The transplanting of the young tobacco plants continues until some time in early June. These plants are transplanted at intervals so that the crop will mature over a period of time and can be harvested properly at the right moment. Corn and potato cultivation begins or continues in June, and the operation is repeated from four to six times. Potatoes need to be sprayed about once a week.

In early June, alfalfa is ready for the first cutting. A week later, the mixed clover and timothy hay may be ready to cut. This crop is generally cut only once, whereas alfalfa is usually cut three times in the season. As soon as the hay is dry it is baled in the field and stored in the barn. None of it is stacked outside. Barley is generally ready to be harvested by the middle of June. Wheat, if it matures early, is ready to be harvested late in June. The grain is shocked in the field after it is cut so that it will dry thoroughly. After a few days it is threshed in the field or in the barn. The straw, however, is nearly always stored in the barn, whether baled or unbaled.

In July, the cultivation of corn and potatoes continues. The whole tobacco patch is thoroughly hoed early in the month and this work engages the entire family. The threshing of small grains begins early in July and may continue into August. Threshing is accompanied through work exchanges with extended families or neighbors.

August is often a slack month, and family members may travel to visit distant relatives. Sometime in August, tobacco-cutting gets into full swing and the alfalfa is ready to be cut the second time. Some early potatoes are dug in the latter part of this month.

September and October are very busy months. In September the silos are filled and the cutting and storing of tobacco is completed, safely ahead of an early frost. During the latter half of the month potatoes are dug and the corn is harvested. Each of these tasks generally requires several days of work. Farmers begin to buy steers for winter feeding. The digging and marketing of potatoes may well last until the middle of October.

The corn harvest may continue until November. Generally the corn stalks are shredded during November to be used as feed. In this month some farmers will remove loose stones from the fields. December is the month for stripping tobacco, and the feeding of steers may receive attention. A good deal of butchering is done. Visiting is frequent and perhaps prolonged. With few exceptions, weddings are reserved for November and December.

THE NONFARMING AMISH

Although the Amish excelled as agriculturalists in Europe, not all made their living from the land. On early American tax lists some were listed as operators of grist mills, sawmills, and quarries, and others were tanners, brewers, and blacksmiths. It appears that the sturdy farming tradition emerged in America with the second generation of Amish. When some of the family members worked as hotel-keepers, clerks, and merchants, the conservative elements of the Amish regrouped and clung to farming as the approved form of occupation. Other occupations were extremely limited from about 1830 to 1950.

In the wintertime, sleighs are used to transport families
to church and social gatherings.

Every newly married couple of able body and mind was expected to
operate a farm.

Squeezed Off the Farm. With the increasing cost of farmland, the
diminishing availability of good farmland, decreasing farm profits,
and the increase in costs of farm machinery and supplies, the occupational pattern has changed. Prior to 1954, Amish fathers in Lancaster
County, Pennsylvania, who sought employment in factories were
excommunicated. Today many are forced to work off the farm or to
move to areas where cheaper farmland can be secured. The proliferation of nonfarming employment occurred very rapidly after 1960. The
economic pinch the Amish find themselves in today is different from
that of a half-century or more ago. The old assumption that "if you

Home of an Amish factory worker. Only a small barn
is needed, for the horse and carriage.

work hard you can survive" is no longer true. No matter how hard a
family works, today man and wife cannot assure their sons and daughters that they will be able to start housekeeping on a farm.

This conclusion is based on a series of interviews with two generations of Amish farmers who were asked, "What are the most serious
problems confronting a young Amishman wishing to enter farming?"
The overwhelming responses from the younger men were "money
problems," "finding a farm," "high interest rates," and "the high cost
of equipment."[30] Responses from the older farmers were no different.
They stressed the important function of a father, as in this comment:
"The only way he can start is if his father helps him, moves on and
works, and maybe he can buy it for half of what his daddy paid. If he
hasn't a daddy to help he just can't get started."

Today roughly half of the Amish households are engaged in farming
(Table 5). Of the three main settlements, Ohio has the largest per-

30. Eugene P. Ericksen, Julia A. Ericksen, and John A. Hostetler, "The Cultivation of the Soil as a Moral Directive: Population Growth, Family Ties, and the
Maintenance of Community among the Old Order Amish," *Rural Sociology*, in
press.

Table 5

Occupations of Amish household heads in the Pennsylvania,
Ohio, and Indiana settlements

Type of occupation	Pennsylvania (%)	Ohio (%)	Indiana (%)
Farming	49.5	41.3	49.0
Farming and second occupation	0.7	2.3	9.1
Farm laborer	1.7	0.1	—
Nonfarming	34.6	44.8	36.0
Retired	7.9	9.5	3.2
No information	5.6	1.1	2.7
Number of household heads	2,034	2,680	1,360

Sources: Pennsylvania Amish Directory (1973); Ohio Amish Directory (1973);
Indiana Amish Directory (1970).

centage of nonfarmers. Very few of the Amish household heads work as farm laborers. Single men, if they are the sons of farmers, typically work on the farm of their father or on another Amish farm.

Diverse New Occupational Patterns. A large proportion of the non-farming Amish work in shops and trades within the Amish community as carpenters, cabinet-makers, carriage-makers, blacksmiths, harness-makers, and lumber workers. Traditional occupations that are useful to the Amish community but do not involve group participation are butcher, sheep-shearer, shoe repairman, broom-maker, beekeeper, plumber, horse-trainer, bookbinder, tool-sharpener, orchard-grower, and carpet-maker.

Since about 1960, newer occupations have emerged, as indicated in the Amish *Shop and Service Directory,* which covers the major communities.[31] The listings include accountants, appliance stores, bake shops, bee supplies, butcher shops, cabinet shops, canvas products, carpentry supplies, casting and foundry work, chair shops, cheese houses, clocks and watches, country stores, dry goods, engine shops, farm equipment and repair, farm markets, farm wagons, feeds, furniture shops, greenhouses, hardware, harness shops, hat shops, health food stores, machine shops, locksmiths, print shops, refrigeration, shoe shops, silos and silo equipment, sporting goods, tailor shops, tomb-

31. *Old Order Shop and Service Directory of the Old Order Society in the United States and Canada,* 1st ed. (Gordonville, Pa.: Joseph F. Beiler, Compiler, November 1977). The publication is, in effect, a "yellow page directory" without telephone numbers.

stones, upholstery, and woodworking shops. The shops are generally located on farms and are neither obvious nor advertised. On many farms such activities supplement farm income. It may well be that modest yields and a limited scale of farming are maintained by income from commercial activity.

The above list does not reflect some of the more specialized types of farming such as broiler-, chicken-, turkey-, and hog-raising. Another is raising trout fish. Many specialty shops and services have sprung up. They support the diverse needs of the community and also provide economic support and employment within the Amish community. The multiplication of these small enterprises, commensurate with the growth of the Amish population, is one of the most important changes that have taken place in Amish society in the twentieth century. Now that the Amish can buy and sell to members of their own faith and community, they are less dependent on the outside world for their survival. Interaction with the non-Amish is also thereby greatly reduced.

Work in Small Industries. Amish breadwinners who work for non-Amish employers constitute a small percentage in some Amish settlements and a large percentage in others. In 1970, less than 5 percent of the Amish household heads in Lancaster County, Pennsylvania, were employed by "English" employers. In the Nappanee community of Indiana 71 percent were employed by non-Amish.[32] The Amish prefer to work close to their homes, and with the trend toward ruralization of industry, they have begun to work in mobile-home industries or boat factories. Some of these industries locate near Amish communities in order to recruit the Amish as workers. Employment is seen as an opportunity to save money toward the purchase of a farm. Often an Amish father will work as a laborer until there are several children under the age of six in the family, and then he will make serious efforts to locate on a farm. There are, however, an increasing number who have no intention of locating on a farm.

A marginal occupation may be tolerated by the Amish community for good reasons, or as long as it does not constitute a direct threat. However, when an individual takes his marginal occupation seriously and wishes to excel by outside standards, the distress to the community may exceed toleration limits.

Amish Industries and Professions. When Amish enterprises become large—successful by worldly standards—they also constitute a liability

32. Rechlin, "The Utilization of Space," p. 79.

An Amish carriage shop

to the Amish way of life. The determination to maintain a small-scale operation dictates that if the business becomes "too large," it must be sold to an outside company. One Amish plant employs twenty-eight people, which is considered exceptionally large. Steel-fabricating plants or machine shops require large sources of energy, the movement of large quantities of raw material, and transportation. These plants may employ a diesel-powered generator as an energy source. For the delivery of their products they will hire non-Amish trucks and drivers. One Amish company makes, delivers, and installs farm silos, often within a radius of 200 miles. Another makes steel grain bins and delivers and installs them according to specification. The delivery and installation of these products requires a crew of several persons and from one to five days of labor. These firms typically hire trucks with non-Amish drivers and single Amish boys as laborers.

One of the new professions is school teaching. Most Amish children went to the public school thirty years ago, and thus the Amish did not train their own people for this vocation. Teaching is learned by apprenticeship and is normally done by single girls, never by a wife and mother of small children, and rarely by a married man who depends on teaching as a source of income. There are no Amish physicians, and there will be none so long as college training is forbidden. A few Amish girls have become practical nurses. Again, this activity is regarded as a calling to a community need and is not pursued as a means of livelihood.

Amish Prestige and Management Patterns. The measures of social class in terms of income, education, and material possessions have little relevance in Amish society. The goals of an Amish person are obedience, humility, and brotherly love, and thus are very different from those in a competitive and consumer-oriented society. Persons having the highest prestige in Amish society are those retired couples who have trained their children well, have remained with the Amish church, and have provided their children with farms. Such a retired couple will have very modest savings, a small income, but will have earned great respect in the Amish community. In a study of Amish fertility patterns no relationship was found between income and family size.[33] The best indicator of Amish prosperity is the labor-force activity of the male household head. The highest prestige activity is farming, the second highest is self-employment in a nonfarm business, and the lowest is day labor.

Among young Amish couples today, farming is a highly cooperative enterprise between husband and wife. Wives are frequently book-keepers and are in close control of the flow of information on finances. Farm schedules of harvesting, meal preparation, and sleeping often require adjustments involving a high degree of understanding and commitment. In this respect the Amish are a stable asset for land invest-ment firms. The Farm Credit Service in some areas regards its loans to Amish customers as a sound investment. If the crops are poor in one year, the Amish are not inclined to quit the farm, but will expect a better crop the next year. They will have family help, for farming is made into a family enterprise. A loan from a young operator's father or a relative, combined with a mortgage, will often make the differ-ence. Amish farm enterprises are not suddenly disrupted by divorce.

Good management is an important differentiating quality in Amish life. By "good management" the Amishman means acquiring a whole complex of attitudes and resources, including the following: willing-ness to start the day early, working cooperatively within the family, knowing how to include children in family work, maintaining punc-tuality and orderliness, having equipment and tools in place and in good repair, maintaining good livestock and horses, working the soil and harvesting at times when the weather is right and the labor is available, learning to preserve food and conserve material supplies and

33. Julia A. Ericksen et al., "Fertility Patterns and Trends among the Old Order Amish," *Population Studies* 33 (July 1979).

An Amish blacksmith replacing the shoes
on a road horse

energy, and not shrinking from the demands of hard work. When the members nominate persons for church leadership and ordination, they choose persons who they believe have practiced these values, and they invariably choose farmers rather than laborers and business persons.

The Amish themselves recognize differences in style and tidiness among family lines. Amish genealogists refer to a "classy style of life" and "an extraordinary trim impulse" in the Lapp family line in the Pequea Valley and the Mast family in Conestoga Valley.[34] This finery is manifest in well-bred horses, spacious and well-ordered farm dwellings, many varieties of flowers in the garden and at the windows in the home, regular sweeping of the walks and driveways with a broom, and decorative china in the cupboards. There are also family lines that have a reputation for being slothful. However, since unity and brotherly love are the overriding goals, these differences are deliberately minimized and generally not vocalized.

How do the Amish justify living on some of the highest-priced agricultural land in the nation? To them the land is a trust to be shared and to be made productive for the needs of many, and to be passed on to generations to come. By exercising a variety of skills, they attempt to improve the land before passing it on to the next generation. An enormous variety of practical skills is needed on their part

34. *The Diary* 10 (April 1978): 32.

to maintain this goal. Although the Amish might be classed as small-scale capitalists, they differ greatly from Max Weber's description of the Protestant ethic as expressed in Calvinism, Pietism, and Methodism.[35] As in Weber's thesis, manual labor, frugality, industry, and honesty are valued and may be useful, but unlike his thesis, such moral virtues do not give assurance of salvation for the Amish. Wealth does not accrue to the individual for his enjoyment, or for the advancement of his social standing, but rather enhances the well-being of the community. The Amishman is, in fact, embarrassed by outward signs of social recognition. Similarly, the Amish calling is not that of seeking worldly success, for the Amishman does not depend on material success for his sign or assurance of salvation. The ascetic limitations on consumption, combined with the compulsion to save, make possible an economic base for a people "in the world, but not of it."

35. Max Weber, *The Protestant Ethic and the Spirit of Capitalism* (New York: Charles Scribner's Sons, 1958), pp. 144–54.

CHAPTER 7

The Amish Family

ꕥ

PROCREATION, nurture, and socialization are the major functions of the Amish family. The central role that the family is given in Amish culture can be illustrated in many ways. The family has authority over the individual not only during childhood but also during adolescence and later life. Certain loyalties to parents, relatives, and grandparents may change, but they will never cease. The size of the church district is measured by the number of families (households), not by the number of baptized persons. It is the families that take turns having the preaching service. Maps and directories of settlements made by Amish persons list the households and often the names of the parents, their birth and marriage dates, and the birth dates of the children as well. After marriage it is recognized that the most important family function is childbearing. Parents stress not their own individual rights but their responsibilities and obligations for the correct nurture of their children. They consider themselves accountable to God for the spiritual welfare of their children.

MATE-FINDING

The young Amishman's choice of a wife is limited or conditioned by his value system. He must obtain a partner from his own Amish faith, but not necessarily from his own community. Because of minimum contact with Amish young people of other communities and

147

states, marriages in the large settlements have for the most part taken place within the immediate community. The choice of a mate is also governed by the rules of the church. First-cousin marriages are taboo, while second-cousin marriages are discouraged but do occur infrequently. Forbidden in Lancaster County is marriage to a "Swartz" cousin—that is, to the child of a first cousin.[1]

There are certain exceptions to the rule that marriage must be endogenous with respect to group affiliation. It is always permissible to marry into a more orthodox affiliation if the more liberal party joins the conservative group. Young people intermarry freely among Amish districts and settlements that maintain fellowship with one another.

The occasion that provides the best opportunity for young people to meet is the Sunday evening singing. The singing is usually held at the same house where the morning preaching was held. The youth from several districts usually combine for the singing. This occasion provides interaction among young people on a much broader base than is possible in the single district.

On Sunday evening after the chores are done, the young folks make preparations for the singing. The young man puts on his very best attire, brushes his hat and suit, and makes sure that his horse and buggy are clean and neat in appearance. He may take his sister or his sister's friend to the singing, but seldom his own girl friend. If he does take his own girl, he will arrange to pick her up about dusk at the end of a lane or at a crossroad.

A singing is not regarded as a a devotional meeting. Young people gather around a long table, boys on one side and girls on the other. The singing is conducted entirely by the unmarried. Only the fast tunes are sung. Girls as well as boys announce hymns and lead the singing. Between selections there is time for conversation. After the singing, which usually ends formally about ten o'clock, an hour or more is spent in joking and visiting. Those boys who do not have a date usually arrange for a *Mädel* ("girl") at this time.

Although there are other occasions when young folks get together, such as husking bees, weddings, and frolics, the singing is the primary occasion for boy-girl association. Both the boy and the girl look upon each other as a possible mate. A boy or girl may "quit" whenever he or she pleases. The usual age for courtship, called *rumspringa* ("running around"), begins for the boy at sixteen, and for the girl between fourteen and sixteen. Secrecy pervades the entire period of courtship

---

1. The nickname "Swartz cousin" originated with Jacob Swartz, who was excommunicated for marrying Magdalena Stoltzfus (b. June 18, 1832). She was his "first cousin once removed" (the offspring of his first cousin).

Friendship groups offer the opportunity for meeting
prospective mates. Courtship requires a spirited horse
and usually an open (topless) buggy.

and is seldom relaxed, regardless of the length of the association. If a boy is charged with having a girl friend, he will certainly be very slow to admit it. Courting that cannot be successfully disguised becomes a subject for teasing by all members of the family.

Among themselves, young people seldom refer to their boy or girl friends by first name. The pronoun "he" or "she" is used instead. The terms *beau* and *Kal* ("fellow") are used in general conversation. The term *dating* is used, but has no dialect equivalent.

Besides taking his girl home after the singing on Sunday evening, the young man who has a "steady" girl will see her every other Saturday night. When Saturday evening comes, he dresses in his best; he makes little ado about his departure and attempts to give the impression to his younger brothers and sisters that he is going to town on business.

Before entering the home of his girl, he makes sure that the "old folks" have retired. Standard equipment for every young Amishman of courting age is a good flashlight. When the girl sees the light focused on her window, she knows that her boy friend has arrived, and she quietly goes downstairs to let him in. The couple may be together in the home until the early morning hours on such occasions. The clatter of horses' hoofs on hard-surface roads in the early hours of the morning is evidence of young suitors returning home.

The old way of spending time together was for a boy and girl to lie on the bed fully clad. The Amish have no uniform word in their speech for this practice, which to them in earlier times was very ordinary. *Bei-schlof* ("with sleep") is the term used in one area. In English this behavior pattern is known as bundling. It is an old custom, having been practiced in Europe and in early American colonies, especially in large, unheated houses. Unfortunately the subject has been exploited by pamphleteers and story writers. The practice has been sharply condemned by most Amish leaders, though it is defended by some. In the nineteenth century new settlements were started by families that wanted to get away from the practice. Those communities that assimilated most to the American society have sensed the misinterpretations of outsiders and thus tend to oppose the practice of bundling. Those groups that have consistently retained their traditional culture with its very rigid sex codes have been least opposed. The practice has disappeared without argument in other areas with the influx of modern home conveniences (living-room suites, etc.) and a wider range of social contacts with the outside world.

Mate-finding takes places in the confines of the little community rather than outside it. Conflict and casualties resulting from mismating are absorbed by the culture. Conflicts are less obvious here than in the

Newlyweds receive many gifts and substantial help
from their families in the process of establishing
a new home.

greater society. The wedding is a climactic experience for family and
community, and the families of both bride and bridegroom take an
active part in helping the newlyweds to establish a home.

It is an important task of the family to provide a dowry. Homemade
objects and crafts are the usual items. Furthermore, it is understood
that each person invited to a wedding will bring a gift for the new
couple. These tokens of friendship, which are usually displayed on the
bed in an upstairs bedroom, consist of dishes, kerosene lamps, bed-
spreads, blankets, tablecloths, towels, clocks, handkerchiefs, and small
farm tools.

The parents of the bride and bridegroom also provide furniture, livestock, and sometimes basic equipment when the couple moves into their home. For instance, one bridegroom, an only son, had the farm deeded over to him together with the farm machinery and livestock. The bride received from her parents a cow, tables, chairs, a new stove, dishes, bedding, and many other items. The dowry of the bride was in this case not unusual. All mothers by tradition make a few quilts and comforters for each child. These are usually made years in advance so that they will be ready when needed. One housewife made three quilts and two comforters for each child; she had seven boys and three girls. The wedding ceremony will be discussed in Chapter 9.

MARRIED-PAIR LIVING

Social roles are well defined within the Amish family. The force of tradition, religious teaching, and emphasis on the practical help to make it so. Family organization is strictly monogamous and patriarchal. Overall authority tends to belong to the father, but there are varying degrees of practice in specific families. In keeping with a biblical teaching (I Cor. 11:3), the man is the head of the woman just as Christ is the head of the church. The wife has an immortal soul and is an individual in her own right. Although she is to be obedient to her husband, her first loyalty is to God. In marriage husband and wife become "one flesh," a union which is terminated only with death. There is no provision for divorce. The wife follows her husband's leadership and example but decides as an individual whether she is ready for communion. In church council she has an equal vote but not an equal "voice." Should her husband sin to the extent that he is placed under the ban, she, like all members, will shun him. The husband would do the same if his wife were under "the ban." Important family decisions typically are joint decisions. The Amish wife participates actively in any decisions to move to a different locality, which may not be true of today's "corporation wife."[2]

Cooperation between husband and wife prevails in differing degrees, depending somewhat on the make-up of the personalities and their adjustment. The line of authority is not rigid, however, as an example will indicate. A man and his wife called at the home of a neighbor to see a bed that was for sale. He remained seated in the

2. An observation made by Gertrude E. Huntington in "The Amish Family," in *Ethnic Families in America*, ed. Charles H. Mindel and Robert W. Habenstein (New York: Elsevier Scientific Publishing Co., 1976), p. 307. I am indebted to Gertrude E. Huntington for assistance in clarifying the nature of family structure and roles in Amish society.

The married pair upholds community rules
and sets an example for the children.

buggy while she entered the house and inspected the bed. Undecided, and not willing to commit herself without the encouragement of her husband, she called him. After both had looked at the bed and pondered over the price, she said, "What do you think?" He replied, "You are the boss of the house." After a few gestures that indicated she approved of the purchase, he wrote out a check for the amount asked.

The wife is often consulted when family problems arise, and she exercises her powers in rearing the children, but her husband's word is regarded as final in domestic matters. She is her husband's helper but not his equal. An Amish woman knows what is expected of her in the home, and her attitude is normally one of willing submission. This is not to suggest that there are no exceptions, for the writer has known families where the wife exerted influence out of proportion to the usual pattern. In practice, the farm is the Amishman's kingdom, and his wife is his general manager of household affairs.

Property, whether household goods or farm equipment, is spoken of as "ours" within the family. In actuality, however, any transaction involving the sale or purchase of property is made through the husband or has his approval. Farms are usually owned jointly by husband and wife to ensure legal ownership in case of the death of the husband. In public affairs men are regarded as more fit than women for leadership. Banking, writing checks, and depositing money are done by both in many households. Women and men bid for household items at public sales. The experienced housewife generally has the authority to make decisions pertaining to the house, but husband and wife usually confer with each other before making any large purchases, and the considerate husband will consult his wife before purchasing any household item. The wife generally has a purse of her own that is replenished periodically by her husband for the purchase of household supplies, groceries, and clothing. When her supply of money is exhausted, she asks for more.

Major household expenses or anticipated medical expenditures are usually discussed mutually, and if the wife decides she would like to patronize a certain doctor, her husband is likely to consent. The husband, on the other hand, may purchase farm equipment or livestock without seeking the advice of his wife. The wife often keeps the income from vegetables or produce sold on the farm.

The extent to which the farmer aids his wife in household tasks is nominal. He helps on special occasions such as butchering and cooking apple butter, but he does not help in the routine preparation of food, nor does he wash dishes. At weddings, the men serve as cooks and table waiters with their wives. Guests at an Amish table are often addressed by the husband: "Now just reach and help yourselves."

The wife's duties include care of the children, cooking and cleaning, preparation of produce for market, making clothes for the family, preserving food, and gardening. Typically, washing will be done on Monday, ironing on Tuesday, baking on Friday, and cleaning on Saturday. There are no special shopping nights, as purchases are made in the village store during weekdays. Women and adolescent girls frequently help with the harvest of crops, especially cornhusking. In one family, each of the older girls manages a team of horses during the summer months. They plow the fields, cultivate the soil, and do the work of adult males. This is exceptional, however, since women are not generally called upon to help with the heavier jobs in farming. It is the woman who sees that the fences, posts, grape arbors, and frequently the trees about the farm buildings are whitewashed in the spring. The appearance of the lawn and the area surrounding the house is largely the responsibility of the wife, and she feels obligated to keep the inside as well as the outside clean and neat in appearance.

The wife aids the husband in chores that are not usually considered household tasks more than the husband helps his wife in household work. In one home, while the men and carpenters were remodeling the barn in anticipation of the oldest son's marriage, the mother arranged to have neighbor women and relatives come for a day to paint the barn's window sashes.

Gardening, except perhaps for the initial spading in the spring, is the sole responsibility of the wife. The Amish wife usually raises a large variety of edibles, often as many as twenty kinds of vegetables. She makes sure that there are plenty of cucumbers and red beets because they are part of the standard lunch at Sunday services. Typical Amish gardens abound with flowers. Some gardens have as many as twenty varieties. Order and cleanliness tend to be distinctive features of Amish gardening. Orchards are a part of the typical Amish landscape, and spraying, if done at all, is the man's job. More often than not, fruits are purchased from commercial sources because expensive equipment for spraying is considered too costly for a small orchard.

Almost all women's and children's clothing is made at home by the wife or her relatives. Food-processing consumes a large part of the wife's time. Meat-curing may be done by the husband, often at the suggestion and according to the plans of the wife.

With regard to the woman's role in religious services, the teaching of the Apostle Paul is literally obeyed: "Let the woman learn in silence with all subjection." In leadership activities, the woman is not "to usurp authority over the man." At baptismal service, boys are baptized before girls. Women never serve as church officials.

Amish parents try to be of one mind when dealing with their children and to discuss any differences between themselves privately and prayerfully. Marriage partners are taught to be considerate of each other and never to disagree in public.

PERSONAL RELATIONSHIPS

The personal relationship between husband and wife is quiet and sober, with no apparent displays of affection. The relationship is in striking contrast to the expectation of a romantic ideal expressed in popular American culture. Patterns of conversation vary among Amish mates, but terms of endearment, or physical gestures of affection, are conspicuously absent.

The husband may address his wife by her given name, or by no name at all. He may merely begin talking to her if he wants her attention. In speaking about his wife to others he may use "she" or "my wife," but rarely her given name. The mother of the family in like manner may refer to him simply as "my husband" or "he."

Irritation between mates is expressed in a variety of ways, but is conditioned by informally approved means of expressing dissatisfaction. As a rule, institutional patterns override personal considerations. Little irritation is observable among the Amish. Displeasure or disapproval is expressed by tone of voice or by gesture. The husband may express disapproval by complete silence at the dinner table, in which case the wife is left to guess what is wrong. The usual conversation may lag for several days before it is completely restored to a normal level. Harsh and boisterous talk between mates is rare.

Roles of the parents are defined in terms of traditional familial patterns and to some degree by kinship ties. The husband and wife are not only individuals connected by personal sentiments, but as members of a group must maintain the standards and dignity of that group. This tendency toward the consanguineal system compares favorably with the findings of Thomas and Znaniecki in their study of the Polish peasant family, in which, they say, "the marriage norm is not love, but 'respect.'" As they explain:

The norm of respect from wife to husband includes obedience, fidelity, care for the husband's comfort and health; from husband to wife, good treatment, fidelity, not letting the wife do hired work if it is not indispensable. In general, neither husband nor wife ought to do anything which could lower the social standing of the other, since this would lead to a lowering of the social standing of the other's family. Affection is not explicitly included in the norm of respect, but is desirable. As to sexual love, it is a purely personal matter, is not and ought not to be socialized in any form; the family purposely ignores it, and the slightest indecency or indiscreetness with regard to sexual relations in marriage is viewed with disgust and is morally condemned.[3]

The Polish pattern of marital relationships compares favorably with the Amish. The Amish are in addition very conscious of the biblical pattern: "Wives, submit yourselves unto your own husband, as unto

3. William I. Thomas and Florian Znaniecki, *The Polish Peasant in Europe and America* (New York: Alfred A. Knopf, 1927), 1: 90.

the Lord. . . . So ought men to love their wives as their own bodies. . . . and the wife see that she reverence her husband" (Eph. 5:22, 28, 33).

The Amish are strongly opposed to premarital sex and extramarital affairs, and any transgression among members must be confessed to the church assembly whether or not pregnancy occurs. Males and females have equal responsibility to confess. After a period of punishment (by excommunication), repenting individuals are received back into the church. They are completely forgiven. Pregnancy is not always considered sufficient reason for the offending couple to marry, but if the couple decides to marry, the wedding is held before the birth of the child. If there is no marriage in such cases, the mother may keep the baby or the baby may be adopted by an Amish couple.

CHILDREN AND PARENTS

Amish children appear innocent and unspoiled by the things of this world. The birth of a child brings joy to the family and community, for there will be another dishwasher or woodchopper, and another church member. Thus, children are wanted. At no time in the Amish system are they unwelcome, for they are regarded as "an heritage of the Lord."

The first two years of life are happy ones. Baby obtains what he wants. He is given permissive care with great amounts of love from mother, father, brothers, sisters, aunts, uncles, grandfathers, grandmothers, and cousins.

After about the second year, restrictions and exacting disciplines are continuously imposed upon the child until adolescence. He must be taught to respect the authority of his parents and to respond properly to their exactness. The child is considered sinless since he does not know the difference between right and wrong. It is the duty of parents to teach him this difference so that he will realize his moral inadequacy and choose the "right way" of the Amish religion.

The Amish home is an effective socializing agent that is directed at making the child a mature person in the Amish way of life. Early in life the child learns that the Amish are "different" from other people. Thus, he must learn not only how to understand to play the role at home and in the Amish system but also how to conduct himself in relation to the norms of his "English" neighbors. He cannot have clothes and toys just like the "English" people have. He soon learns to imitate his parents, to take pride in the "difference," and appears no longer to ask "why" until adolescence.

Amish children are raised so carefully within the Amish family and community that they never feel secure outside it. The faces of many

Strong ties are maintained
between generations.

Amish boys and girls reflect pure intent, a sincere, honest, cordial, and well-bred disposition. The extraordinary love and discipline they get prepares them well for Amish womanhood and manhood.

The family is expected to transmit to the child a reading knowledge of German. The Amish school also aids in this process. The family members may gather about the sitting-room table, each with a German Testament, and take their turns spelling, enunciating the alphabet, and reading. In some families, this exercise is carried out daily in connection with morning and evening prayers. Even preschool children, ages four and five, take their turns by repeating words or syllables as they are pronounced by the family head.

Amish children do not receive regular allowances from their parents. A young person who works a day or half a day for a neighbor is often permitted to keep the earnings, but is expected to save the money. When parents take their children to town they may give them a small sum for buying candy. Early in life parents may provide a "bank" in which to save pennies. The necessity of taking good care of one's clothing and other personal items is strongly emphasized to the child.

Just as the parents are to be examples to their children, so the older children must be good examples to the younger ones. Among children in the family, age is more important than sex in determining authority, accountability, and work. The older ones care for and help the younger children, but they do not punish them physically. Normally they persuade and wheedle them into obedience. In late adolescence masculine dominance becomes more evident in brother-sister relationships.

Teaching the child to work and accept responsibility is considered of utmost importance. The child begins to assist his parents at the age of four and is given limited responsibility at the age of six. The boy learns to feed the chickens, gather eggs, feed the calf, and drive the horses. The girl is trained to perform small jobs for her mother and to learn early the art of cooking and housekeeping. Some parents give a pig, sheep, or calf to each child with the stipulation that he or she tend the animal and take care of it. In this way the child is motivated to take an interest in the farm.

The role of children and the work performed by each is well illustrated in the following description of a family of six children, five boys and one girl, between the ages of three and twenty-two.

The girl (aged twelve) enjoys helping her mother with the household duties, especially setting the table and preparing meals. She and her younger brother (aged eight) help their mother with the garden. When the time comes to do the chores, each has a specific assignment, but their duties also overlap. The four oldest children and the father milk fifteen cows regularly. The oldest son feeds and beds the horses, hogs, and calves. The second feeds the laying hens, and the third tends the pullets on range and carries wood for his mother. The girl milks three cows, feeds the rabbits, and gathers the eggs. The eight-year-old boy has no regular work assignment but assists his mother or one of the older members of the family. The two older sons frequently help on washday with heavier tasks such as carrying water. The third son has a decided dislike for housework.

In many farm families each child will be given an animal, usually a calf or heifer, which will become exclusively his. The boy or girl will choose and name the animal. Typically this may occur as early as the seventeenth birthday, and the family may gather to watch the young person choose his animal from among the herd. When the animal matures and has a young calf, the calf may be sold and the proceeds will go into the savings account of the child. The fate of the animal is linked to the care and attention it is given by the owner. The child as owner learns the consequences of feeding, neglect, growth, birth, sterility, disease, or death. After the young person marries, the animal is taken to the farm home of the new couple.

In the Amish family, sons who reach the age of twenty-one are paid

Young children acquire familiarity with farm animals and the natural environment while learning Amish rules of behavior.

monthly wages if they are unmarried and continue to work at home. A young man may hire out for the summer, but this practice has almost completely disappeared among those Amish who farm with tractors. Farmers who need assistance frequently request help from a neighbor or a relative for a few days. Single girls occasionally work as maids in other Amish homes. A *Maut* ("maid") among the Amish enjoys the same privileges as a family member would.

The ability of the family to act as a unit in an emergency is illustrated by what happens when the livestock breaks out. Charles P. Loomis, who worked at an Amish place as a farm hand, describes such an incident. As the family was seated at the suppertable,

Mattie got up to get some milk and saw that the cows were getting through the gate. She screamed and the whole family dashed to the door. Mother hurriedly put the baby into the carriage. We ran after the 22 cows. The big family encircled them, one girl having run over a mile on plowed ground. We got them back in. They had not been out this spring and were wild. Mother said she had read in books about stampedes in the west. Chris and I put them back in their stanchions after supper. He fed them grain first, but still we had a job. He said, "They're out of practice. When they get to going to the meadow each day they will do better."[4]

Strict obedience to parents is a profound teaching stressed over and over by Amish parents and by the preachers and is a principle based upon several passages in the Bible. An Amish lad who runs away from home, or even an adult who leaves the Amish church, is held guilty of disobedience to his parents.

Amish children, like all children, manifest resentments by pouting or by responding negatively. But when these manifestations are overt, "smackings" are sure to follow either with the palm of the hand, a switch, a razor strap, or a buggy whip. Temper tantrums, making faces, name-calling, and sauciness among youngsters are extremely rare, for the child learns early that his reward for such rebellion is a sound thrashing.

Disputes between boys are perhaps as frequent in Amish as in non-Amish families. The manner of expressing dissatisfaction is mostly verbal, especially among youngsters, but noses occasionally do get broken. Profanity is not permitted, and if discovered by the parents, is usually promptly treated with punishment. Resentment toward a brother or sister is expressed only mildly in the presence of older

4. Charles P. Loomis, "A Farmhand's Diary," *Mennonite Quarterly Review* 53 (July 1979): 248.

persons. In the presence of parents, a quarrel may be expressed by silence, hesitancy, or by completely ignoring the situation.

The subject of sex in Amish life is regarded as a purely personal matter. Adults purposely ignore any mention of the subject, especially in the presence of children. Very little sex instruction is given to the ordinary Amish child. In spite of this suppression, the child acquires gradually, piece by piece, an elementary knowledge of the process of biological reproduction. The Amish child most certainly does ask questions about the sexual behavior of animals on the farm. To satisfy his curiosity, the child more often than not talks such matters over with associates his own age. The jokes of young men show that sexual interests have developed long before courtship and marriage. Any remark about sex in private conversation between a boy and girl of courting age is inopportune, but an indecent joke is not uncommon among a group of men.

FOOD AND TABLE

In the Amish home a "place at the table" is symbolic of belonging. When a place is vacant due to death, marriage, sickness, father's having gone to town, the discipline of the ban, or a runaway child, all are deeply aware of the empty place. The seating is traditionally arranged with father at the end of the table and the boys to his right from youngest to oldest. Mother is seated just to the left or right of father with the girls on her side of the table. Figure 10 shows the seating arrangement of a typical family—father, mother, and children, with their ages—before the marriage of any of the nine children.

The family table becomes the scene for the evaluation of behavior, for expressing personal likes and dislikes before the group, and for group participation and decision-making. Conversation for its own sake is not encouraged. Conversation at breakfast is typically about the work that needs to be done, how and who should do it. The mother may indicate that certain decisions need to be made relative to preparing the brooder house for the chicks, or about the apples that need to be picked. The father may delegate such a task to one of the sons, directing that it be done after school or when there is time. At noon, the absence of the school-age children makes possible a more intimate conversation between parents and older children. A progress report on the work accomplished thus far is often the topic of conversation. Father and mother may evaluate the products of a salesman who called during the morning hours. In the evening the entire family gathers about the table. Silence during this meal is often interrupted by an occasional belch, a question from a child, or the bark of a dog.

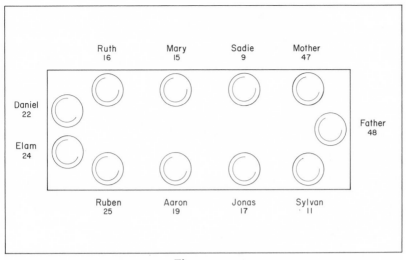

Figure 10.
Seating pattern at the Amish family table

Amish women spend much time cooking, baking, and canning foods. They take advantage of the growing season by serving vegetables from the garden and fruits and berries when they are ripe. They use canned foods when necessary and convenient. They also shop in small supermarkets for specific kinds of food. The old-fashioned Amish maintain ice boxes for cooling in the summer. Others have kerosene-operated refrigerators. At the table their portions of food are generous and the flavor is often excellent.

The Amish work hard and eat accordingly. The standard breakfast in Pennsylvania may include eggs, fried scrapple or cornmeal mush, cooked cereal, and often fried potatoes. Bread, butter, and jelly or apple butter are served with every meal. The standard diet is rich in fats and carbohydrates, consisting of potatoes, gravy, fried foods, and pastries. There are traditional foods like home-cured ham, chow-chow, pickled beets, shoo-fly pie, apple dumplings, bean soup, rivel soup, green tomato pie, and stink cheese. The Amish diet is also influenced by contemporary foods like meat loaf, bologna, and pizza. Cakes, pies, and puddings are numerous. Amish gardens are a good source of fresh vegetables, but the Amish tradition of overcooking and oversweetening probably cancels out much of the natural vitamins and minerals. In recent years health foods, vitamins, and food supplements have been much in evidence. Some Amish operate health-food stores.

The outdoor bake oven has disappeared in most Amish communities. Earlier it was preferred for drying fruits and vegetables and for baking

The family garden is an important economic and cooperative
enterprise. Some families preserve as many as 800 quarts
of fruits and vegetables each year.

pies in large quantities for the preaching service. Field corn is dried
and browned in the oven before it is ground into cornmeal. Amish
cooks prefer winter wheat for making pies and pastries and spring
wheat for baking bread. Ground cereals—cornmeal, wheat hearts, and
whole wheat flour—are still available in some village stores.

Among outsiders, especially tourists who flock to Lancaster County,
there are many myths about Amish foods. There is the legend of "seven
sweets and seven sours" on Amish tables. The only place I have ever
eaten the seven sweets and sours is in a tourist hotel. The tourist
industry has done well in capitalizing on myths, judging by the number of restaurants that cater to "Amish" foods. Advertised items such
as "Amish soda," "Amish highball," or some kinds of pastries are
obviously an outsider's capitalization on the tourists' determination
to find something distinctively Amish. Over fifty "Dutch" restaurants
have emerged in Amish localities. Some of them have Mennonite or
former Amish cooks in their kitchens. Most outsiders are not able to
distinguish between restaurants that serve "real" Amish dishes as
opposed to "fake" ones. There are forty Amish-type cookbooks. Al-

though many are small and localized, a few have enjoyed extensive distribution.[5]

Family ceremony is minimal, for social order and social roles are clearly defined and effective. According to older Amish informants, the only religious rite observed by a family in bygone days was silent prayer before and after meals. Bedtime prayers were repeated silently in bed. This is the traditional pattern still practiced by the most orthodox groups. Some families kneel together before retiring while the father reads a prayer from the prayer book.[6] Rarely is there a spontaneous audible prayer. The Amish have retained some of the ceremonial practices of the Reformation, such as the use of prayer formularies and prayer books, silent prayer, and Luther's German translation of the Bible.

At mealtime each member at the table repeats silently his memorized meditation. Children, upon reaching the age of puberty or earlier, are expected to say their own prayers. These prayers are memorized, in German, and they may consist of the Lord's Prayer or a prayer of about the same length taken from a prayer book. The following are examples.

Gebet Vor Dem Essen

O Herr Gott, himmlischer Vater, Segne uns und Diese Deine Gaben, die wir von Diener milden Güte zu uns nehmen werden. Speise und tränke auch unsere Seelen zum ewigen Leben, und mach uns theilhaftig Deines himmlischen Tisches durch Jesus Christum. Amen. Unser Vater, etc.

Prayer before Meal

O Lord God, heavenly Father, bless us and these the gifts, which we shall accept from thy tender goodness. Give us food and drink also for our souls unto life eternal, and make us partakers of thy heavenly table through Jesus Christ. Amen. Our Father, etc. [Lord's prayer is repeated].

Gebet Nach Dem Essen

O Herr, wir sagen Dir Lob und Dank für Deine heilige Speis und Trank, für Deine vielfaltige grosse Gnaden und Gutheiten; Herr, der Du labest und regierest, ein wahrer Gott bis in Ewigkeit. Amen. Unser Vater, etc.

5. *Amish Cooking* (Alymer, Ont.: Pathway Publishers, 1977) is the major publication of the Amish themselves. (The original collection of recipes for this volume was compiled by Joseph N. and Sylvia Peachey of Belleville, Pa., under the title *Favorite Amish Family Recipes*.) See also Bill Randle, *Plain Cooking* (New York: New York Times Book Co., 1974).

6. The standard prayer book is *Christenpflicht*. Prayers on pp. 124 and 126 of the book are typically used in the morning and evening.

Prayer after Meal

O Lord, we give praise and thanks for your sacred food and drink, for your manifold great grace and goodness; Thou who livest and reignest, a true God till eternity. Amen. Our Father, etc. [Lord's Prayer is repeated].

The Amish home is the center of life and place of belonging for all the family members. Home is a place of security. It is a center for decision-making with respect to work, play, and exposure to the wider community and to the outside world.

RECREATION AND LEISURE

Recreation and leisure are informal and related to work; they are not entered into as pursuits in themselves. Homemade rather than store-bought toys are typically provided. There are certain games which Amish children and young people play. Clapping games are a common form of indoor play among adolescent girls and they are frequently played at informal family visits. It is called "botching." There are several ways of playing the game. Two people, seated on chairs and facing each other, clap the palms of their hands together alternately, then alternately strike each other's lap until there is a decided loud clap. The feet may be used to keep proper timing. If several are efficient, a vigorous contest will ensue to see who can go the fastest. These clappings are sometimes played to the tune of "Darling Nellie Gray" or "Pop Goes the Weasel."

Much of the leisure time of the Amish is spent visiting relatives, the older members of the community, and the sick, and attending weddings in the fall. Easter and Pentecost, observed not only on Sunday but on Monday as well, provide long weekend occasions for visiting. In large settlements where distances to be traveled are as great as forty miles, a family may start early on a Sunday morning and attend church in a neighboring district. They will drive still further in the afternoon, stop for Sunday evening supper with a family, and continue their journey after supper until they reach their destination.

Weekly auction sales and household auctions are a common form of recreation for many family members. For some boys and men, hunting is a favorite sport in season. Softball is rarely played on Sunday. Young people of courtship age play ball on special weekday holidays such as Ascension Day or Easter Monday. Hiking is a common activity among boys.

The use of tobacco can be classed as another form of pastime. Its use varies from one area to another and with *Ordnung*. Many districts have officially discouraged its use and will excommunicate a persistent smoker, but conservative groups have tended to have few or no scruples against its use. Among the Lancaster County Amish, who themselves raise tobacco as a cash crop, single and married men, including preachers, use it. In those districts where it is permitted, there is no effort to conceal smoking, except in the case of cigarettes, which are viewed as "worldly." Where forbidden, it is often done secretly. Older men appear to have more of a "right" to chew or smoke than young men. Pipe and cigar smoking is the accepted practice. Modern lighters are used by some. Older informants among the very orthodox Amish say that as far back as they can remember the people have used tobacco.[7] It was formerly common for older women to smoke a pipe and a few of them still do, but this is not done openly.

THE MATURE YEARS

Respect for the elders, already obvious among children, is even more pronounced with regard to mature Amish people. All age groups in both sexes revere parents, grandparents, and great-grandparents. The duty to obey one's parents is one of the main themes in Amish preaching. Perhaps the verse most often repeated on this point is one of the Ten Commandments: "Honor thy father and thy mother, that thy days may be long upon the land which the Lord thy God giveth thee" (Exod. 20:12; Eph. 6:2; Col. 3:20).

Not only is there respect for the aged, but authority is vested in the old people. This arrangement naturally lends itself to control of life by the aged. Preservation of the religious ideals and mores is thereby ensured, and the younger people who are inclined to introduce change can be held in check.

A strong consciousness of kinship is peculiarly favorable to gerontocracy, or social control by the older members of society. This control is informal rather than formal, but is, nevertheless, "closer to us than breathing, nearer than hands or feet."[8] The part that old people have "in drawing forth and molding the character and life-policy of every younger person in the kinship group makes the necessity for direct control much less frequent in isolated culture than in more accessible communities."[9] The relatively integrated community is associated with effective rules imposed by the aged, be they parents or church leaders.

---

7. Additional sources on the use of tobacco appear in John Umble, "The Amish Mennonites of Union County, Pennsylvania. Part I: Social and Religious Life," *Mennonite Quarterly Review* 7 (April 1933): 71–96; and in the *Mennonite Encyclopedia*, s.v. "Tobacco."

8. Howard Becker and Harry E. Barnes, *Social Thought from Lore to Science*, 3rd ed. rev., 3 vols. (New York: Dover, 1961), 1: 11.

9. Ibid.

Thus deference to age pervades not only familial relationships but also the religious leadership of the group. Furthermore, the counsel of the older bishop or minister carries more authority than that of younger ones.

The Amish farm typically contains two dwellings, one of which is the *Grossdaadi Haus*, which houses the grandparents. At retirement the older couple moves into this house and a married son or daughter falls heir to responsibility for the farm. The grandparents may retain some type of control of the farm until the younger couple demonstrate their ability to manage the farm. The grandparents have not only a separate household unit but a horse and buggy of their own. Instead of two houses, many farms have one dwelling that is large enough to accommodate two separate household operations. When there are no grandparents to occupy these quarters, they are sometimes rented to other Amish people, or occupied by the hired man and his wife. Some of the Amish who retire in or near a village will erect a small barn beside their dwelling so that they can feed and maintain a horse.

By the time they are sixty, many Amish have accumulated enough wealth for a satisfactory retirement. Traditionally, the Amish do not accept old-age assistance or public assistance of any kind. Neither do they buy life insurance. Needy older persons are aided by relatives. Should such close relatives be incompetent or unwilling, the church will come to the assistance of the elderly.

The retirement of father and mother from active life on the farm stabilizes the social organization of the entire Amish community. While the young man is free to make his own decisions, the very presence of the parents on the farm influences the life of the younger generation. The young couple is not obligated to carry out the wishes of the parents, yet an advisory relationship stimulates not only economic stability but also religious integrity.

The final stages of life are characterized by integrity rather than despair. Amish attitudes and practices with respect to aging constitute a sound system of retirement.

Age at Retirement. The age at which Amish retire is not rigidly fixed. Health, family needs, and the inclination of the individual are all considerations in determining the proper time. A couple may retire anytime between the ages of fifty and seventy. Moving "off the farm" provides opportunities for the young who need a farm. By providing a farm for their offspring, the older couple advances their standing in the community. They also do not have to choose between full-time work or doing nothing. They continue to work at their own pace,

Many Amish farms have double or triple dwelling units,
one of which serves as the "grandfather" house
for the grandparents.

helping their married children to become established on the farm.
Many continue to work in small shops of their own.

Prestige. In community and church activities older men and women
keep their right to vote, and their influence or "voice" increases.
Ordained leaders never retire from their positions. Wives have an
important influence on their husbands. Long periods of visiting friends
and persons of the same age, and exchanges before and after the
preaching service, help to form an informal consensus on any subject.

Housing and Transportation. Private housing is provided in the
"grandfather" house, the dwelling unit adjacent to the main farmhouse. This arrangement allows for independence without sacrificing
intergenerational family involvement. By having their own horse and

Older Amish people usually gain respect and status
with age and are remarkably independent.

buggy, both couples may travel at will. There is no fear of losing a
driver's license.

Functional Traditions. By living in their own house, a retired couple
can maintain personal customs and living arrangements. This includes
furnishings, guest rooms for visitors, shop tools, facilities for making
toys for children, quilts, and rugs, and maintaining Amish standards.
Old-fashioned ways are preferred and perpetuated voluntarily. The
slow rate of technological change allows social bonds to take priority.
In an institution for old people or in an apartment, the same sense of
living comfortably with an unchanging social structure would not be
possible.

Economic Security. Amish retirees are with few exceptions not wealthy.
Income, however, is not a serious problem. Economic subsistence is
maintained without government aid of any kind. Life earnings, rentals
from farms, carpentry, or part-time work provides some income. They
do not seek or need counsel with respect to maintaining their human
rights. The community's sensitivity to sharing and practicing mutual
aid and its abiding interest in the well-being of those in need are
great assets to older people.

Social and Family Continuity. Transgenerational contacts are maintained with relatives. There is little problem with loneliness. Older

people are assured of meaningful social participation, in work and in community activities, in seasonal frolics, auctions, and in the activities of weddings and holidays. Travel to distant places may also constitute a significant pastime for older people. Contentment with helping the married children, whether in work, in times of sickness, or in crisis, constitutes a basic attitude and expectation. The young ask their parents about farming methods or for advice on rearing children. This does not mean that their advice is accepted, but their views as parents are recognized and respected.

Health and Medical Care. Good nutrition and health care are readily at hand. Years of physical labor and exercise have kept the body active. When health fails, relatives and friends come to visit frequently. There is no stigma attached to being sick. In case of financial need, either the relatives or the church will pay unmet medical bills.

CHAPTER 8

Child Nurture and Training

🌿

TRUE EDUCATION, by Amish standards, is "the cultivation of humility, simple living, and submission to the will of God." The single most important goal is eternal life. The Amish do not believe in predestination—that some persons are born to be saved and others are born to be damned. Children are believed to have an inherited sinful nature through no fault of their own, and they are therefore lovable and teachable. Given the proper environment, they are capable of assuming right conduct by the time they become adults. Parents are responsible for training their children, and they are morally accountable to God for teaching them right from wrong. Obedience to parents and ultimately to God is a fundamental virtue. Children are taught to be well-mannered, quiet, and humble in the presence of others. Children must not be idle. They must learn useful manual skills, learn to read and write, and acquire some knowledge of the Scriptures.[1]

1. Gertrude E. Huntington provided assistance in the development of this chapter. Amish socialization is discussed in greater detail in John A. Hostetler and Gertrude E. Huntington, *Children in Amish Society* (New York: Holt, Rinehart & Winston, 1971). The material in this chapter is based on our joint publication, with revisions, and is used with the permission of the publishers.

THE GOALS OF EDUCATION

The family, and to a lesser extent the Amish school, are believed to have the primary responsibility for training the child for life. The child also has an explicit relationship to a wide social fabric within his culture—his parents, siblings, extended relatives, church, community, and the school—all of which help to equip him for adult life. Schools are expected to teach the children literacy, cooperation, and the skills needed to live productive lives in keeping with values taught in the home and in the church. On reaching physical and social maturity and demonstrating sincerity and a knowledge of Amish religion, the young people are baptized into the believing community, where they will choose their spouse. Their willingness to suffer persecution or death in order to maintain their faith is made explicit in baptism.

AGE STAGES

From birth to death the Amish person passes through a series of stages in keeping with his age and sex. The social functions of each age group are delineated and determined by the Amish culture. These age groups or stages are: babies, little children, "scholars," young people, adulthood, and retirement. To become an Amish person, the individual must learn the appropriate attitude and behavior patterns in each of these stages. School is only one of many influences in the life of the individual. The socialization patterns of the first four stages will be discussed here; adulthood and retirement have been described previously.

Babies—from Birth to Walking. Babies are regarded as a gift from God and are welcomed with pleasure into the family and community. A baby is considered blameless, can do no wrong, and if he cries he is in need of comfort, not discipline. Babies are rarely fed on a strict schedule but are fed when hungry. The baby is included at the family table during mealtime, for the attitude of the family is one of sharing. Eating is an important social activity.

During the first year the baby receives solicitous care from persons of all ages. Babies are enjoyed, they are believed to be gentle and responsive. A baby can be spoiled by improper handling, especially by nervous, tense handling, but that is not the fault of the baby. The infant is secure within the home and the Amish community, and this equips him to trust himself and those around him. At this age babies are not scolded or punished. Although a baby may be difficult, he is not considered bad. The baby stage ends when a child begins to walk.

Children are included in important farm activities
after school hours and on Saturdays.

Little Children—from Walking to Entering School. Parents create a
safe environment for their children, protecting them from physical
and moral danger. The preschool child learns to respect and obey
those in authority, to share with others and help others, to do what he
is taught, and to enjoy work and perform it pleasantly.

Respect for authority is shown through obedience. The relationship
between authority and responsibility is learned very early. Although
the younger children must obey the older ones, the older children
may not make arbitrary demands on the younger. The four-year-old
is expected to hand over his toy to a younger child if he cries for it,
but in the absence of the parents the younger one must obey the
older.

Parents teach obedience by being consistent and firm. The use of
a switch may be used, but not harshly. Parents vary in their handling
of the disobedient child, but they will not tolerate stubbornness or
defiance. Generally the Amish are matter-of-fact rather than moral-
istic in dealing with their children. Work is viewed as helping others,
and children are trained to help one another rather than to be independent. There is little difference in the tasks done by preschool girls
and boys. Children are not thanked for carrying out responsibilities

expected of them. Crying and deep emotion are not discouraged except in the case of physical pain or self-pity.

Amish children experience great freedom of movement as they accompany older persons around the farm. They are encouraged to be useful but are not pushed to perform tasks beyond their ability. Initiative in the physical world is encouraged, but asking questions of an intellectual nature is strictly channeled. Instead of asking how or why, the child learns to observe and imitate on a behavioral level. The presence of a father is considered necessary for the proper up-bringing of the preschool child. Little children sit through the long preaching service, girls with their mothers, and boys with their fathers. Here they learn to be quiet and patient. The Amish do not sanction kindergartens, believing that the child should be under the care of the parents in the home. Small children are kept away from the outside world as much as practical. They are not usually intro-duced to non-Amish people.

"Scholars"—Children between the Ages of Six and Fifteen. During the school years the family continues to be the primary agent of a child's socialization. The family protects the child, supports the

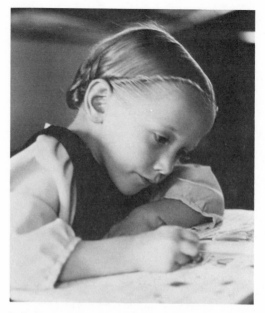

A young "scholar." Amish children receive strong support from their
families in learning basic educational skills and acquiring the attitudes
of humility, forgiveness, and appreciation.

training given in school, and punishes and forgives the transgressions
of the child. Punishment is for the safety of the child—for physical,
cultural, moral, and legal safety. School children are motivated primarily by concern for other people and not for fear of punishment.
Rewards are used to develop the attitudes of humility, forgivenesss,
admission of error, sympathy, responsibility, and appreciation of
work. Parents are responsible for seeing that the children stay within
the discipline of the church. The school supports the parents who
teach their children by example to become Christians, and who
teach them the work skills they will need to live in the Amish community.

The function of the school is to teach the children the three R's
in an environment where they can learn discipline, basic values, and
how to get along with others. There is concern that the home, school,
and church teach the same things. Most children attend Amish
schools. Here the teacher is an Amish person, and emotionally the
school belongs to the Amish community. Amish children must learn
to understand something of the world in order to reject it selectively.
They are expected to master the English language and to learn the
skills that will enable them to transact business with outsiders.

During his school years, the Amish child spends most of his non-school time with his family. The family attends church and visits many friends and relatives as a unit. The child spends much time with a mixed group when he chooses. In addition to his parents, he knows many adults who have an interest in him and his development. When not in school, girls learn to cook, bake, sew, and make things for their playhouses. The boys help with the farm work, but they also build toys or birdhouses, and they trap fur animals or fish in streams. Boys and girls are rewarded for the work of their hands and for their sense of industry. The child has many role models and informal teachers.

Young People—from Adolescence to Marriage. At the end of the school years, the peer group, rather than the family and the church, become the young person's reference group. The individual chooses his "crowd" or "gang" of friends. If a youth makes friends with outsiders and is governed by an alien peer group, he is likely in danger of leaving the Amish faith. Earlier in life the young person accepted being Amish as part of his identity. He must strive to determine what it means to be Amish. By working at various jobs—for other Amish families or away from the community—both boys and girls gain a knowledge of the wider community and the world outside their home. Some adolescent rebellion is to be expected. During working hours the young people are respectful of community standards. During free time with their peers there may be considerable testing of boundaries. But if the young Amish person is physically removed from the community, he may become susceptible to alien religious influences.

During this period the young person must come to terms with two great decisions: whether he will join the Amish church, and whom he will marry. To make these decisions, the individual must establish a certain degree of independence from his family and his community. The family relaxes some of its control. The church has no direct control over the young person who has not voluntarily become a member. Sampling the world and testing the boundaries may take the form of owning a radio or camera, attending movies, wearing non-Amish clothes, having a driver's license or owning an automobile— all more or less in secret. If these deviations are managed discreetly, they may be ignored by the parents and community. The young person is thereby allowed some freedom to taste the outside world he is voluntarily expected to reject when he becomes a church member.

Generally Amish young people discover continuity between what they were taught as children and what they experience as adolescents.

Intense play and group cooperation are part
of growing up.

What the young person learns about himself as a person, a worker, a
member of a peer group, and a member of a family, he is able to
integrate with who he is, where he has come from, and where he is
going.

SCHOOLING

Today most Amish children attend Amish schools, though a few in
rural areas still attend public schools. A half-century ago all Amish
children attended public schools. The Amish built their own schools
and staffed them with their own teachers in response to state consolidation of small country schools. In the one-room country schools,
children were taught largely by oral means and by example; discipline
and basic skills were stressed. Those aspects of schooling that were
not considered relevant were tolerated. With consolidation, all this
changed. The Amish have struggled to retain a human rather than an
organizational scale in their schools, to make them complementary to
their way of life.[2] In 1972, thirty-five years after the Amish first opposed the consolidation of schools, the Supreme Court upheld the
validity of Amish schools.

2. The school conflict is discussed in Chapter 12.

Setting and Organization. The Amish have two types of schools—the elementary school, consisting of the first eight grades, and the vocational school.[3] The latter, not held uniformly in all settlements, is on-the-job training that combines instruction and farm work for pupils who have completed the elementary grades but are not old enough to obtain a working permit. Amish schools are built and operated by the parents of a local church district or districts and not by a centralized organization.

Most school buildings consist of one or two classrooms, often with an entrance room, sometimes a bookroom, and newer schools may have a finished basement where the children play during inclement weather. In earlier times rural one-room schoolhouses were purchased from the state when they became available. They were remodeled extensively. The high ceilings were lowered to create a cozier, more homelike atmosphere. Today most school buildings are built by the Amish themselves. Building committees have their blueprints approved by state fire and health officials. The land for the building is often donated by an Amish farmer. The schoolhouse is well constructed, made of glazed tile, cinder block, brick facing, stucco, or aluminum siding. The Amish schools do not have electricity. They are built in such a way as to take full advantage of available natural light. In certain communities schools have indoor lavatories, but in most areas outhouses are preferred. Many schools have old-fashioned rope-pulled school bells. Inside, colorful drawings and charts made by the "scholars" may be found on walls and windows. Every schoolyard has a ball field. A few have swings or seesaws. Sledding and ice skating are considered when a site is located for a school.

Most Amish pupils walk to school. In those settlements where distance is a problem, the Amish hire a school bus to transport their children. They are opposed to accepting transportation services or school subsidies from the government.

Elementary schools are administered by a school board. In most communities each school has its own board, but in some places several schools are administered by a single board. Members are elected by the patrons or appointed by the church. A board consists of from three to six members, one of whom serves as president. There is usually a clerk or secretary who keeps records, and a treasurer. The treasurer collects the funds for the operation of the school, issues the teacher's pay check, and is responsible for the bills. An attendance officer is responsible for seeing that attendance records are forwarded

3. The vocational school is described in Hostetler and Huntington, *Children in Amish Society*, pp. 71–79.

to state officials, although in some schools the teacher performs this function. To the outsider these slight variations and overlapping responsibilities may be confusing, but to the Amish such local diversities are respected. Where children from different Old Order affiliations (noncommuning churches) attend one school, the members of each different affiliation may elect one board member.

The school board meets as a unit with the teacher, ideally once a month. These are open meetings, and parents and other church members are encouraged to attend. The school board is responsible to the patrons and the local church district for the smooth functioning of the school. The board hires and fires the teacher, pays the teacher's salary, and keeps the building and playground in good condition. It must also set the tuition fee and assess the school tax. For patrons who cannot pay their share, the church may be asked to eliminate any debt at the end of the school year.

Statewide Amish board meetings are held annually for members of the school boards, committeemen, church officials, and others, including teachers and parents who are interested. Statewide committee members are elected at these meetings. These occasions attract from six to eight hundred people, who usually meet in a large barn. State committees may appoint several subcommittees. When vital issues are at stake, a small committee meets with public education officials to exchange views. The Pennsylvania "Amish Church School Committee," established in 1937, has attempted to clarify the Amish position on education to state education officials. The Old Order Book Society (Gordonville, Pa.), which was organized to print books suitable for use in Amish schools, reports to the several statewide annual meetings. This committee also functions as a treasury to help provide funds for the establishment of new schools.

Schedule. The school day consists of four major periods of about an hour and a half each, a pattern typical of rural schools a half-century ago. There is a recess between periods, including a noon break. During each period there is class recitation, generally about ten minutes for each class. The children who are not reciting know when it will be their turn and what subject they should prepare for.

School typically starts at 8:30 and is dismissed at 3:30. All schools have an opening period that includes the singing of hymns, Bible reading without commentary, and the recitation of the Lord's Prayer. Many schools have a song and silent prayer before dismissal for lunch. In the afternoon session the teacher may read to the children for a few minutes, occasionally from a completely secular book like a Nancy Drew story. The hardest or most important subject is frequently

Sledding and ice-skating are favorite sports
among Amish school children.

scheduled for the first hour of school. Spelling, generally considered
an easy subject, is usually scheduled for late in the afternoon. Spelling
matches are often held at this time. Singing has an important function
in Amish schools, and teachers encourage the children to learn new
songs and to enjoy this group activity.

Curriculum. Local preferences and different state rulings on school
curricula result in slight variations in subject matter taught. The

children learn English (including reading, grammar, spelling, penmanship, and, to a limited extent, composition) and arithmetic (addition, subtraction, multiplication, division, decimals, percentages, ratios, volumes and areas, conversion of weights and measures, and simple and compound interest). Amish schools do not teach "new math." Most schools teach some health, history, and geography; some teach a little science and art. Some substitute agriculture for history and geography. The children learn the letters and sounds of the alphabet phonetically before they begin reading.

Textbooks are chosen by the school board, with or without the consultation of the teacher. The Old Order Book Society publishes a list of books suitable for Amish schools. A special journal for Amish teachers, the *Blackboard Bulletin*, published monthly by Pathway Publishers (an Amish-owned-and-operated company with headquarters in Aylmer, Ontario, and LaGrange, Indiana), contains a variety of aids for teachers. Some of the discarded books from public schools may be used, and are sometimes donated to the Amish by public school teachers and administrators. The old books are preferred because they have less science, fewer references to television, and less discussion of sex education. The Amish are opposed to sex education and to health books that stress how to make oneself attractive.

Finding suitable reading material for Amish pupils has been a difficult problem. Those books that support conspicuous consumption, are superficially patriotic or militaristic, or contain illustrations supporting these values are unsuited for a nonresistant group that tries to live "separated from the world." The classic *McGuffey Readers* have been accepted in a few communities, especially in Ohio. This is not surprising, for they were written by one of the founders of the common-school system in Ohio at a time when the schools stressed proper morality and character development. This philosophy of education coincides with the Amish attitude. The brand of patriotism promoted in the *McGuffey Readers* is also shared by the Amish, for it stresses the beauties of the nation, and not its technological pride and superiority.

In response to the need for good reading books, Pathway Publishers has undertaken the task of producing a series of suitable readers for Amish schools. The Amish have also produced two history books: *Seeking a Better Country* (1963), by Noah Zook; and *Our Better Country: The Story of America's Freedom* (1963), by Uria R. Byler. The Amish do not want their children to read fairy tales, stories in which animals talk and act like people, or stories that involve magic. The stories selected and written by Amish authors are set in rural

America and stress the Christian virtues of honesty, thrift, purity, and love, but without a heavy religious vocabulary.

Amish schools use a limited amount of material in the classroom, but the children learn it thoroughly. The Amish stress accuracy rather than speed, drill rather than variety, proper sequence rather than freedom of choice. The Amish school aids the child to become a part of his community and to remain within his community. The school emphasizes shared knowledge and the dignity of tradition rather than progress. The Amish assume that individuals are weak, that they need help—from one another, from a higher power, and from individual effort—in order to improve. In short, Amish children are presented with certain appropriate facts that they are encouraged to learn thoroughly rather than question critically. These facts form a part of the community's shared knowledge and thereby help the community to remain of one mind. The schools function effectively to maintain the bounds of Amish culture, to prepare the young to live simply, with minimum reliance or middle-class values and the mass communication systems of modern society.

Amish schools support the religion taught in the family and church but do not attempt to interpret or teach religion in the classroom. Only those who are ordained of God should explain the Scriptures to an assembled group. Parents teach their own children within the family, but they do not teach the children of other families. Amish religion tends to be ritualistic and nontheological. Christianity is to be lived and not talked about. The Amish are critical of persons who show off their knowledge of the Bible by frequently quoting passages from the Scriptures. This is considered a form of pride. Although German verses are memorized in school, teachers do not teach religion or induce the children to be "scripture-smart for religious show." Teaching is by example. Self-denial, humility, and forbearance are the approved form of religious behavior.

The Teacher and Teaching Methods. Amish teachers are selected on the basis of their aptitude for and interest in teaching children. They have no formal training beyond the elementary grades. This fact is appalling to public school administrators, but the Amish feel that certified college teachers are "unsuitable" as teachers in their schools. If we compare the role of the teacher in two cultures, the Amish and a typical suburban school, the very different functions of the teacher become apparent.[4] Middle-class teachers are too far removed from

4. Ibid., pp. 107–8.

Young people progress toward adulthood
in an orderly pattern. Loyalty to a peer group
is an essential stage.

the oral tradition to identify with the Amish, and in most cases they
are unsuitable as examples.

The Amish teacher teaches with his whole life. He must be a
person who has integrated his life with that of the community, for
every aspect of behavior and personality is related to teaching. He
must be well grounded in his religious faith, exemplifying the Amish
traits of steadfastness and love of fellow man. In addition, he must
be interested in education and have sufficient factual knowledge to
keep ahead of the scholars. One becomes a teacher by being asked
to teach, by serving as an apprentice for a specified period. After
three years of teaching, a person is considered qualified by Amish
standards.[5] Teachers attend annual statewide teachers' meetings and
local meetings in their community for the purpose of lending one
another support and advice. The *Blackboard Bulletin* provides stimu-

---

5. *Guidelines in Regards to the Old Order Amish or Mennonite Parochial
Schools* (Gordonville, Pa.: Gordonville Print Shop, 1978), p. 29.

lation and discussion of school projects. Teacher-training is primarily informal and personal.

The school has the atmosphere of a well-ordered family. The teacher represents a parent or an older sibling. The pupils and teacher call each other by their first names. The classroom typically runs smoothly, for the teacher does not pretend that the children make the decisions. Orderliness, supported with appropriate biblical mottoes on the wall, is stressed. The Golden Rule, "Do unto others as you would have others do unto you," is to be followed. The children encourage one another's good performance so that the whole class or school may do well. Individual responsibility, not individual competition, is encouraged. Since a person's individual talents are God-given, no one should be praised if he is a fast learner, nor should he be condemned if he is a slow learner. There is a place for each person God has created. Such differences are acknowledged and respected by the teacher and children.

Teachers are not confronted with a room full of waving hands competing for the chance to give an answer. Grades conform to an absolute rather than a relative system of grading. Grading on the curve, where one child's good grade depends on another child's poor grade, is unacceptable. Grades are not manipulated to motivate the student. Rather, scholars are taught to accept the level of work they are able to do and always to work hard to do better. The discussion method is not considered appropriate for academic subjects, for every child is expected to learn and to be able to recite the facts.

Teachers use encouragement and rewards much more than punishment. The child in need of discipline is usually first spoken to in private. A teacher may ask a child to apologize to the group, or to remain in his seat during recess or at noon. Corporal punishment is sometimes used for serious or repeated offenses. Teachers aim never to belittle their scholars or to use sarcasm or ridicule as a means of controlling them. They try to make the offending child understand the transgression and to accept punishment willingly because it is deserved. Teachers feel emotionally very close to their scholars and the children in turn admire and want to please their teachers.

THE AMISH PERSONALITY

Amish schools stress social responsibility rather than critical analysis. Factual material, though somewhat circumscribed, is learned thoroughly. The children are taught both by practice and by example to care for and support the members of the school and community. Typically the Amish personality may be described as "quiet, friendly, responsible, and conscientious."[6] The model Amish person is loyal, considerate, and sympathetic. The Amish person "works devotedly to meet his obligations," and although careful with detail, "needs time to master technical subjects." How other people feel is important to him. He dislikes telling people unpleasant things.

When asked about their vocational preferences, Amish school children generally name occupations requiring service and manual labor.[7] Boys prefer farming or farm-related work. Girls prefer housekeeping, gardening, cooking, cleaning, caring for children, or some type of humanitarian service such as nursing or teaching. Their vocational aspirations are realistic and attainable within the limits of Amish culture. An analysis of drawing exercises done by Amish children reveals a strong awareness of other people. Work apart from play is not sharply delineated, nor are there rigid differences between the sexes in the leisure-time preferences of the children. Amish children show a remarkable ability to conceptualize space at an early age, and the inclusion of others in their drawings suggests the importance of the family and of group activities.

On several standardized tests, Amish children performed significantly higher in spelling, word usage, and arithmetic than a sample of pupils in rural public schools.[8] They scored slightly above the national norm in these subjects in spite of small libraries, limited equipment, the absence of radio and television, and teachers who lacked college training. The Amish pupils were equal to the non-Amish pupils in comprehension and in the use of reference material. They had lower scores in vocabulary. In those aspects of learning stressed by the Amish culture, the Amish pupils outperformed pupils in the control group.

Children of both sexes identify with the goals of their parents and generally accept these role models for themselves. Several studies of parent-child relationships support these conclusions. Sons identify closely with their fathers;[9] the child "knows exactly who he is and

6. The descriptions of Amish personality are based on the results of the Myers-Briggs Type Indicator (Isabell Briggs Myers, Educational Testing Service, Princeton, N.J.) as reported in Hostetler and Huntington, *Children in Amish Society*, pp. 80–81.

7. Hostetler and Huntington, *Children in Amish Society*, pp. 85–88.

8. Ibid., pp. 91–95.

9. Joe Wittmer, "Homogeneity of Personality Characteristics: A Comparison between Old Order Amish and Non-Amish," *American Anthropologist* 72 (October 1970): 1063–68.

Saturday work includes cleaning and refilling the kerosene lanterns.
© National Geographic Society.

Harvesting corn. With other members of the family,
young adults learn to work with machines
adapted to scale.

where he is going to fit when he grows up."[10] Amish children in the
eighth grade rate their families more positively than do non-Amish
children.[11]

By outside standards Amish culture provides an environment that
is limiting and restrictive. To the Amish child it provides reasonable
fulfillment and a knowledge of what is expected of the individual.
Learning is directed toward conformity with what is right, not
toward discovering new knowledge. The wisdom of the ages is for
the Amish more important than the pronouncements of modern
science. It is more important to do what is morally right than to
win acclaim, popularity, or riches, or to survive physically. Within
the clearly defined boundaries of the culture, there is a certain richness

10. M. L. Lembright and K. Yamamoto, "Subcultures and Creative Thinking: An
Exploratory Comparison between Amish and Urban American School Children,"
Merrill-Palmer Quarterly of Behavior and Development 11 (January 1965): 49–64.

11. Mervin R. Smucker, "Growing Up Amish: A Comparison of the Socialization
Process between Amish and Non-Amish Rural School Children" (M.S. thesis,
Millersville State College, Pa., 1978).

and diversity of experience in the small Amish school where long-term intimate relationships are formed.

The Amish Dropout. It is extremely rare for a child who has completed the Amish elementary grades to enter high school and continue formal schooling. The child who continues his formal schooling will not remain Amish and hence is a "dropout" from the Amish way of life. By not entering high school, Amish children are all classed as dropouts in public school statistics. If a family changes church affiliations by joining a liberalized group, the children are more likely to continue formal schooling. Some Amish resume their formal education in their late teens or after the age of twenty-one. An insatiable motivation for learning is manifest in a few. The belief advanced by some educators, that the Amish should be forced to complete more years of schooling so that in case they should leave the faith they would not be disadvantaged educationally, has no foundation. Lack of formal schooling is no problem for the Amish person who seeks employment. In many communities, both Amish and former Amish persons are in great demand as farm tenants, carpenters, painters, builders, housecleaners, and baby-sitters.

CHAPTER 9

The Life Ceremonies

BIRTH, coming of age, marriage, career achievements, and death are marked by appropriate ceremonies or rites of passage in most societies. Such major changes "are not accomplished without troubling social and individual life, and it is the purpose of a certain number of rites of passage to check their noxious effects."[1] This chapter examines Amish ceremonies as they relate to three major turning points—birth, marriage, and death.

BIRTH

In many societies the ceremony associated with birth is formal and elaborate, but in Amish society it is barely visible. Some folk beliefs about pregnancy and birth exist, but birth is marked by neither sacred nor kinship ceremonies. The addition of children to the society is not "troubling" in any way, and their coming is not regarded as an economic burden. In fact, the birth of a child enhances the standing of the parents in the community. An Amish couple may expect to have several, possibly many, children, for children are wanted.

The majority of babies are born in the hospital because most

1. Arnold van Gennep, "On the Rites of Passage," in *Theories of Society,* ed. Talcott Parsons, 2 vols. (Glencoe, Ill.: The Free Press, 1961), 2: 951.

doctors will not make home deliveries, but with the help of a few sympathetic doctors and midwives, some of the Amish are able to have their children at home. One obstetrician in Pennsylvania observes that she is making more and more home deliveries and that the present ratio is about three to one in favor of home deliveries. There are no taboos against good medical care, but home births are preferred. Amish women view birth not as a threat but as an experience that affirms them as part of the community. No social ceremony is needed to "check any noxious effects," because there are none.

Secular rituals such as baby showers, with their consumer orientation, have no place in the Amish family. Infants are dressed functionally, as are adults, and they are not lauded with fancy or expensive clothing or equipment. And because the Amish family is so effective in socializing the child for adult life, there is scarcely any need for a religious rite. The Amish believe in adult baptism; there is no occasion for infant baptism. Godparents are not assigned; the care and concern of the community for the children is assumed. It is only after the child has been raised to "a way of life" that he is brought into formal relation to the religious community through baptism. Baptism is, of course, a very awesome experience and admits one to a new state. It logically belongs in a discussion of the life ceremonies, but because of its religious significance I have treated it earlier as part of the Amish charter.

MARRIAGE

A wedding is an elaborate affair, for the whole community has a stake in marriage. It means a new home, another place to hold preaching services, and another family committed to rearing children in the Amish way of life. Marriage also means that the young man and young woman are ready to part with their sometimes wild adolescent behavior, to settle down and become respectable members of the community. Marriage is a rite of passage marking the passing from youth to adulthood.

Amish courtship is secretive, and the community at large is not informed of an intended wedding until the couple is "published" in church, from one to four weeks before the wedding. Signs of an approaching wedding, however, provide occasion for joking and teasing. Since there is nothing among Amish traditions that corresponds to the engagement period, other signs of a wedding are sought. An overabundance of celery in the garden of the home of a potential bride is said to be one such sign, since large quantities are used at weddings. Another cue may be efforts on the part of the father of the potential bridegroom to obtain an extra farm, or to remodel a vacant dwelling on one of his own farms.

Weddings are usually held in November and December, since this is a time when the work year allows community-wide participation. The great amount of preparation involved requires that weddings be held during the week, traditionally on Tuesday or Thursday.[2] Second marriages involving widows or widowers may be held anytime during the year and do not involve such elaborate preparations.

Shortly before a young man wishes to be married he approaches the deacon or a minister of his choosing and makes his desire known. The official then becomes the *Schtecklimann,* or "go-between." His task is to go secretly, usually after dark, to the home of the bridegroom's fiancée, verify her wishes for marriage, and obtain the consent of her parents. The girl and her parents have by this time already given formal consent, so the duty of the intermediary is little more than a formality.

The deacon reports his findings to the ministers and announces or "publishes" the intent of the couple at the preaching service in the girl's district. If the bridegroom-to-be is from the same district, he leaves immediately after the important announcement, just before the last hymn is sung. He hitches his horse and is off to the home of his fiancée, where she is awaiting the news that they have been "published." The bridegroom then remains at the bride's home until the wedding day. They are busy during this time with the innumerable preparations that must be made. Walnuts and hickory nuts need to be cracked, floors scrubbed, furniture moved, silverware polished, and dishes borrowed.

The bridegroom's first assignment is to invite personally all his relatives to the wedding. The parents of the couple also do some inviting. Relatives at a distance are notified by postcard or letter. No printed wedding invitations are mailed. Invitations are addressed to entire families or to certain members of the family, such as the husband and wife only. Some invitations are for the evening festivities only. Honorary invitations are extended to uncles, aunts, and special friends to serve as cooks and overseers. Both men and their wives serve in this capacity. The parents of the bridal party decide who will have the honor of serving the meal; on the wedding day they themselves do not work.

Wedding customs vary from one ceremonial and ecological com-

2. The practice of holding weddings on Tuesdays and Thursdays, according to William I. Schreiber, is a vestige of ancient peoples that predates the Christian Era. See *Our Amish Neighbors* (Chicago: University of Chicago Press, 1962), p. 186.

munity to another, especially in menu, physical arrangements, and social activities. The following are observations made by the author at a wedding in central Pennsylvania.

Food preparations began on the day before the wedding. The cooks—married couples numbering thirty persons in all—began arriving at the bride's home at seven o'clock in the morning. Custom required that the bridegroom cut off the heads of the fowl. Men picked the chickens, ducks, and turkeys. The women washed and dressed them. The women prepared the dressing, stuffed the fowl, washed dishes, baked quantities of pies, peeled two bushels of potatoes, and cracked nuts. The men cleaned celery, supplied plenty of hot water from large kettles, emptied garbage, and constructed temporary tables for the main rooms in the house. Six tables, made of wide pine boards and trestles, were set up around three sides of the living room, in the kitchen, and in one bedroom, to create a seating capacity of one hundred (see Figure 11). The dressed, stuffed fowl were placed in a large bake oven outdoors on the evening before the wedding.

The wedding day itself was a great occasion, not only for the bride and bridegroom, but for the kinship community and guests, especially the young people. Before daylight on the day of the wedding the bride and bridegroom and their two attending couples went to a neighbor's place a mile from the bride's home where the preaching and ceremony were to take place. This service was open to the public, but was attended chiefly by those who were invited to the wedding.

As wedding guests arrived for the service the bridal party was already sitting in the front row. At nine o'clock, when the house was filled, the singing began, and the ministers proceeded to the council room and the bride and groom followed. Here they were given instructions concerning the duties of marriage while the assembly below sang wedding hymns (*Ausbund*, selections 97, 69, 131). Upon returning to the assembly the bridal party (holding hands) took their seats near the ministers' row, the three young men facing their partners. Their clothes were new, but in the style of typical Sunday garb. The main sermon delivered by the bishop focused on marriages in the Old Testament: the story of Adam and Eve; the wickedness of mankind after the Flood, in that wives were chosen foolishly; the uprightness of Noah's household in not intermarrying with unbelievers; the story of Isaac and Rebekah, and the adulterous plight of Solomon. The sermon was concluded with a recounting from the Apocrypha (Tobit, chapters 1–14), indicating how Tobias carefully obeyed his father's instructions in obtaining a wife of his own tribe in spite of enormous stumbling blocks.

Near the hour of twelve noon and at the end of his long sermon, the bishop asked the couple to come forward. The marriage ceremony was carried out without the aid of a book or written notes. It consisted of a few questions and responses and concluded with the bishop placing his hands on the clasped hands of the couple as he pronounced a blessing upon them. The vows appeared to be similar to those of other Protestant groups, but no special prayer was offered. The vows, in translation, were as follows:

"You have now heard the ordinance of Christian wedlock presented. Are you now willing to enter wedlock together as God in the beginning ordained and commanded?"

"Yes."

"Do you stand in the confidence (*Hoffnung*) that this, our sister, is ordained of God to be your wedded wife?"

"Yes."

"Do you stand in the confidence that this, our brother, is ordained of God to be your wedded husband?"

"Yes."

"Do you also promise your wedded wife, before the Lord and his church, that you will nevermore depart from her, but will care for her and cherish her, if bodily sickness comes to her, or in any circumstance which a Christian husband is responsible to care for, until the dear God will again separate you from each other?"

"Yes."

"Do you also promise your wedded husband, before the Lord and his church, etc."

"Yes."[3]

The couple then clasped their right hands together and the bishop continued: "So then I may say with Raguel (Tobit 7:15), the God of Abraham, the God of Isaac, and the God of Jacob be with you and help you together and fulfill his blessing abundantly upon you, through Jesus Christ. Amen." The bishop pronounced them husband and wife. Many, including the bishop, wiped away their tears, for all understood that the marriage would remain unto death.

Near the end of the ceremony several close relatives and table-waiters left the service. The bridal party remained a full half-hour for the closing formalities and then left, walking briskly in couples to the yard gate, where they were met by three hostlers, each with a buggy ready to go. Each hostler remained in the buggy and sat on the lap of the couple as he drove them to the bride's home for the wedding dinner.

At the bride's home the couples alighted from their buggies and

3. Translated from a nineteenth-century source; see *Mennonite Quarterly Review* 33 (April 1959): 142.

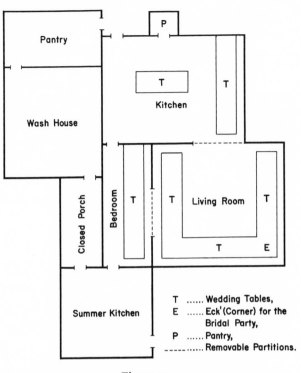

Figure 11.
Floor plan showing arrangement of tables
for an Amish wedding

walked quickly to an upstairs room. Their mood was most serious; no shouting or handshakes of congratulations greeted them. The tables were loaded with food, ready for the large crowd that began to gather about the house and barn. The cooks had already eaten, so that they would be ready for the afternoon's work of serving tables. Two couples were assigned to serve each table.

Guests were seated under the supervision of the bride's father, who ranked all but the young people of courting age according to kinship. The bridal party sat at the *Eck* ("corner table") located in the most visible part of the living room. The bridegroom sat to the right of the bride, with attendants on either side. The unmarried girls (cousins and friends), with backs to the wall, filled the wedding table(s) around three sides of the living room. The young men sat on the opposite side facing the girls. In the kitchen and bedroom the married women took seats in similar fashion at the table(s) around the wall and the men sat opposite. Facing the bride and bridegroom sat the

Schnützler ("carver"), who was to carve the fowl for the *Eck* and see to it that the bridal party was well served.

When the places at the tables were filled the bishop gave the signal for silent prayer. *Wann der Disch voll is, welle mir bede* ("If the tables are full, let us pray"). All bowed their heads in silent prayer. The wedding dinner consisted of roast duck and chicken, dressing, mashed potatoes, gravy, cold ham, cole slaw, raw and cooked celery, peaches, prunes, pickles, bread and butter, jams, cherry pie, tea, cookies, and many kinds of cake. The meal was a jolly occasion with plenty of opportunity for visiting. All were expected to eat well. Some brought tablets and mints to aid digestion.

The *Eck* did not contain flowers, but fancy dishes, cakes, and delicacies were abundant. No less than six beautifully decorated cakes (baked by friends) and numerous dishes of candy were displayed there. One large bowl of fruit was in the center of it all. An antique wine flask (containing cider) and matching goblets were used by the bridal party.

When the first group had finished eating, the dishes were quickly removed, washed in portable laundry tubs, and replaced for a second sitting. The bridal party did not leave the table. When most of the people were through eating, a hymn was announced by one of the singers. All heartily joined in singing except the bride and bridegroom, who by custom do not sing at their own wedding since it is considered a bad omen. Each guest had brought his own song book, the small *Lieder Sammlungen*. There was a considerable amount of singing until about five o'clock in the afternoon, when many older people went home. Some slow tunes were used, but most of the hymns were sung to the fast tunes. Women, who ordinarily do not assume leadership in religious services, frequently announced hymns and also led the singing. During the afternoon the young people left the tables to gather outdoors and in the barn for their own visiting and festivities.

It is the custom at the wedding supper for the young people to sit in couples; thus each boy was forced to bring a girl to the supper table whether he wanted to or not. The older boys who had "steady" girls had no difficulty in pairing off, but young boys with little or no experience in courtship showed great timidity in finding a partner. Those who refused to find partners were seized and dragged to the door, where they were placed beside a girl. Once in line, all resistance ceased and each couple went to the table holding hands, following the example of the bridal party. The supper included roast beef, roast chicken, noodles, beef gravy, chicken gravy, mashed potatoes, cole slaw, prunes, fruit salad, potato chips, cookies, pies, cakes, and for the bridal group and cooks there were, in addition, baked oysters and ice cream.

Hymns were sung during the supper hour, which continued until ten o'clock. The bride and bridegroom during this time sent plates of extra delicacies—cakes, pie, and candies—from the *Eck* to their special friends seated in various parts of the house. The final selection sung after the evening meal was *Guter Geselle* ("good friend"), a religious folk song. This selection cannot be found in any of the Amish song books. It is largely sung from memory, although it has been printed in leaflet form. The first verse reads:

Guter Geselle, was sagest du mir?	Good friend, what do you say?
O guter Geselle ich sage dir,	O good friend I tell you—
Sage dir was eins ist.	I tell you what one thing is;
Eins ist der Gott allein,	One is God alone,
Der da lebet und der da schwebet,	He who lives and He who soars,
Und der den wahren Glauben führet	And He who leads the true Faith
Im Himmel und auf Erden.	In Heaven and on Earth.

After supper the young folks again went to the barn, where they played games until midnight. At this point most of the married people returned to their homes, but the cooks stayed to wash dishes and take care of the remaining food.

The bride and bridegroom spent the night at the bride's home, but no pranks were sprung on the couple. Although there is no immediate honeymoon, the custom of visiting uncles, aunts, and cousins for a few weeks following the wedding is expected.

The parents of the bride and bridegroom were not present at the ceremony, nor were they given special recognition at the celebration. They were constantly supervising and managing the kitchen and entertaining, seeing that the supply of food was adequate and that the serving was progressing according to schedule. They ate with the cooks and played a subordinate role.

The bride and bridegroom were highly esteemed as they sat at the *Eck*. The occasion was geared for their full enjoyment. However, when they mixed in the crowd separately, between meals, they were treated as ordinary individuals. There was no expression of best wishes. This seems to have been taken for granted. The wedding gifts displayed on the bride's bed consisted chiefly of kitchenware and farm tools.

Barn games are commonly played at weddings, and husking bees take place in some of the most conservative groups. In some settlements games have "gotten out of hand," so that there are weekly hoedowns or "hops." The traditional games played include "Bingo" (not the conventional game but the singing and marching game), "Skip to Ma [My] Lou," "There Goes Topsy through the Window," "O-Hi-O," and "Six-Handed Reel." These and the following games have on occasion been played at weddings: "Little Red Wagon Painted Blue," "Granger," "Charlie Loves to Court the Girls," "We Will Shoot the Buffalo," "The Needle's Eye," and "Six Steps Forward-I-do-I-do." These games, also known as party games, involve holding hands and swinging partners.

Many families and church leaders are opposed to barn games, not because they are wrong in themselves, but because they have led to excesses, and often attract nonmembers with musical instruments. Their opposition is based upon the conviction that it is unnecessary, hilarious conduct, and does not conform to the Christian standard of good behavior. These party or "ring" games were characteristic not only of the Amish but of settlers in the colonial period in America. The Amish kept them alive in their traditions.[4] Although the Amish are opposed to dancing, they never reasoned that the "singing games" were a form of dancing.

The "infair," a distinctive institution in Lancaster County, is an event that formally recognizes the relationships formed between two new kinship systems. A few weeks after the wedding the parents of the groom entertain the bride's parents and all their married and unmarried children on a special day of visiting. The day is celebrated by a large, family-style dinner.

In summary, marriage in Amish life is not simply a romantic affair. The preoccupation with personal taste that is so common in Protestant weddings, where the ceremony and the content of the sermon are dictated by the couple, is not a factor in Amish weddings. The clothes of the bride and bridegroom are made in traditional styles. Marriage is bonded by the community and symbolizes the couple's acceptance of mature values. Community and personal expectations allow no room for divorce, and separation is almost unknown. The ceremony is elaborate because much is expected in the way of community conformity and responsibility.

DEATH

Death is a sober occasion. In some respects, however, it is taken as a matter of course, as the Amish person lives his life in the shadow

---

4. Several games played by the Amish appear in an album entitled *Colonial Singing Games and Dancing* (No. WS 107), produced by the Colonial Williamsburg Foundation, Williamsburg, Va.

of death and in conscious submission to the forces of nature. The Amish community is very sensitive to sickness among its members, and if someone is seriously ill, a sense of religious duty compels members of the church and community to visit the sick person's home, though it may be only a five- or ten-minute call.

When my father's cousin, "one-arm" Joe Byler, was on his deathbed with cancer, I visited his home with my sister. His children were all present. The women, dressed in black, were washing dishes and seemed busy with work. Evening callers entered the house without knocking, whereupon they were invited to enter the sitting room. The visitors, consisting of neighbors, friends, and relatives, extended the usual handshake with all the others in the sitting room and quietly found seats. Only a word or two was exchanged with the wife of the sick man when she came out of his room. She, as spokeswoman concerning the current condition of her husband, conversed with one of the women seated in the circle of visitors. All others, particularly the men, were quiet and resigned. An air of seriousness prevailed during the long periods of silence.

The Amish die in the hospital only when it is necessary or unavoidable; they prefer to die at home.[5] News of a death spreads throughout the Amish community very rapidly. Following a death a list is immediately made of persons who are to be notified personally and invited to the funeral. Next, nonrelatives are appointed to take full charge of all the work and arrangements. Relatives who live at a great distance are notified from the telephone of a non-Amish neighbor.

When death overtakes a family member, few decisions need to be made for which tradition has not provided. Neighbors and nonrelatives relieve the bereaved family of all work responsibility. The family is not confronted with the numerous decisions faced by the typical American family at such a time. Community responsibility relieves the Amish family of the tension and stress of such decisions as choosing a coffin and a place of burial, as well as the financial worries associated with death.

Young men take over the farm chores and an older married couple takes on the honorary position of managing the household. They appoint as many other helpers as they need for cleaning, food preparation, and burial arrangements. The closest kin spend their time

---

5. For observations on death and dying in Lancaster County, I am indebted to Kathleen B. Bryer, "Attitudes toward Death among Amish Families: Implications for Family Therapy" (M.A. thesis, Hahnemann Medical College, Philadelphia, Pa., 1978). For Iowa customs, see Melvin Gingerich, "Custom Built Coffins," *The Palimpsest* 24 (December 1943): 384–88.

in quiet meditation and in conversation in the living room. The bier is located in an adjacent or back room. Still other friends come to the home, and a few sit up all night while the closest kin retire. Some Midwestern Amish still observe the old custom of the wake by sitting up all night around the deceased, and young people gather at the home in the evening to sing. Generally, funerals are held on the third day following death.

Traditionally the dead are dressed in white. For a man this includes a white shirt, trousers, and socks. A woman is clothed in a white dress, cape, and organdy cap. The cape and apron are frequently those that were worn by the deceased on her wedding day.

Amish coffins and wooden vaults are made by an Amish carpenter or by an undertaker catering to Amish specifications. Formerly they were made of walnut, but due to the scarcity of this lumber, pine is now used. A coffin consists of a plain-varnished, stained and oiled wooden box without side handles. The coffin design varies among Amish settlements. The inside is lined with white cloth by some groups, but a lining is not used by the more traditional Amish. Some groups prefer to have the lid all in one piece; for viewing the body, the lid is slid back about two feet. Other groups have a two-piece lid, and the upper part of the lid is fastened with hinges and is opened for viewing. In both types the lid is fastened with wooden screws.

Most Amish groups have the body embalmed, though a few very strict groups do not. The undertaker never sees the body of the deceased person in the latter case. In some communities the body is not taken away from the home until the day of the funeral. The undertaker executes the burial permits. From four to six pallbearers, depending on the need, are selected by the family. One pallbearer may assist with the seating arrangements at the funeral and open and close the coffin for viewing at the funeral. All help to close the grave.

The funeral and burial are strictly "plain." There is no modern lowering device, artificial grass, carpet, or tent at the grave, nor are there flowers. The expenses of an Amish funeral would hardly exceed the cost of a wooden coffin and embalming fees. Simple obituaries, if requested by the local newspaper staff, are sometimes published in the village newspaper.

In Lancaster County, Pennsylvania, the Amish use several funeral directors. One is a native of the area and speaks the Amish dialect, and all provide the funeral wagon, the team of horses, and the driver for transporting the body to the cemetery. In such a densely popu-lated Amish area certain customs are unique as well. During the

On the death of a member, many Amish come to the aid
of the bereaved family. The grave is prepared
by members who are not close relatives.

wedding "season," November and December, weddings take prece-
dence over the dates set for funerals. Inside the burial grounds the
coffin is again opened for a brief viewing.

When a death occurs the funeral director is notified by telephone
by a neighbor. Upon his arrival at the home, the funeral director
often finds forty or fifty people who have gathered to see the deceased
person just as he or she was when death occurred. These gatherings
are an expression of sharing and of support for the family. The body
is then brought to the funeral home for preparation, dressed in appropriate undergarments, placed in a coffin, and returned to the
home. The work of the funeral director does not involve contacting
the ministers or pallbearers, or preparing the grave. Young men called
leicht-ah-sager go from place to place extending invitations to the
funeral. Members within the church district of the deceased are welcome to attend without an invitation. But relatives must be invited,
and the cutoff point for relatives is usually cousins of the same age
as the deceased.

Great respect is shown for the dead in many ways. The burial
garments are made by the family. Members dress the body and comb
the hair. Manners and comments all indicate great respect, love, and
concern. Traditional mourning garments also indicate such respect.
Black (among women) will be worn for one year when there is a loss
in the immediate family, for six months for a grandparent, three
months for an uncle or aunt, and six weeks for a cousin.

The following is an account of the funeral of an Amish patriarch that was held at nine o'clock in the morning on a February day at his old homestead in Mifflin County, Pennsylvania:

On our arrival the barnyard was already full of black carriages. People were gathering slowly and silently in the large white house, first removing their overshoes on the long porch. Inside there were three large rooms. The wall partitions had been removed so that the speaker could be seen from any part of the three rooms. Benches were arranged parallel with the length of each room. About three hundred people were present. The living room held sixty-two persons, including the fourteen ministers (many of them guests) seated on a row of chairs down the center of the room. The large kitchen seated probably eighty persons, and the third room held about fifty persons, including children. Of the remaining people, some were upstairs, others were standing in the summer kitchen, and more were outdoors.

The third room, ordinarily the master bedroom, had been used as the living quarters of the deceased grandfather. It was in this room that the body of the deceased was resting—in a coffin that had been placed on a bench against the wall. Relatives sat facing the coffin, with the next of kin closest to it. They had their backs to the speaker.

The house gradually filled. The head usher was a friend of the family but not a close relative. With hat on his head, he seated incoming people and reserved special space for relatives. When every bit of available bench space was full, and chairs had been crowded in at all possible odd corners, the audience waited in silence for the appointed hour.

After the clocks in all three rooms struck nine the minister at the head of a long line of preachers removed his hat. At once all the other men removed their hats in perfect unison. The first minister took his position at the doorway between the kitchen and the living room. His message, similar to an ordinary introductory sermon at a regular worship service, was full of biblical admonitions, largely from the Old Testament. This gathering, he reminded his hearers, was special. God had spoken through the death of a brother.

He made reference to the life and character of the deceased, but these remarks were incidental to the sermon, which continued: "The departed brother was especially minded to attend worship services the last few years of his life, in spite of his physical handicaps. Those who ministered to his needs have nothing to regret because they have done their work well. His chair is empty, his bed is empty, his voice will not be heard anymore. He was needed in our presence, but God needs such men too. We would not wish him back, but we should rather prepare to follow after him. He was a human being and had weaknesses too, but his deeds will now speak louder than when he lived."

After thirty minutes the first speaker sat down. He was followed by a second minister, a guest in the community, who delivered the principal address. He too reminded his hearers that a loud call from heaven had come to the congregation, and that the Scriptures warn every member to be ready to meet death. "We do not know when 'our time' will come, but the important thing is to be ready," the minister warned. "Death is the result of Adam's sin. Young people, when you are old enough to think about joining the church, don't put it off." (Such direct admonitions to the young, linked with intense emotional appeal, provide motivation for conformity to traditional Amish values.)

Two passages were read, one near the beginning and one near the close of this second address. The readings were from John 5 and Revelation 20. The sermon was far from a eulogy. The emphasis was personal and direct. It was an appeal to the audience to live righteously, inasmuch as a day of reckoning comes for all people. The minister said he did not wish to make the sermon too long because the weather was unpleasant for the horses standing outside in the rain. After speaking for forty-five minutes, he read a long prayer as the congregation knelt. At the conclusion of the prayer the audience rose to their feet and the benediction was pronounced.

At this point the audience was seated and a brief obituary was read in German by the minister who had preached the first sermon. In behalf of the family he also thanked all those who had shown kindness during the sickness and death of the departed one and invited all who could to return to the home for dinner after the burial. The assisting minister read a hymn. There was no singing.

The minister in charge announced that the boys could retire to the barn. The reason was apparent, as rearrangement was necessary to provide for the viewing of the body. Except for the ministers, the living room was entirely vacated. Next, the coffin was moved to a convenient viewing place into the main entrance. Everyone present formed a line and took one last look at the body of the departed brother. Sorrow and tears were evident, but there was little weeping. The closest relatives stood in back of the coffin during the viewing and followed it to the grave.

Meanwhile friends and helpers had prepared the hearse for transporting the body to the graveyard. The hearse consisted of a one-horse springwagon with the seat pushed forward. Because of the

After the funeral service, relatives and friends drive in procession
to the burial grounds. Most then return to the home
of the deceased for a meal.

rainy weather, a canvas was placed over the coffin to keep it dry. The
horses of the mourners were hitched to their carriages by the many
helpers. Relatives of the deceased entered their buggies and formed
a long line to follow the body to the *Graabhof* ("graveyard"). The
procession traveled very slowly, seldom faster than the ordinary walk
of the horses.

Upon arrival at the graveyard the horses were tied to the hitching
posts. The coffin, supported by two stout, rounded, hickory poles, was
immediately carried to the open grave and placed over it. Relatives
and friends gathered near. Long, felt straps were placed around
each end of the coffin. The pallbearers lifted the coffin with the straps
while a bystander quickly removed the supporting crosspieces. The
coffin was then slowly lowered into the grave and the long straps
were slowly removed. Standing in the grave on the frame that surrounded the casket, a man placed short boards over the casket as they
were handed to him. Nearby a father clutched his four-year-old son
and whispered something into his ear, hoping that some recollection
of his grandfather would remain in his consciousness. With shovels
the four pallbearers began to fill the grave. Soil and gravel hit the

Walking to the preaching service on Sunday morning

single-file into the long farm lane, and the sound of still other horses trotting on the hard-surface road over the hill, evokes deep sentiments among the gathering community. Neighbors and those nearby usually walk to the service. No driver would think of passing another "rig" on the way to the service.

On arriving at the place of worship, the carriage halts in the barnyard, where the mother and girls dismount. Father and sons drive to a convenient stopping place, where they are met by hostlers, often sons of the host household, who help unhitch the horse and find a place for it in the stable. The horse is given hay from the supply in the barn. Meanwhile the men cluster in little groups in the stable and under the forebay of the barn, greeting one another with handshakes and in subdued voices.

Finally the preachers observe that it is time to withdraw to the house. In winter the men remove their heavy overcoats and hang them in the barn, frequently on the same hooks where the harness is hanging; there are no closets in Amish houses, and thus there is no place to hang so many clothes. In summer the service may be held in the barn. The order in which worshipers gather is determined by sex and age, a principle that is evident in the entire social life of the society. First the ordained men enter, followed by the oldest men. They are leisurely followed by the middle-aged. The last to enter the assembly are the unmarried boys, who come in single file according to seniority. The age grouping holds also for the meal that follows the service.

The women and girls place their shawls and bonnets in the wash-house or the woodshed. In summertime the girls remain here until it is time to join the assembly. In winter they gather in the kitchen. They usually take their seats before the boys come in from the barn; the latter, incidentally, in some districts remain in the barn until the service has begun. The girls also enter single file, generally according to age, shaking hands with the ministers as they enter. The baptized single women head the line as a rule. Visiting young people who are members are frequently given the privilege of following the lead person in the procession.

Amish houses are specially built to accommodate the many people, often 200 or more, who gather for worship. The houses have wide doors, and in the Eastern states there are removable partitions so that people seated in almost any part of the main floor can observe the preacher. Each church district owns benches and hymnals, which are transported from one meeting place to another. The furniture is removed or stored in such a way that rooms can be filled with benches.

The seating space consists of backless benches, which occupy the kitchen, sitting room, and main bedroom. A center row of chairs is reserved for the ordained. Older men take benches next to the wall, but the feeble ones are given rocking chairs. Chairs are frequently given to the ministers' wives and the oldest women. The preacher, who stands at the doorway between the two largest rooms, has no pulpit, but occasionally a chair upon which to lean. Women and men are seated separately, though they are not in separate rooms. Several rows of unmarried women occupy the sitting room with the men, and men who arrive late remain in the kitchen with mothers and infants. Preschool boys sit with their fathers and girls with their mothers. Infants, a month or six weeks old, also are brought to the service. Being present is important.

The customs of one district or settlement may differ slightly from those of others. The symbols that bind a group into a unified whole differ from Pennsylvania to Kansas, and even within the state of Pennsylvania. While the order of service is almost uniform, the manner of informal behavior, as well as the extent to which informal behavior is ritualized, differs. For instance, men in some districts leave their hats on in the house until the hymn is announced. Then, with one uniform swoop, off they come; they are put under the bench, piled on empty benches, or hung on hooks. In other districts hats are taken off as the men enter the house. The boys may pile them on the porch. In some groups men leave their hats on during the meal, taking them off only for the silent prayer at the beginning and at the end of the meal.

The preaching service may be three hours long and there are a variety of forms which the order of service may take.

ORDER OF AN AMISH PREACHING SERVICE

1. Hymns (several) are sung while the ministers retire to an upstairs room for counsel. The *Loblied* (*Ausbund*, p. 770) is always the second hymn. (The singing of a hymn may take from twenty to thirty minutes.)
2. *Anfang*, or "introductory sermon"
3. Prayer (assembly kneeling, and in most localities silent)
4. The assembly stands while the *Armen-diener* ("deacon") reads a chapter from the Bible.
5. *Es schwere Deel*, or "main sermon," which is concluded by the reading of a chapter from the Bible.
6. *Zeugniss*, or "testimonies," to the main sermon are given by other ministers present as requested by the one who preached. Other lay members are frequently asked to give *Zeugnis*.
7. Closing remarks by the minister who preached
8. All turn and kneel while the minister reads a prayer from *Die Ernsthafte Christenpflicht*. (The prayer on p. 55 is commonly used.)
9. Benediction (assembly standing)
10. Announcement: where the next meeting will be held; whether members should remain after dismissal for a members' meeting.
11. Closing hymn
12. Dismissal, with the youngest leaving first, followed by the older ones in the order of their ages.

After the rooms have been occupied and everyone is waiting for the service to begin, an elderly man announces a hymn number. The old man begins to sing what seems like a solo, but after the first syllable the whole assembly joins in unison. The *Vorsinger* or *Vorstimmer*, the one leading the singing, may be any male member who has had the informal training required. He is not formally appointed, nor does he stand or sit in any special place. The *Vorsinger* continues to sing the beginning of each new line of a hymn in a trembling falsetto. The tunes are extremely slow, with the voices of the old joining those of the young in unison.

With the singing of the first hymn, the ordained men withdraw (oldest first) to a room upstairs for *Abrot* (*Abrath*, or "counsel"), for prayer, and to arrange who will preach the sermons. When there are applicants for baptism, they appear before the ministers upstairs. On entering, the oldest applicant says, "It is my desire to be at peace with God and the Church." Each of the others in his or her turn says, "That is my desire too." After instruction they are dismissed and the ordained proceed with their business.

While the preachers are in the council room, the assembly continues to sing hymns, which are interspersed with long periods of silence. With a nod the elderly *Vorsinger* passes to another the responsibility for leading the next hymn, and frequently a young man is nudged by an older one to take over in the middle of a familiar hymn. Should a young man lose the melody and his courage, an older member will come to his rescue. Considerable talent is demanded of the song leader to sing the tunes from memory.

When the preachers descend the stairway the singing stops at the end of the verse. The preachers shake hands with latecomers and with any whom they had not greeted earlier in the morning. After the ministers are seated, one of them rises and stands between the two large rooms to deliver the first sermon. With hands folded beneath his full-grown white beard, a preacher typically begins to mumble in a low tone, gradually building up to an audible and rhythmic flow of words in mixed Pennsylvania German, German, and English:

Liebe Brüder und Schwestern und alle die womit versammelt sin, zum erschde will ich eich die Gnade Gottes winsche und die mitwirkente Graft des heiligen Geistes, un wie Petrus sagt, "Gelobet sei Gott und der Vater unsers Herrn Jesu Christi, der uns nach seiner grossen Barmherzigheit wiedergeboren hat zu einer lebendigen Hoffnung, durch die Auferstehung Jesu Christi von Toten, zu einem unverganglichen und unbefleckten und unverwelklichen Erbe." (I Pet. 1:3–4)

Dear brothers and sisters and all who are assembled here, first of all I wish you the grace of God and the accompanying power of the Holy Ghost. As Peter says, "Blessed be the God and Father of our Lord Jesus Christ, which according to his abundant mercy hath begotten us again into a lively hope by the resurrection of Jesus Christ from the dead, to an inheritance incorruptible, and undefiled, and that fadeth not away, reserved in heaven for you." (I Pet. 1:3–4)

In a typical opening sermon, the minister reminds the congregation of the purpose of their meeting—to listen once again to the Word of God. He brings to the attention of all some Scriptual teachings, pointing out the importance of obeying the commandments. For instance, he admonishes the worshiper: "schaffet, das ihr selig werdet, mit Furcht und Zittern" ("Work out your own salvation with fear and trembling" (Phil. 2:12). This is a favorite quotation. Before bringing his half-hour introduction to a close, he mentions the importance of prayer and of trust in God. Appreciation for freedom of worship is typically expressed. After a few words of apology for his weakness, he informs the congregation that he does not wish to take the allotted time away from the brother who is to bring the main message: "Auch ich will die Zeit net lang verbrauche in mein grosse Armut und Schwachheit und die Zeit wegnehmen von der Bruder wo es schwere Deel hat." He asks the hearers to pray for the minister who is to bring the main message and then quotes a favorite verse: "Kommt, lasst uns anbeten, und knieen, und niederfallen vor dem Herrn, der uns gemacht hat. Denn er ist unser Gott, und wir das Volk seiner Weide, und Schafe seiner Hand, Heute, so ihr seine Stimme horet, so verstocket euer Herz nicht." (For translation, see Ps. 95:6–8.) He then closes with the words, "Und wann dir einig sind lasset uns bede" ("If you are all agreed, let us pray"). All kneel together for a period of silent prayer.

The signal to rise from prayer may not be apparent to the visitor. When the preacher feels that enough time has been allotted for individual prayer, he gets up from his knees. Those who hear his foot scraping the floor as he rises know that it is time to stand.

All remain standing while the deacon reads the Scripture. The deacon may offer several remarks, after which he admonishes the congregation to be obedient to the Lord. The entire chapter is read in a singsong, chantlike fashion. After the last verse of the chapter, the deacon concludes: "So weit hat die Schrift sich ersteckt" ("Thus far extendeth the Scripture"), and all are seated. The Scriptures read at the preaching services follow a seasonal pattern.[2] The register of Scriptures begins at Christmas time with the birth of Christ and concludes with the New Testament account of the judgment and end of the world. Selections from the hymnal (*Ausbund*) are integrated with the register of Scriptures and hymns.

Now the time has come for the main sermon. The preacher begins with the usual greeting: "Gnade sei mit euch und Friede von Gott unser Vater. Wir sin schon viel-feldich vermanhnt wore auf dem meiget Stund bei dem Bruder." ("Grace be with you and peace from God our father. We have been admonished many times this morning hour by the brother.") He reminds his hearers of the importance of obedience to the vow of baptism, of obedience to the Bible and par-

2. Registers have been published on many occasions. Aside from pamphlets and those published by J. A. Raber in his *Der Neue Amerikanische Calendar*, a few have appeared in the *Mennonite Quarterly Review* 15 (January 1941): 26–32, and in Joseph W. Yoder, *Amische Lieder* (Huntington, Pa.: Yoder Publishing Co., 1942), p. xii.

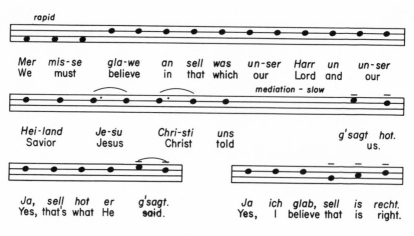

rapid

Mer	mis-se	gla-we	an	sell	was	un-ser	Harr	un	un-ser
We	must	believe	in	that	which	our	Lord	and	our

mediation - slow

Hei-land	Je-su	Chri-sti	uns	g'sagt hot.
Savior	Jesus	Christ	told	us.

Ja,	sell	hot	er	g'sagt.		Ja	ich	glab,	sell	is	recht.
Yes,	that's	what	He	said.		Yes,	I	believe	that	is	right.

Figure 12.
Intonation of an Amish sermon

ents. *Das alt Gebrauch* (equivalent to "the old way of life") sums up a major aspect of moral emphasis. This phrase embodies the principle of separation from the world, the *Regel und Ordnung* ("rules and discipline") of the church, and the idea of strangers and pilgrims in an evil world. Innovations that are unacceptable are labeled *eppes Neies* ("something new") and are met with the force of *das alt Gebrauch*.

Delivery of the sermon falls into a stylized pattern.[3] Somewhat like a chant, the preacher's voice rises to a rather high pitch; then, at the end of each phrase, it suddenly drops (see Figure 12). Babies who fall asleep in their mothers' arms are carried, sometimes directly in front of the preacher, into the next room and up the stairway, where three or more may sleep on the same bed. Other children lean on the arm of the parent, or pass the time with a handkerchief, making such objects as "mice" or "twin babies in a cradle." In the kitchen, mothers are nursing their new babies. Not only do the babies tire; the singsong sermon and the stuffy atmosphere and warmth of the packed room frequently put many of the hard-working men to sleep. Some who appear to be nodding or swaying in sleep are just changing their posture, since there are no backrests.

The service is orderly and reverent. On rare occasions humorous incidents occur, like the forgetful mother who put her baby to sleep and upon descending the stairway had the baby's little white cap on her own head.

---

3. Although characteristic of the traditional Amish preacher, chanting is not unique to the Amish. See Bruce A. Rosenberg, *The Art of the American Folk Preacher* (New York: Oxford University Press, 1970).

Meanwhile, as the preacher goes on with his singsong sermon, the backless benches seem to get harder and harder. The children begin to get restless. The mother of the house may pass a dish of crackers and cookies to all the mothers and fathers having youngsters at their side. The dish is passed down the aisle, across, and over to the next room so that no child misses this treat. Moments later a glass of water is passed for the same youngsters. The long sermon has just started and there may be two more hours of sitting still. The host of the house may bring a glass of water for the preacher.

The preacher relates first the Old Testament story from Adam to Abraham, and second the account from John the Baptist to the end of Paul's missionary journeys. The earnestness with which he speaks produces drops of sweat on his face, and every few minutes it is necessary for him to reach to his inside coat pocket and draw out a handkerchief to wipe his forehead. He holds the white handkerchief in his hand and occasionally waves it through the air as he illustrates a point.

He concludes the long sermon with the reading of a chapter from the Bible, but interrupts the reading with comments. Then, with a long sigh the preacher sits down and asks other ordained men to give *Zeugnis* ("testimony") to the message and to "bring anything up which should have been said," or to correct any mistakes. Those offering comments (ranging from three to five minutes in length) remain seated.

After the testimonies are completed, the main preacher rises to his feet for some closing remarks. He is thankful that the sermon can be taken as God's Word and he further admonishes the congregation to give praise to God and not to man: "Ich feel dankbar dass die Lehr hat erkannt sei kenne fer Gottes Wort. Gewet Gott die Ehr nicht Mensche." He thanks the congregation for being quiet and attentive. As a guest, he admonishes all to be obedient to the home ministry, and in speaking to the ministers he advises them to visit other districts. This, he says, strengthens and builds up the church. He asks the congregation to kneel for the closing prayer. Except for three or four mothers who are holding sleeping babies, all kneel while the minister reads in chant style from the prayer book.

When the minister is through chanting the long prayer, everyone rises for the benediction, which he recites from memory:

Zuletzt, liebe Brüder, freuet euch, seid vollkommnen, trostet euch, habt einerlei Sinn, seid friedsam; so wird Gott der Liebe und des Friedens mit euch sein, grüsset euch unter einander mit dem heiligen Kuss. Es grüssen euch alle Heiligen. (II Cor. 13:11–13)

So befehle ich noch mich, mit euch, Gott und seiner Gnadenhand an, dass er uns walte in dem seligmachenden Glauben erhalten, darinnen stärken, leiten und bewahren bis an ein seliges Ende, und das alles durch Jesum Christum, Amen.

Finally, dear brethren, rejoice, be perfect, be comforted and be of one mind; be peaceful, and the God of love and peace shall be with you. Greet each other with the Holy Kiss. You are greeted by all the saints. (II Cor. 13:11–13)

So I submit myself, with you, to God and his gracious hand, that He please to keep us in the saving faith, to strengthen us in it, to guide and lead us until a blessed end; and all this through Jesus Christ. Amen.

When the minister says the words "Jesum Christum" at the very end, all in complete uniformity bend their knees. This genuflection may come as a surprise to the visitor, but to the member it is an intense experience indicating full obedience and reverence. It symbolizes unanimity with the group.

When the assembly is again seated, the deacon announces the place of the next meeting. In the event that business pertaining to discipline is to be taken up, the deacon also asks that after the singing of the closing hymn, members remain seated: "Was Brüder und Schwechdre sin, solle wennich schtill sitze bleiwe." On such occasions, all the unbaptized boys and girls and nonmembers are dismissed.

When a members' meeting is not scheduled, the congregation is dismissed with the closing of the hymn. The youngest leave the service first, with the men and women marching out separately.

The men remove some of the benches, passing them through a window and the door, to make room for tables, which are formed by setting benches together. Soon the women and girls have set the tables with pies, bread, butter, jam, cheese, pickles, red beets, and coffee—a a standard menu that varies slightly with local custom. Each place setting consists only of a knife, cup, and saucer. The pies are baked firm enough so that each person can cut his own piece and eat it while holding it in the hand. This meal is not supposed to be a feast, but just a "piece" to hold one over until he returns home. The ordained, regardless of their age, always eat at the first sitting, and visitors are often asked to come to the first table. Otherwise age determines who should come to the table. It is usually necessary to set the tables three or four times, with the boys and girls and youngest children eating last. When preaching was held in my home, my brother and I hid some "half-moon pies" in the barn (with mother's permission) and with our best buddies ate them right after the dismissal.

The afternoon is spent in conversation about religion and other matters of mutual interest. To rush away from the service or to leave immediately following the meal is considered somewhat rude. The